To J

with l

from the author.

Sept 1998.

CW01642232

LATIN WEEKENDS

Flying Visits to South America...

Robert Johnson

MINERVA PRESS
LONDON
ATLANTA MONTREUX SYDNEY

To Elaine, Sally and Nina,
and the Latin Americans

Contents

Chapter One

Weekend in Mexico

Quetzalcoatl. The Feathered Serpent. The Lord of Time. Who was he?

How did such a strange creature come to dominate the northern lands of what was to become known as Latin America? There was nothing of Quetzalcoatl in Venezuela or Colombia. If he ever reached out to Cuba or Hispaniola no trace now remains. Those places were not his world.

His world was on the western rim of the Caribbean and in the mountains beyond. Two worlds, in fact. One that the first Spanish arrivals found still thriving and highly organised; one just a folk-memory, some indecipherable books and a series of ruined cities largely abandoned to the tropical rainforest. The Aztec and Maya worlds – those were the societies over which Quetzalcoatl extended his rule: sometimes clearly; sometimes obscurely; sometimes under a different name and guise. The Feathered Serpent was not the god of primitive hunter–gatherers or fishers, but of places where the new arrivals from Europe were staggered at the complexity of urban life. Cities had populations larger than those of any in sixteenth-century Castille; vegetable gardens fed a million or more and huge markets allowed up to 60,000 people to barter and exchange their products and crops: textiles; tobacco; tomatoes; chilli peppers; cacao; peanuts and the many varieties of potatoes. They were places where (from twentieth-century observations) a constant tracking was made of the movements of the planet Venus, of Orion, of the Pleides and of other stars. They had a golden calendar measuring the days of sowing and the days of reaping. People offered strange homage to this Lord of Time; people hid from the power of a Lord of the Dawn.

★

Mexico City is a place unmistakable from the air. It is reached from Caracas by a great dog-leg route around the south-western coastline of the Caribbean. Northern Colombia at 33,000 feet, just a green haze of tropical vegetation framed by a glittering sea. Then over the Atrato swamp of the north-west; the seventy-five mile gap in the land-route down the Americas that is too wet, too difficult and too expensive to bridge. Then Panama, over the low 'peaks' of Darien and down into the suffocating damp heat of the Canal Zone. Suffocating, damp heat kept out by the air-conditioning, the plate glass and the international modernity of Tocumen airport.

Panama – a place unseen. A place represented only by duty-free shops offering electronics; cameras; shoes; scarves and crocodile handbags. A terminal where lines of tiny children are being led up and down the concourse like little ducklings – each holding on to the shoulders of the one in front – with a nun at their head. A terminal with a slight sense of overstatement. A small plaque commemorates the role of the USAF Tactical Air Command, the Strategic Air Command and the Military Airlift Command in a twentieth-century engagement. Not the War of the Pacific, the Korean War, the Gulf War or even the Cold War, but the Arrest of Noriega, 27th December 1989 to 24th January 1990!

Mexico City is reached from Panama up the 1,900 mile spine of Central America, across Nicaragua, Honduras and Guatemala. A slow descent beginning towards the interior plateau of Mexico and the huge rectilinear sprawl of one of the modern world's largest cities. Losing height as its ragged edge begins to sweep under the aircraft's wing. Then an absolutely level spread of pale, washed-out urban colours made up by the roofs of many small houses lining straight streets. Outer suburbs but few trees and few gardens. Houses built over the long-drained floor of Lake Mexicali. Strips of bright red and pink – the plastic awnings of street markets. Strips of bright orange – pencil-like commuter trains moving slowly about in the vast metropolitan area.

A flight beginning just north of the Darien peninsula and the Atrato swamp – an area inaccessible, unexplored and largely uninhabited. A flight ending in the world's fourth largest megacity – twenty square miles in area, 7,000 feet in altitude and with a million people per square mile.

A flight ending, moreover, right in the middle of that densely-packed megacity! Rather than the final descent gliding low over buildings that were beginning to space themselves out ever more widely in an attempt to turn away from the roar and fumes of touchdown and takeoff; these buildings grew closer and higher. Urban expansion almost overwhelmed the runways of Benito Juarez airport. Factories, office blocks, suburban streets and busy motorways – all appeared in such close view that the last few satellite dishes and penthouse rooftop plants were seemingly knocked aside by the aircraft wheels. A dark haze of polluted air lay over more distant parts of the city. The flight rolled to a halt in the thick atmosphere of one of the most industrialised countries in Latin America.

★

'VIOLENT ATTACK ON TRAIN AND PASSENGERS' shouted the headlines of a newspaper. An express train connecting Guadalajara with the Mexico/US border town of Mexicali had been held up. 'THREE DEAD – FIVE INJURED – HAUL OF MORE THAN $266 MILLION BY BAND OF DELINQUENTES'.

The booty was not quite as large as it at first seemed: $266 million in Mexican pesos was $86,000 in United States dollars. Robbing a train in 1992 and escaping north was obviously less profitable than robbing a train in 1892 and heading south, but if you picked the right *cambio* it was obviously worth the risk. And this was the Mexico every tourist had a right to expect. Nobody landing at Benito Juarez wanted reality – certainly not to be plunged into twenty million inhabitants coughing their way about in an environmental nightmare. No – arriving in Mexico was supposed to be arriving into a living myth. A nervously-deserted terminal building; a couple of drinkers hunched over their tequilas in a bar at the far end; a glass mirror behind the bar; the occasional squint up from a broad-brimmed hat; a puff of smoke from a chewed cigar; a slow movement of the arm; a twitch of the poncho; a turn to face the arrival of *gringo* strangers; a '*Hold it right there – amigo*' as a safety catch clicks open in the sudden hush of confrontation.

That was the 'real' Mexico, after all. Everybody knew that. The thunder of mounted riders raising dust clouds amongst the sage-brush, cactus and rocky desert landscape of the border. A row of sombrero-clad bandits on the skyline. Bandoleers, drooping moustaches and bells tolling over the rooftops of the pueblo. The Cisco Kid, the Alamo, the Rio Grande, the Monterreys, the Laredos, the treasure of the Sierra Madre. And now – according to *El Nacional* – outlaws still holding up a northern train for a fistful of dollars!

Sombreros hung next to the newspapers but they didn't look quite right. A bit grubby. The pollution had caused the brims to sag and a limp sombrero was definitely not the right image for a megacity. And checking up on the *El Nacional* index of air quality for its north-east, north-west, central, south-east and south-western sectors seemed more pressing in a daily paper than finding out whether *delinquentes* still wore hats. So much for the good old days of clean and simple dust when they were called *desperados* and used to wave '*adios!*' from the ridge before galloping off into the sunset. '*Ah, Cisco... Ah, Pancho!*'

Surprisingly – considering that dark yellow haze which enveloped the plane in the last moments before wheels touched tarmac – the newspaper's view was that the atmosphere was basically 'satisfactory' around Benito Juarez, despite ozone levels causing longer-term concern on the charts for having dropped (or risen?) until they were halfway to being 'less than satisfactory'. It was a day when the background content of sulphur dioxide, nitrogen dioxide and carbon monoxide – whilst still there – did not seriously threaten the continuation of life in Mexico City. Some days it did.

But could you always believe what the papers told you? That 'satisfactory' air made the eyes sting and the few gulps of it taken whilst changing planes were like taking in a cubic foot of neat exhaust. 'Very bad' must be terrible!

*

The air was distinctly better in the land of the Mayas. A familiar tropical warmth drifted in as soon as the cabin door was opened. Unpolluted but agitated. Something fierce and angry was about to hit the northern edge of the peninsula of Yucatan and the town of Merida. The palms caught it first – their glistening dark green fronds thrashing about ever more wildly as a breeze rapidly became a wind and then a howling gale. The domestic flight from Mexico City had put down just in time. Thunderous grey clouds towered in the east. Cuba had just had another torrential downpour. Now it was Yucatan's turn. Late summer – the season for Caribbean storms. The hurricane season!

But this hurricane touched Yucatan only lightly. Lashing rain and fierce gusts slapped and buffeted the terminal building for twenty minutes or so and then it was all over. Clean, clear 'extremely satisfactory' air followed in the wake of the downpour – made even more delightful by the returning sun steaming out a delicate scent from the moistened vegetation. The departing clouds veered off across the Bay of Campeche and headed north-west towards the Gulf of Mexico. Latin America had seen the last of those clouds – Corpus Christi, Galveston or Houston would be next to get them.

Merida was no crowded lake-bed housing twenty million people. The population of the entire Yucatan peninsula was less than one-fifth of that of the megacity. A quiet, dozy sort of place it seemed. Shady streets leading to quiet, dozy hotels where bedroom doors led on to open balconies which gave a wide view over low rooftops to the western horizon. And that pure coastal air. The peninsula was level country – a near flat limestone plateau one hundred feet or so above sea level. Very different from the atmosphere at 7,000 feet. Funny though – the lowlands with a clean atmosphere and the mountains with a dirty one – it was usually the other way around. Spending more than a few minutes on a balcony near Benito Juarez trying to admire the high altitude view would put you in hospital with severe respiratory and ocular problems.

Yes – Merida seemed a long way from the 'index of air quality'. Even further from a fistful of dollars. The hotel was pink – a colour which made the blue surface of its little pool waiting to refresh weary travellers look like imitation water painted into one of the more lurid Disney cartoons. Real enough, however, and with a rum punch or two taken in the rattan chairs at its side, and an attentive barman who slowly polished glasses and was only to pleased to offer a refill, it was about as far from the madding crowd as you could get. A slow rhythmic wafting of ceiling fans continually pushed back the declining heat of the western Caribbean day. The stupor of late afternoon and early evening settled over a very quiet and tranquil small town. The provinces looked forward to the quick sub-tropical onset of darkness and the coolness of evening. An early night beckoned – there didn't seem much else to do.

Unfortunately, the peace of the provinces was rudely shattered at supper time. A noisy riot blew into the hotel restaurant in much the same manner as the storm had swept across the place a few hours earlier. A large family of small children (under the patchy supervision of two young girls and no adults) settled fractiously into an evening meal of flying bread rolls, musical chairs, table crawling and sporadic howling.

Thirty minutes of that and anyone could see the virtue of child sacrifice!

The Mayans had practised it, of course – child sacrifice. All over the Yucatan peninsula. And in particular – it seemed – at Chichen Itza, one of the nearest of the now-ruined ceremonial centres. Viewed through the eyes of twentieth-century Europeans, terrible things had taken place there and elsewhere. Even viewed through the eyes of sixteenth-century Spaniards, the legacy of the Mayans was something to be treated with abomination and destroyed as quickly as possible.

And yet it was hard to believe of the distant ancestors of the people who still lived all over this part of Central America: in Yucatan; in Belize; in Guatemala; in El Salvador and even in Honduras. The Mayans – those round-headed, dark-eyed, black-haired, likeable people who (to the newly-arrived) all looked the same – it was hard to believe that they had practised child sacrifice.

Nonetheless, there was evidence to show that some kind of sacrificial killing had almost certainly taken place at the Sacred Well of Chichen Itza. This sizeable water-filled, natural limestone solution hole seventy-five miles to the east was where a former American Consul to Merida had spent a considerable amount of effort between the years 1904 and 1907 groping for treasure. He did find treasure in the muddy sediments on the floor of the steep-sided pool, or *cenote* but not much: necklaces; earrings; bracelets; and rings of gold, copper and jade. He also found the bones of fifty human skeletons: some adult males; some adult females (most of whom appeared to have received strong blows to the head). The rest were children. A later dredging of the pool brought up a doll. A tiny figure wrapped in rayon – a material of the second half of the twentieth century.

Despite the doll, dating of the bones had subsequently proved that most of the contents of the Sacred Well belonged to the pre-colonial era of the Mayan world; to that society which had reached its heyday in the seventh and eighth centuries and which had a propensity for human killing only as part of a highly sophisticated culture. Unlike the Aztec and the Inca worlds, that of the Maya was in decline by the time the first Spanish arrivals reached Yucatan. The memories of its heyday several centuries earlier had already grown dim and confused. People had the old books, knew of the old cities and even worshipped the old gods, but they were archivists not creators. The Spanish promptly dealt with the archives. The first archbishop of Yucatan – Diego de Landa – rapidly consigned whatever he could find to the cleansing fire of Christ. The books were heretical and dangerous and the work of the devil. A new start was to be made and the old world destroyed. The anguish this caused gave rise to some surprise.

> *We found a large number of books in these [hieroglyphic] characters and, as they contained nothing in there not to be seen as superstition and lies of the devil, we burned them all, which they regretted to an amazing degree and which caused them much affliction.*

What 'they' – the Maya of the sixteenth century – were 'regretting' was the burning of more than a thousand years of intellectual and spiritual property. It was a heritage which probably linked the several cultures of Central America: Olmec, Zapotec, Teotihuacan, Mayan, Toltec and Aztec. A heritage which seemed bloody and harsh for those on the Earth but one which looked carefully up at the cosmos and found meaning in what it saw. The cosmos was harsh, too, and needed appeasement.

Through all this heritage weaved the strange form of Quetzalcoatl – pointing somehow to that cosmic vision. Sometimes Quetzalcoatl was a feathered serpent, sometimes the being called Kukulcan, sometimes the form called Ehecatl, and sometimes a bearded white man from the east. In the fires of Christ, the Maya thought they were losing for ever the key to the celestial cycles; to their grasp of time. But they had forgotten that there was another part of the heritage left in stone.

The Spanish missed the buildings in the rainforest. Oddly, they even seemed to miss Chichen Itza and the other centres in the more open country of Yucatan. They pulled apart the less massive carvings of the great monuments near Mexico City but were overwhelmed by scale elsewhere. And through nearly all those scattered monuments of the peoples of Central America, there appeared to be that common thread. In the ruins of the Maya, Aztecs and other archives of stone, it was always present. It changed shape, colour and meaning as it snaked through over one thousand years, but it was always somewhere there. It was the thread of Quetzalcoatl.

Who or what was Quetzalcoatl?

★

The plane lifted away from Merida and headed due west – gathering height for its rise over the narrowing spine of Central America, where the Sierra Madre Oriental and the Sierra Madre Occidental came together to form the high rugged interior of Mexico. For maybe thirty minutes before they did so, however, the land below was pale green – the colour of the dense low bush and tree cover of the peninsula. It was land which seemed mostly uncultivated but which occasionally showed rectangular patches where the vegetation had been cleared to reveal a thin, red, lateritic soil. Sometimes even this had been scraped off. The limestone rock surface of the plateau appeared through the redness like bone showing through flesh. Even from the air, it was difficult to escape the darker side of Quetzalcoatl; it was difficult to shale off images of the cosmic demands he had once made on the people far below.

Then came a cliffed edge to the limestone and a strand of white sand. Then the waters of the Bay of Campeche. Then a long coastline running almost north–south. Then the sprawl of a large city with tiny ships riding at anchor off a port area. Then the Sierra Madre Oriental – green forested hills cut by narrow valleys rising and rising from the coast until they were on a collision course with the level path of the Merida to Mexico City flight. But they did stop rising and the aircraft began to wheel above that huge flat area covered to its extreme margins with buildings; the now recognisable lake-bed over which lay a familiar yellowish haze. The metropolitan atmosphere in which twenty million Mexicans were living out their late twentieth-century lives.

The port down on the coast was Veracruz. It was the place – nearly five hundred years earlier – where Hernando Cortés had landed and burnt his boats before turning to face the formidable challenge of the Aztec empire. It wasn't the steeply rising Sierra Madre Oriental that was the biggest problem – although getting cannon and horses up and through such rugged country was difficult enough. Somewhere above, he and his small party of troopers and would-be colonists knew that they would encounter the forces of a large and well-organised military state. Cortés was heading for where rumour and legend had said he would find the capital city of a king whose name was Montezuma. A king who ruled in golden halls. A city capital which stood in a lake and was known as Tenochtitlan.

La Villa Rica de la Veracruz formed a hurriedly founded supply base on the Caribbean shoreline. A Base Camp One. High in the interior lay an opposition that was far more sophisticated than any that the Spanish had come across in their first few island conquests of the New World.

Dangers – and yet riches also, perhaps. Word of a fabulous western kingdom had been filtering back to those in the early Spanish settlements on the Caribbean islands for a few years – settlements which had started to grow a little crowded when the to-ing and fro-ing across the Atlantic began in earnest. Those newly arrived soon felt restless as land and wealth was quickly staked out by others slightly in advance of them. The frontier was moving fast in this New World of which virtually nothing was known and where almost anything seemed possible. As Christopher Columbus arrived back in the Old World after his ill-fated fourth voyage and his failure to find either Cathay or Paradise, a less visionary Hernando Cortés was setting off from Spain to Hispaniola in a more straightforward search of fame and fortune. Columbus found the Americas but less than his dream of a westward route to the Far East; Cortés found Mexico and more than his wildest imaginings.

However, success did not come immediately. Life was unsatisfactory for an unrealised *conquistadore*. The year was 1504 and he struggled to mark out a future in the burgeoning colony of Hispaniola until – in 1511 – Diego de

Velázquez pushed the frontier further west to Cuba. As the tide of conquest once more gathered momentum, Cortés also moved west. Then, in 1517, came tales from slave hunters and the reports of a Juan de Grijalba describing a larger land mass to the west (Yucatan), the inhabitants of which were themselves in awe of a rich but war-like civilisation even further west. Opportunity had at last arrived for Hernando Cortés.

With or without prompting, Velázquez delegated Cortés to investigate whether the frontiers of New Spain were at last somehow touching Cathay – despite Balboa's expedition of 1513 indicating that a great sea also lay in that direction. Cortés sprang into action. In the space of thirty days, he had gathered more than six ships and more than three hundred adventurers from the newly established towns of the largest island in the Caribbean. He let the Trade Winds push him the short distance from Cuba to the shores of Yucatan and then on to the place which was to become Veracruz.

In the end, a full complement of eleven ships, five hundred soldiers, one hundred sailors and sixteen horses were present at the founding of *La Villa Rica de la Veracruz*. It was these six hundred men who – having finished tracing out the *plaza grande*, *casa del gobierno* and *casa episcopal* of their newly christened Rich City of the True Cross – then turned to face Montezuma and the six million people who paid homage to him.

★

The days of wealth and glory had passed but the twenty million up there had to be confronted. And not just the people – they were burning something unpleasant, too, in late twentieth-century Mexico City. That notorious Pemex refinery? Old rubber tyres? Some kind of chemical waste? Fuel from rubbish? Whatever it was, the air around the terminal building was struggling under the burden.

And everyday life in Mexico City was more complex than Cortés had found for most of his stay in Tenochtitlan. The hire and use of a car in the capital, for instance, was carefully regulated so as to not overburden an atmosphere already weighed down with petrochemicals. One day of each week was a 'no go' day for drivers – the selected day being determined (rather in the cryptic fashion of a Mayan stela) by reading number plates. All those with nine-endings were off the road mid-week, those with three-endings had Mondays out and those with number fives could come in on Fridays. Hire cars were mostly out on Wednesdays.

It was perhaps fortunate, in one sense, that it was Sunday. In another sense, however, this ecological day off meant that the full complement of the capital's drivers was out on the road and moving about. A great stream of private and commercial vehicles moved fast down an Avenida Oriente. Entering its flow was like launching a coracle in a tide-race. The main thoroughfare, called Insurgentes Norte, seemed no better. Indeed, that formidable torrent – which gathered up the cars and trucks of the Avenidas and then allowed them to thunder north and south on a wide passage through the city – made you wonder whether twenty million people living cheek-by-jowl on only twenty square miles of lake-bed was really a good idea.

The land beyond the lake-bed rose up as dry hills. These loomed above the city's edge – an industrial fringe of ramshackle sheds, workshops and manufacturing plant clinging to the northwards exit to the metropolis. This gave way to an inevitable halo of *ciudadas perdidas* – that ragged, poverty-stricken hem around nearly all Latin American cities. Bare earth glittered with fragments of broken glass. Drifts of rubbish smouldered amongst primitive breeze-block or corrugated-iron-and-cardboard shacks. There was no sign of water, sanitation, roadways, electric lighting or anything else that made being part of the great metropolis marginally worthwhile – and all this in the cool but tainted air of 7,000 feet.

Surely, life must have been better two thousand years ago in the ancient city of Teotihuacan which lay in the undulating country thirty miles to the north of Mexico City.

But were those ruins of Teotihuacan really once a city? There was no doubt that it must have once possessed a first or second century equivalent to the fringe of sheds and workshops, 'cottage industry' and *ciudadas perdidas* that had finally given way to farmland on leaving modern Mexico City. Teotihuacan stood at the heart of a society which appeared to have derived a great deal of wealth from making and trading useful artifacts and such activity inevitably created the litter of industry. Craftsmen were producing useful things in Teotihuacan and putting their cultural stamp all over Central America at the same time as the Romans in the Old World were putting theirs over north-west Europe and the fringes of the Mediterranean. The city's pottery and figurines were widely sought after in the area which later became Mexico. Obsidian objects were even more widely prized: blades, knives, dart points and scrapers from far and wide have been traced back to Teotihuacan. Cultural complexity and trading links (as has been suggested by recent studies of the ruins) could have been as diverse as not only those of the Roman Empire but the more varied relationships of Renaissance Venice or modern Hong Kong.

A sort of second-century Hong Kong with pyramids? No, that didn't seem to fit – not after seeing the scale of Teotihuacan's monumental buildings. These spread over a huge site and suggested an ordered metropolis planned around a ceremonial axis – an axis which ran like an avenue towards two great pyramids. In the green hills and rough grassland which now surrounded Teotihuacan, they were monumental structures seemed oddly out of place.

The Aztecs had called these structures the 'Pyramid of the Sun' and the 'Pyramid of the Moon'. Not original names and now applied to rough-surfaced rock mounds which reflected back only their vast elemental mass and little of their original glory. Once upon a time, bright paintwork on stucco or plaster had probably given these steeply stepped surfaces an added power and symbolism, but only traces of this surface covering now remained. Early twentieth-century 'renovation' had – for the most part – devastatingly and inexplicably chipped it off. Shorn of their outer layer, the pyramids presented only a rusty-coloured undersurface on each side. From a distance this made them look like massive, bevelled slag heaps.

But sheer man-made mass is always impressive. The pyramids in reduced circumstances still made Teotihuacan seem a very different place from Chichen Itza in Yucatan: a bigger place; older; more ordered; more megalithic. A city that was ancient when the Mayan cities were being built and even more ancient when the Aztecs began their rule not so very far away in Tenochtitlan. A city now hidden and only briefly glimpsed behind the romantic but rather trite names which the Aztecs had put to its site and its main features in an attempt to embrace its builders as part of their ancestral heritage. Teotihuacan – 'the place where the gods were made'. That was not what the original inhabitants had called it. They were the gods. When the Spanish first arrived, huge stone idols of a 'sun god' and a 'moon goddess' stood on the summits of Teotihuacan's pyramids. In being awed by these great carved figures, Montezuma and his priests were much further in time from the people who had placed them there than he was from the traffic which now roared unceasingly across the buried foundations of his city of the lake.

Spanish priests later had the idols destroyed, but the tops of the ancient structures were by no means empty. Sunday in nearby Mexico City meant that it was everybody's turn to contribute to that traffic flow pouring out of the lake bed and away from sector counts of sulphur dioxide, nitrogen dioxide or carbon monoxide. The once sacred summits of their ancestors' monuments were beset with visitors: grannies arrived breathless; mothers chatted together; fathers took photographs of the view; sons raced each other up and down the pre-summit terraces; daughters changed the cassettes on their walkmans and the metropolitan world had its picnic lunch wherever space was available. It was curious to find the top of a pyramid so crowded. There was something of 'The Raft of the Medusa' in it. At the very top, a small lad was even waving a tee-shirt and pointing into the far distance.

At ground level, a similar bustling scene took place where ceremonial processions had once wound their way towards what must have been regarded by the original inhabitants of Teotihuacan as celestial stairways to another, cosmic world. But now that twenty million people lived close by and it was a long way to the sea, a sense of spiritual reverence for the cosmos was difficult to sustain. Especially as, amongst the families eating lunch and the constant coming and going of visitors, the *ambulantes* swarmed like flies – the wandering vendors of obsidian, peddlers of flutes, hawkers of silver bangles who buzzed like bees around a huge honey-pot.

However, through such low-grade and chaotic commercialisation, the power and scale of the place insisted on emerging wherever the eye left the obvious monuments and swept across the rise and fall of the surrounding countryside. Teotihuacan was everywhere: some parts half-excavated and stretching away to the west as a pattern of huge geometrically-ordered squares, rectangles, shallow steps and wide stone plinths; other parts – further away and under land that was still cultivated – revealed by grassy humps suggesting more of the city extending below the surface for several miles. Looked at in its entirety, the site seemed as if it had been built as a single entity – a planned metropolis like Brazilia – worked out on some second-century drawing board and then constructed on the Central American scene where no metropolis had ever been built before. There was the shadow of a huge grid plan in which modern research had detected precise astronomical alignments. It appeared that Mexican Teotihuacan – like Egyptian Giza – pointed to certain star patterns.

A ceremonial centre, then. But how did it feed its workers – those who made all the knives and other artifacts, and created its wealth? Who were the overseers who organised such urbanity and who set and enforced the rules which allowed it to flourish from the second century to the eighth century? Priests? Ministers of a king? A mix of both? Did some kind of theocratic aristocracy live an easy life amongst shrubs and fountains, cushions, courtesans and private courtyards, whilst others toiled in shacks? Was existence for some measured in obsidian chips and for others in sips of chocolate and nibbles of the cooked flesh of a special breed of dog? Was the place riddled with treachery and intrigue? How did those in Teotihuacan get on with those from the emergent Mayan culture further south? Were they all the same people and all really part of the same culture?

Insufficient knowledge has been passed down the centuries to tell a clear story. Only stones which indicate the common thread of Quetzalcoatl link the beliefs of the people of Teotihuacan with those of the Mayas. A link manifest in a large temple dedicated to the Feathered Serpent which has been excavated in Teotihuacan and lies at a central point near the pyramids of the Sun and the Moon; its presence shows that there was undoubtedly some kind of cultural continuum in the history of the Central American peoples.

Another common thread was that Teotihuacan and the Mayan societies all appeared to have collapsed about the same time. Perhaps the former disappeared slightly earlier and the latter lingered on somewhat later in remote spots (or was taken over by others), but their joint disappearance remains a curious historical fact. Was it due to an early wave of smallpox sweeping across the Americas? Had an Old World ship carrying infection been blown by the Trade Winds across the Atlantic in the centuries before Columbus and never returned home? Did disease spread southwards down the Pacific coast from what is now the Far East of Russia? Did pestilence move slowly into Central America from some animal-borne source – like rabies or bubonic plague? Was it something else – climatic or cultural?

Whatever it was, in the eighth century it emptied the obsidian workshops and the palaces, the temples and the ceremonial and cosmological structures. All over Central America, too, Quetzalcoatl was left almost alone.

Another rainstorm swept across Mexico on the route back to the twentieth-century metropolis. It was – after all – the hurricane season in the Caribbean and such storms had to go somewhere. Like the axis of the ancient city which had been given the name 'Avenue of the Dead', the axis of Insurgentes Norte (the modern Mexico City's avenue of the struggling-to-live), quickly turned into the site of heavy traffic splashing through cascading waters. Traffic moved across the city until it reached the major crossing point of the Paseo de la Reforma. There all came to a stop. At the point where southbound traffic on Insurgentes Norte met east or westbound traffic on Paseo de la Reforma one of the world's worst urban nightmares began to unfold. The rain was falling vertically on twenty million people of Latin temperament squeezed into polluted air hanging darkly over a former lake-bed whose main traffic-light system had suddenly stopped working. At the junction of Insurgentes Norte and Sud with Paseo de la Reforma, a kind of arrested whirlpool of road users developed which gradually edged itself into an immobility so dense that it seemed as if only a fleet of tank-lifting military helicopters could ever succeed in untangling the mess. It was a jam you could spend the night in.

*

It eventually untangled before night fell. Not far away, the resinous pinewoods of Cuernavaca replaced the noxious fumes of the capital of Mexico with their sweet evening fragrance. Even Cortés had opted for the place. It was on the old colonial trade route from the Caribbean to the

Pacific – from Veracruz to Acapulco. Westwards through Cuernavaca went settlers, and the necessities of life in the Far East; eastwards came Chinese silks and spices from the furthest frontier of the Spanish New World. From the Philippines. After Mexico and the Americas, the *conquistadores* had made the greatest leap of all. Across that huge ocean which Balboa and de Bastidos briefly glimpsed from Darien. The fearsome ten thousand mile journey. The real journey off the edge of the Earth that Columbus had half-expected.

Somehow, it was all different in the mid 1500s, things had changed a lot in fifty years. An enormous confidence had grown. Convoys were already bringing back the gold from Cartagena to Seville. The silver was beginning to flow out of Potosí. The first exploratory voyages had begun on the huge ocean, whilst the news of far shores and a circumnavigated world had been stirring the minds of adventurers ever since the remnants of Magellan's expedition arrived back in Seville port in 1522.

It was not long after that momentous voyage into the unknown that the crossing and recrossing of the Pacific began and the great maritime leap to the islands of the South China Sea was finally made. Columbus had been right after all. By sailing west it was possible to reach the east; to reach the wealth of Cathay and the islands of spice. The islands which were named after the Spanish king. By ship to Hispaniola or Cuba or Yucatan was only part of the route. By mule train backwards and forwards on the road over the Sierras from Veracruz to Cuernavaca and down to Acapulco was only another part. A new ocean had then to be crossed as well as a New World; an ocean passage which was three times the distance that the *Santa Maria* had nervously sailed across the Atlantic those few decades before.

Cuernavaca lay forty miles south of Mexico City and 2,300 feet lower. It was still raining there. The town spread down a long hillside. As the storm increased, so did the downpour. So heavily were sheets of water surging through the lower part of the town that most streets were soon seriously awash. Cuernavaca's narrow lanes became mountain streams; torrents swirled around the wheels of parked cars as if they were boulders in the stream-bed; waterfalls cascaded down steps and over low walls; dips and twists in the road became swelling pools of uncertain depth. Night decided to fall. There was no room at any of the inns.

*

Well, there was a room at one: an establishment hidden behind a nondescript door opening off a nondescript backstreet and charging ferociously high prices. There was no choice. It even appeared to be raining inside the building.

Somehow – as Robert Frost once wrote – that made all the difference! The shabby exterior hid a magical interior. An interior which had changed little since the eighteenth century. A stone-flagged, timbered passageway leading around two sides of a luxuriant garden. A colonial inn whose interior space had somehow turned the coarse wet storm beyond its outer perimeter into a harmless shower. Rain was entering inside the building but it did so only on best behaviour – pattering and dripping quietly off leaf and blossom until delicately soaking away amongst the clipped turf of a well-cut lawn. A lamp shone through bougainvillaea blossom. There was a fountain. Red tiles and ancient wooden beams roofed the passageway. Rooms with shuttered doors led off on the side opposite the garden. Earthenware pots caught the merest drip on the open side. Chests of dark oak lined whitewashed stonework – furniture with a long pedigree and which could well have received boots and mud-stained cloaks from the ride up through the high sierras; the ride from the Pacific or the climb from the Atlantic. Another Mexico. Not the fistful of dollars Mexico – a gentler and more civilised Spanish-American country.

The place was even more beautiful when seen by the fresh sunlight of early morning and over a breakfast table partly shaded by the slatted light of old wooden shutters. Bees hummed in the flowers just outside; the ripple of the fountain could be faintly heard now the pattering and dripping of rain was no more; the delicate perfume of pine resin was again in the air; the intensely purple and deep claret red of the bougainvillaea glowed in its frame of greenery. A morning bell tolled in the direction of Cuernavaca's cathedral. Was this garden really in the New World? Was this really New Spain and not Old Andalucia? Was it not in Mexico but in the warm south of Europe?

It was hardly surprising to discover afterwards that even before the days of sector counts and dioxide levels in the city above and to the north, Aztec nobles had – pre-Cortés – chosen to escape the hustle, bustle and market crowds of Tenochtitlan by retreating to the blossoms and pines of Cuernavaca.

Poor old Mexico City up on the lake-bed. Not only was the air still in serious difficulties and the traffic likely soon to tie itself into a permanent gridlock – there was also something wrong with the foundations.

Monday morning and Mass over, its great cathedral in the central plaza looked as if it could hardly hold itself up long enough for the next service to take place. No view of nave, pillars and distant alter met the eye of anyone passing through the massive doors; instead the place was choked with scaffolding. It was the largest and oldest church in Latin America but a sort of internal green lattice framework seemed to be required to hold almost every stone in position and which must have made even the simplest attempt at worshipping a major challenge.

Outside – like dry rot or cracked walls, once an awareness of the problem had been revealed at one location – it was suddenly seen all over the place. Almost every one of the rather dark and grimy buildings around the square either leaned, dipped or bent as the ground on which it stood had either slowly withdrawn its support over the centuries or had rudely lurched up and down in September 1985. The buildings were, of course, suffering from a double problem: not only were they standing on the shifting silts of a former lake-bed; they were also situated on a periodically active earthquake zone.

This sagging *plaza grande* – the Zocolo – marked the centre point of colonial Mexico City. And underneath colonial Mexico City, it had also been the central point of Tenochtitlan – the foundations of the Aztec palaces, temples, libraries, workshops, Montezuma's great halls of justice and all the other structures which the men of Cortés had razed to the ground as efficiently as the first archbishop of Merida had 'culturally cleansed' the written history of the Mayas. The now-buried lake-city of Tenochtitlan was no mean place (although its 500,000 inhabitants paled into the background when confronted by a modern metropolitan overprint of 20 million). Nonetheless, after

Cortés had completed the climb up the Sierra Oriental and first glimpsed its causeways and its many palaces and temples he was totally amazed. So – later – was Bernal Diaz del Castillo who saw Tenochtitlan's ruins in 1568. It was a view which made him exclaim: '*...for it is one thing to read a description like mine of a city such as this and quite another to see it with one's own eyes, in all its strength and grandeur.*'

In the incredibly short time of one hundred years (from 1428 – when they were a subject state to others around them – to 1519), the Aztecs of this lake city capital had developed a vast power structure. They lay at the centre of a spider's web of allegiance which extended their empire over hundreds of vassal states the length and breadth of Central America. Under the colonial viceroy's palace were the three hundred rooms of Montezuma's Palace; under the cathedral was the Aztec Templo Mayor; under the buildings and roads leading into the Zocolo were the three great causeways; ceremonial access routes from the north, south and west which also served as dykes – hydraulic regulators which could be used to control the volume of water in the lake and to inhibit flooding. And under the rest of the early colonial Mexico City still lay the foundations of the houses, libraries, palaces, canals, wide streets and market gardens of Tenochtitlan; all – like nearby Teotihuacan a thousand years earlier – seemingly constructed quickly but gloriously from nowhere. The Aztecs had not built cities previously. Suddenly they conceived and constructed and made reality an urban masterpiece which rivalled the great cities of contemporary Europe.

This magnificent place fell to the Spanish on 13th August 1521, and they took great pains to destroy what was left standing after the fire and pillage of the conquest. The halls of Montezuma crashed to the ground and the stones were re-used in the first buildings of the new Mexico City. The Aztec kingdom died with its king. After presents of precious feathers, gold and silver had failed to send Cortés and his men (and a large body of rebelling anti-Aztec indigenous forces) ignominiously back to Veracruz, Montezuma was lost. His fate had been prophesied. The fall of the empire seemed inevitable. The Spanish had come from the east.

What followed is well-known: the role of the princess Malinche; the death of Montezuma by the arrows of his own people (or, perhaps, the strangling hands of the Spanish); the muddle and near-failure of the grip of the Spanish in the 'Night of Sorrows', and, finally, the street-by-street fighting in the golden city in the lake of the *conquistadores* and their allies as they battled with the Aztecs for final supremacy.

★

Despite the abundant raw materials offered by the dismantling of the Aztec city, some parts of the new Mexico City were an incredibly long time in construction. From start to finish, the cathedral was under construction for an incredible 288 years. Work began in 1525 and finished in 1813. As slow as the monumental growth of the Spanish Empire was; the destruction of the Aztec Empire took only a few short years. In the capital and across Central America, work on massive stone temples to Quetzalcoatl and other gods ceased immediately. All objects of ritual significance were destroyed – this was the time when the idols of sun and moon were pulled down from the pyramids of Teotihuacan. From its primary position in

Montezuma's palace, the 'Stone of the Sun' (the Aztec calendar stone) disappeared for over four centuries – ending up (until recently) as construction material for one of the cathedral towers. The cruelty of human sacrifice also stopped. The gods were dead; the entire world of the Central American societies was passing away.

*

Viewed from a distance, those societies of Central America which ended with the arrival of Cortés seemed all part of the same cultural continuum – a continuum with the fascinating characteristic of suddenly, in a few decades, bursting into cultural flower and creating planned cities where there was no evidence of similar activities preceding them. Montezuma (the ninth Aztec king) occupied the throne at the last cultural flowering. A king who ruled over an ever-expanding empire devoted to appeasing a god who threatened to return some day in the form of a bearded white man arriving from the east. Quite how seriously a constraint this was on his ability to defend the Aztec state will never be known. But it could not be overlooked that – on a date which had apparently been earlier predicted by the Aztec priesthood – a bearded white man did arrive from the east. A man with six hundred followers who, of course, was not Quetzalcoatl but Hernando Cortés. The prophecy was valid but like all prophecies it was also vague and insubstantial and open to many interpretations. Like the forms, power and origins of Quetzalcoatl.

Quetzalcoatl. Who was he? The Templo Major was his temple – a place where it was reported that twenty thousand human sacrifices had to be made each year. It was the building whose distorted stone foundations still underpinned a corner of the main square in colonial Mexico City and which was still visible in the twentieth century. It was less than five hundred years ago, after all, that the Aztec worship of him was in full spate.

But Quetzalcoatl was a god with a history much longer than five hundred years or so. The second century builders of Teotihuacan worshipped his form. And Quetzalcoatl was a god whom the several overlapping but very different societies had all revered. The Maya of Chichen Itza linked him into the ceremony of renewal when they built the dominating two hundred-foot high structure there called '*El Castillo*'. Called a castle but not a castle. More a calendar in stone. Each of the staircases which ran up its four sloping pyramidal sides had 365 steps. The number of stone panels it possessed amounted to 52. There were nine terraces on four faces; its arrangement of 365 steps resulted in eighteen sections. It was no coincidence that there were eighteen months in the Maya calendar. *El Castillo* was a building – like medieval Chartres cathedral – which had a structure suffused with such interlocking cosmic subtlety that the placing of every stone probably had specific meaning. Woven centrally into all this meaning was Quetzalcoatl.

At *El Castillo*, Quetzalcoatl was seasonally resurrected by the sun. The building might well have been built solely to celebrate his rebirth. It joined the cosmos with the society by creating – at the time of the vernal and autumnal equinox and for a period of ten minutes – a great 'serpent' of sunshine and shadow (as two of the faces of the pyramid caught the light), which came gradually into view and slowly undulated down the flank of the structure. (It still does come but induced more regularly by *son et lumière.*) For the reverential Maya watchers, out of the cosmos came Quetzalcoatl to perform a slow dance of light and dark down the slope of *El Castillo* until it joined with the large head of the god carved in stone at its base. At these times, the illusion was complete and very powerful. The Feathered Serpent had come to life.

But how – and why – did this omnipresent Central American god come to demand so much of the lives of those wrapped in its power? Just across from the ceremonial space which surrounded *El Castillo* lay the skull racks of Chichen Itza – a large rectangular platform seemingly devoid of menace until the visitor noticed that it was not human faces but human skulls that were carved on its four sides. And – on now-vanished wooden scaffolding which covered its flat upper surface – the early Spanish also reported real skulls, the preservation of thousands of human cadavers. This was the repository of the sacrificed; the social cost of appeasing Quetzalcoatl. It was apparently the only way that the Mayans (and the overlapping Toltecs) could be the sure that the sun would rise each day and the rains come and the leaves grow and the flowers blossom and the fruit ripen. Death came to play an essential part in life – a belief which could not be regarded as unique to Central America. The process was necessary to ensure that Quetzalcoatl remained in control of the cosmos and thereby continued to come to life each equinox and move down *El Castillo*. For those caught in its awesome mindset, it was the only way of staving off disaster: of keeping the Earth from shuddering and breathing fire and ash; of making the stars maintain their rightful course in the heavens; of holding the universe back from destruction.

Valid fears, of course. But why so strong and all-pervasive? Why did this belief in Quetzalcoatl place such an onerous burden on the peoples of Central America?

The land that is Mexico is racked from time to time by earthquakes. Hoping to appease the random shaking of the earth by close attention to the cosmos could be a contributory factor. But why did the appeasement need to go so far? Other societies coexisted with earthquake and volcanic eruption without need for large-scale human sacrifice. Ancient societies like the Cretans and the Javanese, for example. Much of what is now the Indonesian archipelago was and is a 'ring of fire' – dense populations crowding around the flanks of a chain of volcanoes and supported by the fertility of the weathered ash. But there is no evidence that – through time – those societies felt so precariously balanced in the maw of Nature that enormous human sacrifices had to be made to maintain the *status quo*.

★

Perhaps some pointers lay in other aspects of the Feathered Serpent. Quetzalcoatl was a composite deity. He assumed many forms and many names. To the Maya, he was also known as Kukulcan. Also Ehecatl – the Lord of the Wind. He had an association with the planet Venus which – for the Maya – was the planet above all planets. They called Venus 'the Great Star'. The planet was 'Venus the Red Star'; 'Venus the Bright Star' and '*xux ek*' – 'Venus the Wasp Star'. The first Spanish colonists noticed that the Maya adored and made more sacrifices to that celestial body than to any other deity. Many of those ruins which have recently been identified as possessing a close relationship with astronomical features were concerned with sighting the trajectory of Venus. Venus, Orion and the Pleides were given particular attention and accurately observed and followed. But, for the Maya, it was Venus which rose from the ashes of the sun as the light declined at the ending of day and it was Venus which came again in the darkness before dawn to announce the return of the light.

The movements of Venus could be predicted by the Mayan priests and yet – curiously – when its bright rays appeared in the darkness before dawn they were objects of fear and not reverence. To the Maya, it seemed to be a fear of a light which could pierce the atmosphere like an arrow, of a light which could kill, give rise to pestilence and be a force for destruction. This was Venus the Wasp Star – *xux ek*. According to its changing position in the Maya year, the malevolent rays of this Wasp Star could touch on old men and women at one time; little children at another time; kings at another; the rain at another; youths and maidens at another. Confusingly, these bright rays came from a Venus which was not only known as *xux ek* but also as the deity called Kukulcan. And Kukulcan was another name for Quetzalcoatl.

> *...at a time when the planet was visible in the sky as the evening star, Quetzalcoatl died. And when Quetzalcoatl was dead he was not seen for four days and they said he dwelt in the underworld. And for four more days he was weak. Not until eight days had passed did the great star appear as the morning star. They said then that Quetzalcoatl ascended the throne as god... (Anales de Quauhtitlan)*

The man-god Quetzalcoatl-Kukulcan. Quetzalcoatl – the Aztec counterpart of Kukulcan. Quetzalcoatl identified with Ehecatl, the wind god. Quetzalcoatl identified with Tlahuizcalpantecuhli – 'the Lord of the House of Dawn'. The Lord of the House of Dawn who was Venus; Venus the Morning Star.

★

Quetzalcoatl – to the people of Teotihuacan – was associated with the character of a god who brought notions of universal love, who taught people how to apply the science of agriculture and how to use the calendar, who gave men means to understand the stars.

Quetzalcoatl – to the Maya and the Toltecs – was a god of the morning and the evening star.

Quetzalcoatl – to the Aztecs – was a patron of priests, an inventor of calendars, a source of learning, a lover of books and of writing.

Quetzalcoatl in form was to some a feathered serpent (the *quetzal* being a precious feather and the *coatl* being a snake) whilst to others – like Montezuma – he was a bearded white man who would arrive from the east. And even more strangely, Quetzalcoatl could appear in the guise of the wind god Ehecatl who was a deity uniquely hidden behind a mask from which protruded two short tubes.

Quetzalcoatl as a symbol of death and resurrection. The regular disappearance and reappearance of Venus in the heavens symbolised a departing and a returning. Quetzalcoatl as a god who arrived from the west and departed in the east; a god wandering across the breadth of Central America to the edge of the 'divine water' (the Caribbean/ Atlantic) with a promise of return. Quetzalcoatl as a god who disappeared eastwards on a raft made of snakes.

A shifting and confused picture. Shifting – like something seen through a kaleidoscope. A moving target – changing from one vantage point to another like kaleidoscopic patterns. The same colours making up a myriad of different combinations. Nothing clear, nothing certain. Perhaps – in the case of Quetzalcoatl – made doubly unclear and doubly uncertain when seen across a cultural frontier and when translated across the utterly different cultures of pre-Columban America and the world of Catholic Europe. Some aspects real; some misunderstood; some allegorical; some illusory. Much that became – over the centuries – a jumbled mixture of myth and legend, spiritual insight and real events.

Supposing that kaleidoscopic picture of Quetzalcoatl was shaken-up and searched for meaning; read like tea-leaves or Etruscan chicken livers. What might be there?

For some, perhaps, patterns which spelt out the names of Immanuel Velikovsky or Eric Von Danikan. For others – a fantasy – something closer to the plot of an episode of *Star Trek* or *Dr Who*.

And how much significance could be attached to that sudden growth of the Central American cities; to that central planning of Teotihuacan and to those complex alignments of Mayan cultural centres which facilitated such a sophisticated tracking of the planets and stars? How much significance could be ascribed to a Quetzalcoatl as the god of learning and a Quetzalcoatl – incongruously – as the god of love. How could this god of love be reconciled with a Quetzalcoatl who was a god of punishment; the ominous *xux ek* who could send harmful rays of light to those on the ground, commanding respect and awe.

How much significance could be ascribed to the fact that Quetzalcoatl first seemed to come on to the Central American cultural stage at the time of the Roman Empire – the time of Christ?

Did Quetzalcoatl – seen through a glass darkly – share any parallels with a Christ figure? Or a St Thomas figure – an apostle who appeared to have travelled remarkably far afield and who had somehow inserted himself into the South American pantheon as a credible spiritual force, despite the extreme unlikelihood of his having crossed the Atlantic more than a thousand years before Columbus? Did some form of Quetzalcoatl-worship live on in modern Central America – a worship thinly cloaked in the vestments of Christianity but nonetheless still a spiritual force?

A Quetzalcoatl of love becoming confused with representatives of the Christian message. But what of that darker side to the god's personality. The power to hurt. The association with Venus the Wasp Star. Where did that belief have its origins?

Quetzalcoatl-Kukulcan came from the west and disappeared over the eastern horizon. He came like the Venus which represented him in the cosmos of the Central American societies. But for what?

As a 'god' advising and teaching? As a 'god' – perhaps – who also had a pressing need to uncover the source of life? As a 'god' with a curiosity to understand what lay at the very root of life? As a 'god' seeking knowledge of what cosmic significance lay between the fact of living and the fact of death. Deep questions – still unanswered five hundred years on. Was a probing of the meaning of life the quest that the original Quetzalcoatl – 'the teacher' – might have been on? Did he find the answer?

If such a quest did take place, was it a coincidence that an obvious place to search for the motivator of life was the mysterious energy source which powered the inherent rhythmicity of cardiac muscle? Did Quetzalcoatl demand that the secrets of the human heart be unravelled? Was this process of unravelling the macabre act which caught and embedded itself into the consciousness of the Central

American peoples? Did Quetzalcoatl first select individuals as 'laboratory' subjects. Did Quetzalcoatl the feathered serpent (or, perhaps, Quetzalcoatl/ Ehecatl – the wind deity wearing the mask with the air tubes) demand that many hearts be opened in the search for an answer? And was the diversity of form presented by Quetzalcoatl an indicator that more than one 'god' undertook this quest? Did he (or they) impose a strange legacy of heart removal as a central part of the spiritual process of Central America? Did this search become muddled and incorporated into a monstrous process of appeasement after he (or they) had left?

*

Perhaps he (or they?) found the answer; perhaps not. But the manner of Quetzalcoatl's leaving seemed important. The departure had a relationship with Venus in the heavens. It was a going which appeared to Central American observers like a journey to the east and across the sea. A journey with its beginning on Earth, but where was its end?

After the going, powerful memories were all that was left amongst the Central American peoples. A serpent-like form. A dominant image which then become carved on a thousand stones throughout the region. A returning – some day – from the direction of departure in the east.

A returning of Quetzalcoatl played heavily on the mind of Montezuma and his advisers when he and they first heard of bearded men landing from the east – men from that divine water across which the god had departed. Bearded men with mysterious power and who were approaching through the kingdom of the Aztecs with strange animals, strange weapons and bright armour.

Cortés, however, was not from the stars – he was from Spain. And he had come not to bring the Central American gods to life but to destroy them.

Chapter Two

Weekend in the Dominican Republic and Cuba

Scotland 1881. Grey hills and dark damp trees – a slight winter coolness lingering in the August afternoon air. Hard to imagine the balmy caress of the Trade Winds or the sound of blue water surging through the scuppers under an ocean swell. It was in such a landscape and on a wet August afternoon in Braemar, Scotland, that Robert Louis Stevenson began one of the most marvellous adventure stories ever written. The tale of a map and of a Caribbean island; a tale originally titled *The Sea Cook* and written at the speed of a chapter a day despite interruption caused by illness. A tale which was finished and ready for serialisation in a children's magazine by the beginning of October, 1881.

Treasure Island was published in book form soon after. The narrative quickly captured a wider adult audience with its taste of the roving life, the complex subtlety of Long John Silver, and the sunshine and colour of the West Indies. And with the unfolding of the story of pirates and their treasure came the passages of imagery: the schooner *Hispaniola* 'rolling steadily, dipping her bowsprit now and then with a whiff of spray' as she neared her destination; the first glimpse of a moonlit Spyglass Hill when a belt of night fog lifted and the words '*Land-ho*' reached young Jim Hawkins as he hid in the apple barrel.

★

A Caribbean island – suddenly flashing brilliant green out of an empty sea. Even from the air, such a landfall can still come unexpectedly in the way that Treasure Island appeared to the watchers on the *Hispaniola*. It was Hispaniola which I caught sight of in mid-afternoon, in May 1992 on an Air Dominicana flight from Caracas. The island of Hispaniola, that is – now shared between the Dominican Republic and Haiti and appearing below the starboard wing. Not fog but a high, furrowed cloud parted to reveal its eastern promontory through the port-hole – a finger of land in a deep blue sea. A century had passed since Robert Louis Stevenson set down the tale of Treasure Island and two or three since the real buccaneers roamed the waters and islands which lay partly visible below. The rollicking seventeenth and eighteenth centuries had passed and with them had vanished the rogues of that time. The pirates were no more.

Or had they simply become less obvious? The island of Hispaniola – although second largest in the Caribbean – is just over half the size of neighbouring Cuba. The Dominican Republic occupies almost two-thirds of its land mass, with Haiti taking up the remaining third. Both countries have populations of between five and seven million but the Dominican Republic's GNP per head is twice that of Haiti. The distinction is one of relative poverty – both countries lie at the bottom of the economic ladder in the West Indies. The Cayman Islands has a GNP fifty-six times higher than that of Haiti. In such low income environments do twentieth century pirates still flourish – they have nothing to lose, after all. Even the authorities are loath to miss an opportunity. Passing through such dangerous waters, the lone tourist can do nothing but stand out like a brightly lit galleon did to the likes of Billy Bones or Captain Flint.

With landfall there is always a change of pace – whether arriving from the sea or by air. Air Dominicana was quicker at it than most. The pilot of the Boeing 727 was still at 10,000 ft when the clouds parted, but he had no qualms in getting down on to the runway in the shortest possible time. Instead of the careful circling descent normally expected of a 727, we began a steepish dive which flattened out at 3,000 ft into a tight bend with the port wing dipping steeply towards the banana groves and steamy grassland. Thousands of feet quickly became hundreds. A deathly silence lay over the passenger cabin until – almost imperceptibly – wheels touched tarmac, the brakes were applied and a nervous clapping broke out amongst those who would rather have approached Hispaniola after the fashion of R.L.S.

The Dominican Republic was a stop-over. Getting to Castro's Communist Cuba in the early 1990s still required some circumspection in the countries around the Caribbean. The final leg to Havana was by Iberian Airways and the trans-Atlantic flight from Spain did not put into Santo Domingo airport until the evening. There was an afternoon to spend in one of the earliest of the New World settlements.

*

It was a swelteringly hot afternoon on the ground. The blue Caribbean was no longer the azure and inviting body of encircling water it had seemed from the air. Now it glinted metallically through the palm trees – a sea which had much the same steel-grey look about it as when the first Europeans (led by Bartolome Columbus – one of Christopher's brothers) arrived in 1496 and set about marking their presence in the New World. Before the year's end, the city of Santo Domingo had been founded on what they named as La Isla Española and from this early Spanish outpost the great adventuring began: Diego de Velázquez to Cuba; Cortés to Mexico; Balboa to the Pacific. Those were heroic days in the early sixteenth century – a tide of discovery sweeping over the South and Central Americas in less than fifty years leaving some men rich and famous and many others dead from heat, cold, spear thrust or poison. Its tide also left Santo Domingo in a state of slow decline as the empires of the Inca and Aztec lords drew interest (and greed) further west and south.

Hispaniola in the twentieth century: a pleasant but somewhat tarted-up old city, a ramshackle republic with some true but rather grandiose claims to be the founding state of the Spanish Empire. In more recent years there was also, of course, the uncomfortable history of dictatorships and a poor record in the area of human rights.

Palm trees stretched away landward in all directions. Santo Domingo was clearly more than a short stroll out from the terminal building. This eastern promontory of the large island appeared much more substantial on the ground than when seen from the air. People had become substantial, too. A throng of grandly proportioned Afro-Caribbean ladies milled about expansively on the hot concrete outside the terminal as they and their baggage commandeered every square inch in three taxis which stood waiting somewhat apprehensively for incoming flights. As these vehicles bounced heavily off to the west only Nelly Rent-a-Car was left as an option. A car hire firm but – at first glance – of the type where not only the vehicle was rented but also an attendant mechanic. As I completed the paperwork for a day's hire, the feet and oily overalled legs of one of the Nelly mechanics jerked convulsively beneath the bodywork of a battered Chevrolet as last minute adjustments to the transmission took place. The Chevy was the only Nelly car in sight – an elderly vehicle with an unfinished two-tone cream and brown re-spray and a hole in the exhaust pipe.

It behaved exactly like the raunchy old-timer it looked: well-upholstered, well-used, noisy and with an engine which cut out when it was most needed. The Nelly man waved his spanner encouragingly and made a forwards-pushing movement with one of his feet as the automatic gearing jerked the car away from the office. It was not the first time he had made that gesture. 'Try harder' he could be faintly heard shouting in Spanish as I gingerly circled the palm-lined airport access road before setting off westwards for the city centre.

★

A coastal avenue led sweepingly away from the airport and was marked at regular intervals by concrete plinths which did their best to draw the New World back to this second largest island of the Caribbean. I passed Argentina, embodied as a plinth, then Ecuador, then Colombia, Venezuela and Cuba. The traffic began to increase and buses and trucks must have blotted out Mexico, Chile,

Paraguay and Uruguay. By the time I had managed to catch a glimpse of the next piece of concrete, the Dominican Republic was claiming to be the founding state of the United States and Canada. World aspirations to the Philippines and beyond were cut short by the arrival of the capital. Shacks took over from palm trees and plinths. Diesel fumes pumped into the hot air from a slow-moving stream of overloaded trucks and crammed buses. A long girder bridge spanned foetid-looking dockland waters.

This was the port of Santo Domingo where the ships of the Columbus expeditions had come and gone in the 1490s – probing out from their first Caribbean base for signs that the mainland of China had been reached. Not the *Santa Maria*, of course, which had borne the initial expedition across the Atlantic to reach landfall at the tiny Bahamian island of San Salvador. The *Santa Maria* had then made it to Hispaniola (or *Española* – the Spanish Island – as it was first named by Christopher Columbus) but had run aground on the north coast at midnight on Christmas Day, 1492. The little caravel broke up and never reached the site where the earliest of the Spanish cities of the Americas was founded not long after.

Apart from Santo Domingo, there was not much left of those other early settlements on *Española*: Villa de Navidad; Isabella and Santo Tomas.

Perhaps that was why the Columbus Lighthouse had been sited somewhere just off the Avenida de Las Americas.

★

I should have realised that a turn-off to the left was required before reaching the bridge, but direction-finding was difficult in the midst of conflicting traffic streams. As vehicles converged towards the city centre they met others trying to leave and the result was a great deal of crossing and turning as buses, trucks and more raunchy old cruisers tried to get on or off the narrow span over the river Ozama and the port area. Acting promptly and leaving the main highway then would have been far more cost-effective. But as well as the traffic, the Chevy itself needed a lot of concentration – even though progress had slowed to only a few miles per hour. Pedestrians, escaped bus passengers, motor-cyclists and the occasional hen all took the opportunity to squeeze hurriedly across the bows of a hot and throbbing radiator. No one seemed to notice that the traffic stream was slowly advancing on them as it moved on to the main part of the bridge.

Movement increased beyond the bridge when most of the trucks and buses which made up the major part of the congestion swung away to the right. However, the release was a mixed blessing – I found myself on the west-bound lane of the dual-lane Avenida 27 de Febrero and heading around the city rather than into it. The route had suddenly decided to aim into the Dominican countryside rather than offer direct access to any of the historic or contemporary attractions of Santo Domingo. In the traffic confusion, I'd clearly missed the Lighthouse.

The plane for Havana only stopped briefly in the Dominican Republic and there was little time to get lost down palm-lined back roads and still make the evening connection. A quick glance at a map sorted out some of the difficulty but made it very obvious that I was going the wrong way. Reaching the monument definitely required travelling along the 27 de Febrero in the opposite direction. It required, in fact, a journey back across the bridge.

*

At a traffic light, as the road suddenly cleared and became peaceful, I seized the opportunity to do a swift U-turn and put matters to rights. Both lanes were deserted, the way was open, the lights changed to green, the turn was made and I began to accelerate back towards the distant cloud of exhaust fumes where trucks and buses continued to converge and diverge around the huge roundabout that lay at the city end of the bridge.

This exhaust cloud had grown only a little closer when my musing about whether it represented the start of a Santo Domingo evening rush-hour (and a slower return to the airport) was sharply interrupted. A frantic whirring noise came from behind the Chevrolet. In the rear-view mirror – bent low on a distinctly under-powered motorised cycle but signalling vigorously – was a man who appeared to be trying to race the car. He waved in triumph as I slowed to let him pass. Instead of careering on, however, the stupid fool then lost speed and began to wobble just in front of the bonnet – one gloved hand steering his cycle, the other flapping hard towards the nearby entrance to a used-car lot. With a passing thought that it might be the mechanic with further advice or spares I pulled over and watched the motorcyclist do the same.

Was it a different mechanic? With a sinking feeling, it quickly became apparent that although Nelly Rent-a-Car employees might wear overalls and sometimes a badge, they hardly ever carried pistols in holsters. The motorcyclist was a policeman.

*

He was a policeman who did not seem to relish carrying out his duties under the gaze of a fat bystander whom we both suddenly noticed in the shaded entrance to the used-car lot – a man fanning himself expectantly with a newspaper as he prepared to observe that crime did not pay on the streets of Santo Domingo. With a scowl in that direction, the motorcyclist quickly remounted and, with wavering hand still stretched out behind as if he had handcuffed the Chevy, he moved slowly up the road to a less public spot. It was a place with no spectators. The officer climbed from his bike, gave a stern glance at a shuttered house and then strode towards the car in that slow and rather stiff-legged way beloved of all traffic cops when they have apprehended an offender. He pulled his gloves off as he reached the car, slapped leather on the hot cream roof and motioned for the passenger door to be opened. Once settled in the front seat, he began a pleasant chat.

'*Señor,*' he said. 'Where are you going?'

I showed him the map and pointed out the Columbus Monument.

'Ah yes, down this road and turn to the right past the bridge.'

It seemed a promising start and in English, too. He appeared to be a helpful and friendly man although why he was so eager to act as tourist guide seemed puzzling if that was all the waving and weaving had been for. More light conversation followed: the island; the heat; the history, until the subject matter began to edge gently around to the specific here and now. He asked to glance at my driving licence and passport. Then a black notebook began to intrude on the amicability; then the fact that performing a U-turn in Santo Domingo was – regrettably – not allowed.

It was against the rules. I thought of pointing out that no signs had been visible, and the road had been completely deserted, I was new to the Dominican Republic...

'*Señor,*' he said again, looking into the black book but also taking a studied glance up and down the road. 'It is a matter of a spot fine of 400 pesos. You must pay now in cash. I can take US dollars.'

With another stern glance at the shuttered house, he sat waiting and, in the brief silence which followed (as I mentally calculated that 400 pesos was actually $30 and not going to blow Cuban cash supplies out of the water), his motorcycle slipped from its prop against the kerbstone and rattled to the ground. It seemed like an omen – the sort of natural event that might suddenly increase the seriousness of the infringement unless the matter was settled quickly and the transaction got out of the way.

With a show of chagrin, I gathered the $30 together, passed it over and watched his black book close around the notes. In a country like the Dominican Republic, the sum probably amounted to a significant income supplement.

'Straight on for Columbus,' he said cheerfully as he rose out of the passenger seat. 'Straight on across the bridge. *Buenos dias.*'

I got the feeling he was about to add, 'Thank you very much,' but checked himself just in time.

*

The monument was not ancient, of course. In fact, they were still building it. In distant view and approached from the rear it bore a strong resemblance to a corporate headquarters. A life insurance firm, perhaps – relocated in the mid 1980s from the metropolis to a greenfield site in the suburbs and custom-built. Attention had been given not just to the architecture but to the surrounding land. Carefully planted amenity spaces appeared still young and fresh from the drawing board and the gardener's trowel. It looked a poor show for most of the clerical staff, though. A slightly closer view revealed that the lower floors – where office windows would be expected to offer their incumbents a nice view of well-nurtured plants and trees – were here masked by thick slabs of moulded concrete. In fact, no windows at all appeared to exist for the first few levels and it was only towards the top of the structure that any flavour of the chairman's sumptuous penthouse suite existed. Up there on the eleventh floor, the view must have spread out across the Caribbean – although an even higher and more expansive vantage point could undoubtedly be obtained from the rather odd sculptural basket which sat atop the building. But that could only be the company logo writ large?

The corporate headquarters image faded somewhat as the entrance road began to pass into the landscaped gardens. A clutter of semi-paved pathways and rough concrete steps rose towards what now began to look more like a half-finished sphinx. Knots of resting workmen became visible and it seemed as if all that was needed to make the place complete was some smoothing-off at the back and the addition of huge face at the front. Finished that way, it might have rivalled an Old World monument in its scale.

The New World workforce were hardly straining themselves, however. Speed of construction at the Columbus Memorial Lighthouse looked as if it had been a problem for some time. The date was August 20th, 1992 and the great admiral was due to make his landfall on

October 12th, 1492 – give or take the odd five hundred years. The light that was intended to shine out of the concrete basket on this half millennium anniversary did not seem close to being lit for some months, if not a year or two.

Close up it was such a strange building. Just the sort of thing a pharaoh, absolute monarch or great dictator might put up and then have himself placed inside.

Not that Dr Joaquin Balaquer, the eighty-five-year-old president of the Dominican Republic was a dictator; although he did – as they say – go back a long way. All the way, in fact, to the beginning of the thirty-year reign of the Trujillo family in the days before and after World War II when great strides were made to expand the country's industrial base and to liquidate its debt. Some of the strides involved corruption, blackmail and torture. In 1937, an estimated ten thousand Haitian immigrants got in the way of economic progress and were also liquidated.

Sadly, that was only a later chapter in a long history of repressive governance which haunted the island of Hispaniola. Columbus and his brothers Diego and Bartolome were no saints, either. Diego Columbus – taken by the great admiral on his second voyage – was left in charge of the settlement of Isabella in 1493 whilst Christopher and a party of searchers combed Española for the source of a small amount of gold which the local Caribs had in their possession. The gold-seekers were only away for two weeks but, on their return to Isabella, chaos had already set in under the hot tropical sunshine. The food supplies had putrefied and resentment against the Columbus family had begun to sour relations in the colonial settlement; a resentment which culminated in the hanging of several men.

The executions marked a turning point in the affairs of Columbus. On another exploratory trip, Diego again failed to administer properly the activities of the tiny outpost of New Spain on the edge of the Americas. By 1498 and the third voyage, the Spanish crown began to hear of discontent, more rebellion and more executions and was not pleased to learn that Christopher had made brother Bartolome governor of Española without first seeking royal approval. The grip of the Old World on the New seemed to be loosening. Ferdinand and Isabella decided to despatch Francisco de Bobadilla as governor and chief magistrate of the island – with their wish that the Columbus family should obey his decisions as being those of the Spanish crown.

Unfortunately for the Columbuses – but fortunately for some of the other Española colonists and proto-conquistadores – the arrival of Bobadilla in August 1500 coincided with a short lull in hangings. Although five Spaniards had just been despatched at the gallows, another five still awaited execution. In the south-west part of the island, brother Bartolome had a further sixteen ready for the noose – these sixteen being incarcerated in a well. Matters were clearly out of hand. Bobadilla had not only Diego and Bartolome arrested but also Christopher. The Columbus family left their newly found island of Española in chains and departed for Spain – there to arrive unhappy but alive. Bobadilla, his main task complete, followed later in a ship that was to encounter one of the hurricanes of the late Caribbean summer. Neither the ship nor he was ever seen again.

The situation was somehow resolved in Spain. Columbus was freed but was not the same man. Nonetheless, in 1502, he and his young son Fernando, together with Bartolome, set sail on what was now becoming a well-travelled route across the Atlantic. This was the fourth voyage of 'discovery'. More fierce storms dispersed the four ships of the expedition as they probed the rim of the western Caribbean. Columbus had to be ignominiously rescued by those now established in the main city and port of Hispaniola and returned to shelter and recuperation in the Ozama river which lay only a mile or two from the concrete lighthouse.

★

Geographically, the structure was in the right place to guide hapless seafarers – but it still didn't quite hit the mark. It was like one of those imitation ship's wheels or binnacles which open up into a cocktail cabinet. Incredibly, since only fourteen years had elapsed since the beginning of the discovery of the Americas – those first signs of floating vegetation revealing them to the *Santa Maria* and the other two ships in 1492 – and the death of the great admiral on 19th May, 1506, the monument was taking longer in the building than Columbus had taken in the discovering. Foundations of the sphinx-like corporate headquarters had been laid down in 1948 by '*el Jefe*' himself – concrete first being poured at a time when the iron hand of the Trujillo dictatorship was right in the middle of its thirty years of cruelty. Forty-four years later it was still under construction. Not only had Columbus and others achieved the four or more voyages across the Atlantic in that time, but the conquistadores and the settlers who poured in after them had colonised virtually the entire South and Central American continent.

When finished, the Lighthouse was also intended to be the repository of the bones of Columbus. For whilst, in the flesh, the disaster of the fourth voyage had led to his return to Spain and his death in the Old World (at Valladolid, Castille) the more enduring remains of the Great Admiral seemingly continued their exploratory crossings of the Atlantic!

Quite where they took up final residence was (and is) a matter of some dispute. The Cubans said they were (or had been) in Havana; the Dominicans said they lay in Santo Domingo cathedral; and there is a huge tomb in Seville cathedral which can hardly be empty.

Certainly, the bones in the cathedral of Santo Domingo were the ones which had been earmarked for the move to the Memorial Lighthouse. It was hoped that their presence might lead to it becoming a kind of global pilgrimage centre with the memorial aiming for a high profile in the world of travel brochures. Whilst its real light was sending out a great beam over the sea (no doubt attracting tropical insects from far and wide), a metaphorical beam would be busy brightening up the Republic's tourist sector. Bones had always been a draw and Santo Domingo was not the first city, town or village to come upon the idea. Did it really matter if – behind ornate wrought iron gates and in a black casket – the bones in its cathedral across the nearby Ozama bridge were not those of Christopher! Confused old skeletons were notoriously tricky things to base firm opinions on. And there were so many of the Columbuses: Christopher, Diego, Bartolome, Fernando – probably more. Indeed, the most recent set of their remains had only been unearthed during restoration work on the cathedral in 1877. The main church of Santo Domingo was a place where half the Columbus family might have been buried.

Certainly Bartolome stood a good chance of owning them inasmuch as it was he who had founded the city. Then there was a Diego Columbus (not the brother but a son – not Fernando, either), who organised the building of the cathedral. In all the shipping backwards and forwards across the Atlantic (and certainly in the tumultuous West Indies of the early seventeenth, eighteenth and early nineteenth centuries) it was fairly certain that no one had the foresight to write 'CRISTÓBAL' on the several hundred pieces which might have lain in one box; 'BARTOLOME' on another collection and 'DIEGO II' on a third.

Indeed, the odds were quite short that the fragments that were being so fiercely guarded by the rifle and firm expression of a white-helmetted Dominican marine today, had never travelled beyond the island; were not bones which had discovered America or, quite possibly, belonged to a Columbus who had never left Spain, except in a wooden box.

*

Like the Lighthouse, work was also in progress at the cathedral in Santo Domingo. The ancient church was receiving a face-lift both to the stonework of the outer façade and to the venerable interior as the five-hundredth anniversary grew ever closer. Unlike the Lighthouse, however, men were actually doing things to meet the fast-approaching deadline.

Builders and decorators were everywhere amongst the columns and chapels of the interior – except, of course, the near-sanctified one which held The Bones. To ensure no tricky Cubatur snatch squad grabbed them in the name of the state tourist agency or some such organisation, that white-helmetted marine had to stand fiercely to attention amongst all the clatter and dust of the renovations.

In these circumstances, however, time and not holiness was of the essence; so much so that even on the high altar, two workmen stood squarely on its polythene-covered surface the better to apply gold leaf to an ornate part of the *Redido.* As this was going on, a third – with power tool – sanded something at the base. This task was made no easier by the fact that the heavy altar-cloths were still in place under the polythene, although they did keep in some of the dust.

From a side chapel, loud splintering noises echoed through the vaulting as figures moved above – dimly visible behind more polythene-sheeting and scaffolding. Sizeable pieces of masonry were dropped by whoever was up there – crumbling as they hit the stone flags, and then spreading in a myriad of dusty fragments across the floor of the nave. In one chapel near the altar and at the heart of all this activity stood a cement-encrusted bucket – an attached rope disappearing upwards until it was lost amongst the planks and polythene of the roof.

Suddenly the rope straightened and the bucket swiftly vanished aloft – revealing in its place the faint imprint of a skull-and-crossbones surrounded by what appeared to be a hangman's noose.

Pirates! Was this evidence of an historical reality behind the good ship *Hispaniola* and the days of Treasure Island? Well – not exactly. But not far off the mark, either. This very Caribbean symbol of death was certainly from the days of the Spanish Main but it had been borrowed by the buccaneers and corsairs from the tombstones of the empire on whose wealth they preyed. To the Spaniards of the sixteenth century, the skull-and-crossbones was a symbol of the fleetingness of life and not of Blackbeard and his ilk.

In fact, pirates were johnny-cum-latelys to the Spanish Main. That same sixteenth century was a time when the discoverers and conquistadores enjoyed unimpeded gold and silver extraction before any of the other European maritime nations broke in on the scene and tried to raid the wealth of the empire. The seventeenth and early eighteenth centuries were the times of the English, French and Dutch privateers rather than the golden days of the sixteenth, and it was these sea-going parasites – with their attacks on the Spanish cities and treasure conveys – who then captured and made their own 'the banner of King Death'.

*

So who was the Spaniard buried under the bucket?

Carved on the worn surface of the stone slab, in fact, was the name of a near-contemporary of the Columbus brothers. No less than Don Rodrigo de Bastidos – dean of the first cathedral and first bishop of the young and rapidly expanding New World. A man who had lived and died in the tough early years of its exploration and colonisation – years, moreover, when Francis Drake was still a twinkle in his father's eye (or would have been had that man not been an ardent Protestant lay preacher), and when Teach, Kidd, Bartholomew Roberts, Jean Bart and whoever was the prototype for Long John Silver were two hundred years in the future.

Early days – but times when the whole world was changing as Europeans began their first probing of the lands Columbus had discovered. Indeed, the man whose remains lay under the skull-and-crossbones must have been present in Santo Domingo when ship-borne news of further momentous discoveries first arrived back at harbour. It would be surprising if the young Don Rodrigo de Bastidos had not rushed with the other colonists to meet the ships of Vasco Nunez de Balboa as they entered the Ozama river in 1513; it would be surprising if he had not heard the news from his father (who was on one of the vessels) of land and another sea to the west. Balboa's arrival marked the end of a voyage of exploration in the western Caribbean which had added yet another dimension to the burgeoning European world. Columbus, in 1502, had probed that way but met near disaster; Balboa, in 1513, had climbed the Darien peninsula and found the Pacific Ocean.

The discovery of the Pacific is well-known – how the explorer landed on the coast of what is now Panama, hacked laboriously up the hill-slopes of a densely-forested isthmus of Darien, and found, at the summit of the highest hill, a westwards-looking vantage point. What he saw opened a grander vision of the world, but what he saw also meant the demise of Columbus' view – the one that the admiral seemingly took with him to the grave – that his islands of the Caribbean lay offshore from the continent of Asia (and – somewhat inconsistently – that the Orinoco led inland as one of the Four Rivers of Paradise). The Pacific changed all that. There was further to go before Asia could be reached.

Perhaps the concept of the New World-as-Asia was already being treated with scepticism back in the intellectual centres of the European Renaissance. After all, very little of the information returning with the expeditions and coastal voyages of the first few decades spoke much of Asia. Nothing really fitted; every parallel with China or Japan came unstuck; every pattern of land and sea seemed an uncertain match. But the jury must have remained out until Balboa and his associates reported back what they glimpsed on the far side of the hill in Darien. Then the reality of what the Spanish had begun to colonise and penetrate must have sunk in. It really was a New World that sixteenth century Europe was having to mentally come to terms with. There were no dreamed-of palaces of Cathay visible from that 'peak' in Darien, only a vast unknown expanse of water glittering in the sub-tropical sunlight.

There was the courage to traverse another great ocean to be found before the silks and spices of the East could be gained by voyaging westwards. There was half a world of water to cross before China could be reached.

⋆

The cathedral was not the only old building which had survived the centuries in the historic core of the city of Santo Domingo. Others stood in the surrounding streets: some restored; others still to be attended to. Several were boarded-up or showed crumbling masonry sprouting leafy foliage which, if nothing else, provided a cool retreat for cats from the late-afternoon Caribbean sun.

In the streets, there was no relief to be had for tourists: the glare was intense; the air increasingly hot; and the humidity caused such a state of enervation that only a spell of air-conditioning or a tropical downpour seemed able to make life bearable again. Times must have been difficult for Don Rodrigo and the rest of those early colonisers.

⋆

The heat was disorientating. Beginning the return journey to the airport, I soon realised that, once more, I had missed the route to the bridge across the Ozama and I was somewhere in the western suburbs of the city. The wrong side. Time had begun to close in. A one-way system led inexorably further westwards. Frequent stops at traffic lights slowed progress even more.

At the fifth or sixth set of traffic lights, it was becoming a serious concern. Even finding the Avenida de Las Americas was not the answer. A rush-hour tangle of traffic around its single bridge across the river could well involve more time. The Iberia flight would be starting its descent towards the island of Hispaniola before long. The clock was already ticking. As the tenth traffic light changed from red to green, I decided that an opportunistic right turn was the only way to break the cycle of one-way streets.

The ponderous old vehicle had just completed its swing when there was a muffled shout from behind and a scruffy-looking man stood by his fallen motorcycle simultaneously rubbing his knee and shaking his fist at the rear of the Chevrolet. For an injured party, he then leapt on to the bike with amazing speed and whirred up to the car.

'*Policia, policia,*' he said as he arrived – deftly pulling out a plastic card and motioning me to follow him down a quiet side-road. With a sinking feeling, it looked as if another close encounter (and time-consuming thirty minutes) was about to begin with a representative of the Santo Domingo police force.

The first choice of side-road proved to be a little too busy. Motorcyclist and attendant Chevy then spent the next five minutes making their way like a funeral cortège through several more suburban back-roads. Finally, he signalled a halt well away from passing traffic and nosy pedestrians. The sun beat down fiercely at his choice of location. I noticed that steam was beginning to emerge in delicate wisps from under the bonnet of the Nelly Rent-a-Car.

'*Ow, ow,*' moaned the man as he dismounted from the bike and stumbled up to the car – an approach hindered by his holding on to one of his knees.

'*Mi pierna – Yo necesito la clinica.*' Obviously, we were going straight to the point. '*Quero dolares. Quero dolares estados unidos – ciento dolares estados unidos?*'

Earlier in the afternoon, I had known I'd made a U-turn. This time there was something distinctly phoney about the whole incident. Firstly, I was travelling at a snail's pace as I left the tenth set of traffic lights. Secondly, there was no sense or sign of any scrape or bump sufficient to send a motorcyclist to the nearest hospital. Thirdly, why did we always have to discuss these matters down quiet back streets. Fourth, oily jeans didn't look much like a police uniform. Fifth, his knee...

The knee came to the fore. Settling himself into the front passenger seat with the non-'injured' leg ensuring that the door remained open, he began vigorously to rub it. The motion reminded me of someone desperate to get brass or silver to shine brighter.

'*Mi pierna – ow, ow. Este muy caro. Yo necesito ciento dolares. Yo necesito clinica,*' he intoned. 'I need a hundred dollars.'

I was sure he did – but then it was likely most of the population of the Dominican Republic could probably use the cash, too. And I needed the money since Havana was probably the last place in the world taking American credit cards. One hundred dollars was definitely over the top for a slightly bruised knee. From what I had seen of the visible Santo Domingo economy and the exchange rate of the peso to the US dollar, a person could probably have an arm and a leg amputated at the *clinica* for $100 and still come away with change.

The affair was beginning to drag on and to get rid of someone persistently giving vent to '*Ow, ow*' on a hot afternoon was obviously going to cost something. I tried another tack.

'Okay,' I said. 'I'll drive you to the *clinica* right now. They can look at your knee and we can see what to do then.'

'*No, no – ciento dolares,*' he said, resisting my attempts to lean over and close the nearside door which his non-'injured' leg still insisted on keeping open. '*Yo soy policia,*' he added in a manner which implied that he was at the thin and plain-clothes end of a vast organisational wedge.

'Okay,' I said. 'We'll go to a police station, then.' As I said this, my heart sank as I realised it was a way out that could well cost several more hundred dollars by the time a few other opportunists had climbed on the bandwagon.

'*No, no – soy policia secreto.*'

Just my luck to lightly brush past the knee of a Dominican secret policeman. The incident was getting more and more phoney as the minutes passed and the brass-rubbing continued ever more vigorously, but it was quite possible he could be an undercover agent. After all, the Trujillo regime must have maintained its grip using a whole sub-culture of informers. The island of Hispaniola began its colonial history with the Columbus brothers hanging those who disagreed with them and five hundred years later there were still twenty thousand members of the Dominican armed forces backed up by fifteen thousand paramilitary policemen and women. Many of these probably still held on to very old-fashioned views.

'Okay,' I said, 'I'll give you $30.'

He was about to decline the offer when an unexpected helping hand came from Nelly Rent-a-Car. The engine of the Chevrolet – which had been struggling more and more as the heat became oppressive – suddenly burst out with a loud whining noise. Anyone passing in the nearby streets would have immediately noticed the unusual sound and enjoyed the spectacle of the driver grappling with his problem. They would obviously also notice the discussion between a tourist and a rather scruffy motorcyclist – particularly if they happened to be an authentic part of the thirty-five thousand-member security forces and took exception to freelance activities.

The knee quickly took a lower profile as the shriek continued. '*Okay, okay,*' said the secret policeman, still half in and half out of the car. '*Trente dolares.*'

I counted out the money and as soon as the notes were handed over he was out of the car like a shot – his knee having cleared-up beautifully in the meantime. '*Chiao*' was accompanied by a rapid handshake and the faint words '*Hasta luego*' as the motorcycle kicked into life and roared off to the background noise of the continuing whine.

One problem had gone; another had replaced it. Time was marching remorselessly on. I was still lost in the western suburbs of Santo Domingo, the airport still lay some fifteen miles to the east of the city and the car was playing up. On the assumption that the Nelly Chevrolet might appreciate a short rest out of the sun, I drove the shrieking vehicle slowly around the block until a tree-shaded roadside space became visible. I turned off the ignition. The silence was almost as refreshing as a cool beer might have been.

A few more minutes passed – sufficient for a token gesture at calming down the over-heated system – and I once more turned the key and hoped that the engine would be back to its normal self. There was no shriek. Nothing at all, in fact. The entire ignition system had now gone completely dead.

⋆

The Iberia plane must have landed. It was probably being refuelled. Some early passengers might even have arrived in the lounge and be ready to board. Those who had undergone the long flight across the Atlantic must be stretching their limbs, clutching transit cards and remarking that it would not be long before they were back in the air.

At best, there was probably an hour to go before takeoff. I tried another attempt at starting the old Chevrolet but the key turned on utter silence.

Options. One: telephone the car-hire company so that the resident mechanic could travel down the Avenida de Las Americas and thread his way through the western suburbs of the city until he found me? That scenario looked like taking at least four hours and I dismissed it. Option Two: walk into the centre of Santo Domingo, find a taxi and get the car-hire company to retrieve its vehicle after I'd gone. Expensive – both in relation to the abandoned car and in relation to walking through the back-streets of Santo Domingo. From recent experiences, it would cost $30 every time another motorcyclist whirred past and then halted a few hundred yards ahead rubbing one or more limbs.

The omens were not promising; over the space of several hours, money had begun to disappear into the black economy of Hispaniola as fast as Capt'n Flint's treasure had slipped away to Ben Gunn's cave. By the time I'd gone a couple of streets, no doubt there'd be more Jolly Rogers snaking up the suburban flagpoles than would have been raised aloft on first sight of a Spanish treasure fleet.

There didn't seem to be an option 'Three'. The options had exhausted themselves. I was a bit stuck – like poor old Ben Gunn. 'Were you shipwrecked?' he was asked by young Jim. 'Nay, mate,' came the anguished response, 'I were marooned.'

Marooned on Hispaniola. There was a faint chance Option Two might work. The Chevrolet had stopped a foot or so from the kerb and I thought I'd roll it nearer to the trunk of the shade-giving tree before leaving it locked and awaiting pick-up. The pushing motion brought to mind other old cars which had also gone dead like this. A jammed starter motor had usually been the problem in the past. This often released itself as the car was manually pushed forward. Was it possible...?

It was. The Chevy burst into life – shriek gone and engine throbbing normally. I reached the airport without making further donations to the motorcycling fraternity of uniformed and secret policemen and with a few minutes to spare.

*

The tropical night brought some coolness to the tarmac as transit and newly boarding passengers for Havana were shepherded up to the steps of the waiting plane. It was still humid but perhaps the air would be a little cooler on Cuba – the largest island in the Caribbean. At least, one thing would be different from my recent experiences in Santo

Domingo – there would be no pirates left on that island. Not in Fidel Castro's socialist republic.

A thunderstorm was brewing. The humidity on Hispaniola had been building up for its arrival all afternoon. Like Francisco de Bobadilla, we found trouble not long after setting out from Hispaniola. The plane passed into turbulent air crackling with electrical discharge. Fortunately, most of the force of the storm was moving northwards of the route to Havana; travelling across the Gulf of Mexico and presumably not far from the shores of the southern United States.

On those shores – not more than a few days earlier – hurricane-force winds had slashed their way along the coastal strip with much damage being caused to Mississippi and Alabama. In that direction, as the Iberia flight continued north-westwards, mountainous cloud tops could be seen illuminated in the darkness as they were flickeringly lit from within by each flash of lightning. Now it was here; now it was there. No sound accompanied the discharge of energy from sky to faraway ground. An awesome sight – not least because some of the biggest flashes were originating at about the same altitude as the Cuba-bound aircraft was cruising. For twenty minutes or more it continued; great crooked fingers of power stabbing repeatedly down at a hidden ground or sea like wrathful Olympian gods attempting to extinguish those impudently small creatures who inhabited the lands and waters of the Earth. Uncle Sam was clearly catching the worst of it; Fidel was only on the sidelines.

The storm was over by the time the eastern edge of Havana came into view as a network of dim yellow lights several thousand feet below. Why was low wattage always such a distinctive characteristic of communist countries? They all seemed to run on dim lights.

Cuba was on an absolute minimum of night-time illumination; brightness and colour appeared to be solely for profligate, self-advertising capitalist states. The plane wheeled and descended further as only occasionally did the flash from a car's headlamps indicate that any activity was taking place along what had become discernible as twinkling strands of highway.

Roads cutting through great patches of darkness. Fields? Wasteland? More loss of altitude began to suggest the faint outlines of buildings and palm trees. Those dark areas were the residential suburbs of a city once renowned for its roistering nightlife. It was 10 p.m. and clearly a time when most late twentieth-century Cubans were already abed and conserving their energy.

★

Over the past couple of years, Fidel Castro had become desperately short of energy. There was little petrol to spare for general entertainment and none for staying up late in the tropical night. Along with the petrol had gone the electricity. Communist Europe was no more; the Cold War was over and non-essential lamps had gone out all over Cuba. Supply lines had dried up, Soviet tankers had ceased to arrive and nobody (with Uncle Sam's help) seemed to want the country's sugar and cigars. Fuel was expensive stuff to import when other things took priority.

Even the terminal building was conserving as much power as it could and was dimly lit both inside and out.

There was no flash or hype about Havana airport. It could have been some small stop-over during the early post-war days of commercial air travel. There was Russian lavatorial green paint all over the place and a complete lack of advertisements. The staff were working to a different agenda. It was a curious reversal of Columbus' experience: like him, the Iberia flight had crossed the Atlantic from Spain but once in the New World all the newcomers could think about was gold. Now, it was the locals who were obsessed with gold. Or, in twentieth century terms, United States dollars!

*

It came over as a hindering process. Cuba could not be entered without a hotel room being secured. The only way that rooms might be obtained was through Cubatur. The office of this state tourist agency was open, but only just. Every impression was given that Cubatur might actually be on the point of irrational closure. Re-opening was not necessarily a case of the next day but could be the next week. The office might not even re-open for another year!

Notwithstanding this indefinable impression, a hopeful and growing queue began to form in front of it. Another hopeful and growing queue developed before an immigration cubicle. No one was quite sure which was the best to join. Cubatur's queue-members occasionally slipped meaningfully across to the immigration queue, but began to show doubts there when some immigration queue-members started being turned to Cubatur. Confusion set in: people stood about pointing and consulting leaflets. It seemed that, as much as immigration was particular about those it allowed into the country, Cubatur was equally particular about the currency it accepted. Redirection was taking place to a bank which had earlier seemed closed but then suddenly opened when a face materialised behind glass.

'*Solamente dolares, solamente dolares,*' intoned the face. It was a familiar phrase but...

Only US dollars! But what about the arch-enemy to the north. The nefarious running-dog! Keep your Swiss Francs, German Marks or Japanese Yen. It was dollars which ruled here. Dollars clearly printed with the words 'United States of America' and complete with the face of George Washington as well as the motto 'in God we Trust'.

Cuba-US relations were a curious phenomenon. More Cubans probably lived in Florida than lived in Cuba. The Americans were so close. Key West lay only one hundred miles from the shores of Cuba, but even more incestuous was the fact that the United States naval base of Guantanamo was actually on the island itself. Uncle Sam's ships, guns, armaments, surveillance installations, military personnel and an airfield occupied a strategic position on the eastern tip of Castro's state and had done so since 1903. It had been there since the Platt Amendment gave the US the right virtually to dominate Cuba and had never been ousted. Guantanamo had stayed put all through the Revolution of 1959, all through the Bay of Pigs, all through the Missile Crisis and all through the Cold War.

None of Guantanamo's personnel could bring dollars through Havana airport, however. United States citizens were *persona non grata* in Cuba. Or were they? Immigration was certainly a slow-moving affair.

The immigration cubicles had also received a coat of the light green paint that had been brushed over the rest of the terminal interior. Perhaps the paint was original – put on during what must have been their first incarnation and before they had been dismantled and shipped over from

Moscow airport. Visitors intending to pass through the last stretch of Iron Curtain to linger in the West were still being shown that this was no light matter. The queue funnelled to an entrance. The entrance led into narrow space wherein two forage-capped, khaki-uniformed officials scanned whatever came into their line of vision. It was a job with the objective of filtering out dollars from undesirables. For a brief moment I thought that – like Albania – facial hair might be a problem, but quickly realised that Fidel's chin had remained hidden since the Sierra Maestre.

False beards were taken seriously, however. The scrutiny was no light matter. It was not a brief glance followed by a casual return of a passport. Front and rear of the head and body received close inspection: the former by an intense stare; the latter with the aid of a narrow angled mirror fixed to the ceiling of the cubicle. Two forage caps looked intently into the reflection. They were clearly seeking signs of...

Signs of what: a wig? Tell-tale lumps? An extra person creeping past? Dirty shoes? Dandruff? Then – flick, thump, scribble – with the back of my head seemingly in order, it was suddenly face down and much concentration behind a high counter as the process moved on to the paperwork.

Interestingly, they were not typical Cubans under the forage caps: no Desi Arnez or Fidel Castro lookalikes. In fact, the nearest one had much more the fair hair and pale bony features of some Russians. He and his ferrety blue eyes could easily have come over at the same time as the consignment of dim lights, green paint and old Soviet immigration cubicles – a middle-rank KGB agent straight from Sheremetyevo.

Perhaps that was true. Times must be difficult in this small western outpost of socialism with all the changes since the collapse of the Berlin Wall. Times were difficult enough back in Moscow. Perhaps in the early days of glasnost, the KGB (contemplating future privatisation) had exported men on overseas postings to earn a few dollars and balance its budgets, and now couldn't afford to get them back.

Why Cuba, though – it seemed the last place capable of propping up the Russian security services?

★

The final consultation and thump took place. With one last intent glance at the mirror to ensure nothing had moved or changed in the intervening minute or two, my passport was slapped down on the counter and the terse signal given to proceed into Cuba. I was two or three steps beyond the cubicle when I suddenly realised that they had forgotten to give me back the receipt from Cubatur for the $140 advance settlement of the bill – two nights in an unseen room at the Havana Libre hotel.

I doubled back as the next person was beginning the scrutiny and pointed out that the receipt was needed since – without it – the hotel was likely to query whether payment had really been made on entry. Who knows, I might have to pay $140 all over again!

Ferret-face gave me a long stare as if contemplating a term of imprisonment for insubordination. He then looked shrewdly at his companion and – suddenly breaking into a charming smile – slapped the receipt on the counter.

'*Disculpe señor. Bienvenidos a Cuba,*' he beamed disarmingly. Good try, practical joke, unintended oversight? It could have been any one of them. Odds on that it was the first.

★

Some petrol had been reserved for the tourists. A line of taxis waited outside. Clearly owned by the state, they provided the vital (and only) communication link between Havana airport and the Cubatur hotels of the city centre. I hired one and we set off down the dark road leading to the unseen capital.

The night air was hot, damp and had the fresh odour of the countryside in it. Rain had passed behind the electric storm and pools of water remained. Croaking bullfrogs and the loud rasping of cicadas soon dispelled the atmosphere of Sheremetyevo. How could this be Moscow? Cuba was clearly a Caribbean island.

The driver said nothing as the small Lada buzzed its way further along an empty road. More palm silhouettes showed up against a sky which had now begun to reflect some of the lamplight of Havana. Clumps of bamboo flared briefly out of a less definable tropical foliage. Soon, the outskirts of the largest city in the West Indies began to appear. Low buildings, yards, sheds and the paraphernalia of light industry took over from the palms and bamboo. Patches of dim illumination held people, too – clearly not everyone was in bed although those still up did not seem to be rollicking around. Low factories gave way to more densely populated residential areas – everywhere submerged in the curiously heavy yellow gloom given off by the streetlights.

The bearded and very familiar face of Fidel Castro swept past, stencilled large on a wall. Always the same image. Then administrative buildings. Then a bus moving slowly along like a sweeper – picking up the occasional person still abroad at the late hour of 11 p.m. and carrying them home to bed in some dark suburban side street.

*

There may have been no energy but there was also no litter and no shacks. In fact, for a Caribbean country, it was all rather impressive. Despite the shortages and difficulties since Cuban sugar and other exports were no longer taken at a subsidised price by the USSR; despite the lack of fuel and the desperate belt-tightening which the country was having to go through to preserve its socialism – this was not a ramshackle republic with a happy-go-lucky poverty spreading back amongst the tropical vegetation. Cuba had its expatriate critics and there were probably many more insiders who were equally sick of how the Revolution had turned out but I was nonetheless arriving in a city which was very different from the Santo Domingo I had left only a few hours before. Although threadbare and on its uppers, this place and this countryside seemed to suggest a developed country – not one still striving to achieve development.

*

Being a 'foreigners-only' hotel, the image of a developed country was exactly the impression intended to pervade every nook and cranny of the huge Havana Libre hotel. The taxi arrived in front of its grand foyer. Pre-revolution, it had been the Hilton.

It reared up amongst streets of grand but peeling apartment blocks, empty shops and deserted pavements – an establishment where only 'dollars' were permitted passage through the glass doors. Cuban 'pesos' were discreetly turned away by two men in ill-fitting suits who seemed far more convincing in the role of '*policia secretos*' than any of the motorcycling Dominicans encountered on the next island to the east.

*

A strange mix of people inhabits the hotels of communist countries. Tourists and others who cannot quite be pinned down. Odd nationalities turn up together: Norwegians and Burmese; Serbians and Eritreans. There seemed the possibility that no one was quite what they seemed, but there was the counter-possibility that they were exactly what they seemed although they, in turn, were not quite sure about everyone else. A faint wisp of black-market deals and *agents provacateurs* hung on every chance encounter. The men on the door were not simply there to hail taxis and assist with baggage; they were there to watch those inside going out and to keep those outside from going in – or even seeing in.

Seeing in, perhaps, to the breakfast room where that meal was served in the old-fashioned 'foreigners-to-the-Soviet-Union' way: a kind of surreptitious eating of a square meal behind thick curtains which carefully blocked out any chance of the 'people' seeing what the 'cadres' had as a matter of course.

What they had, in fact, was the product of a Cubo-Soviet style of centrally planned kitchen: fried bananas, scrambled eggs, black beans and bread rolls dished out by a staff lined up like the Politburo on a Moscow march-past. Their less-than-ebullient expressions were infectious. The Caribbean once more faded. Did bright sunshine and palm trees really lie beyond that thick fabric covering the windows? Or was it raining, was the temperature near-freezing and was there a nasty wind sweeping leaves through the peeling kiosks of the Park of Economic Achievement?

*

No, the sun was still shining down on sub-tropical Havana. The taxi ride the previous evening had shown that the city was too large to be visited on foot, and Santo Domingo had shown that the afternoon glare was unbearably hot.

A bus then? Not really an option. The few orange-coloured, single-decker buses which trundled up and down the wide, empty streets had so many people clinging to them that they looked like moving honey pots thick with wasps. A taxi? Bit tame taking a state taxi; I wanted to see Havana without being shepherded through its more instructive parts. Car hire? There had been a car-hire sign dimly shining out from the darkness surrounding the airport terminal – that would be a better way of seeing something of the true Cuba.

An hour later and a taxi ride back down the airport road showed that – even for top dollar – hiring a car during a fuel shortage in Cuba was a naïve idea.

'*Nyet,*' said the heavy-set man who sat in the cabin office clearly advertising cars for hire. Spoken in Spanish, of course, but accompanied by that unmistakable look – the look which the Wedding Guest must have given the Ancient Mariner when the latter first hove into view. 'Hire a car – you must be mad.'

There were, of course, cars all around the cabin – parked on the hot tarmac and all ready for hire. They were probably full of petrol, but it was clear that the normal rules of commercial exchange no longer applied. Some kind of authorisation was needed. It recalled a damp Sunday in the west of Ireland some years earlier. There – on that day – every car in the place was reserved for the clergy. The Church had the place sewn up. Here in Cuba, every car was reserved for the Party.

*

State taxi back to Havana. The mid-morning sun now beat down over the city streets with all the strength of the West Indies. It was hot. I asked the taxi driver quickly to point out some sights.

The Plaza de la Revolution, the José Marti monument, government ministries, the Headquarters of the Central Committee of the *Partido Comunista de Cuba*, Fidel Castro's offices...

The old city began like a crumbling wall just past the Capitol Museum of Natural Science building (a smaller copy of the US Capitol). Then came the harbour fort, then the lighthouse and, finally, the port – for a long time the greatest in the Spanish Americas.

He was proud of it all – that man. White-haired, reserved but with a friendly touch showing through as he took both hands off the wheel to describe the various buildings. He was proud of what had been achieved. For all the tightening of belts and the heavy weight of austerity which had clamped itself over the natural exuberance of a Spanish-Caribbean people (and had soon sent many of them scrambling to the United States and elsewhere), Fidel's dream had not yet turned into a nightmare in his eyes. Perhaps the pride was in being Cuban rather than in being part of the first communist republic in the Western hemisphere, but the clever intertwining of nationalism and politics which followed the revolution of 1959 had placed prime importance in cutting the links with the powerful neighbour to the north.

★

Castro was better than casinos. For most Cubans, the time before land reform and the nationalisation of foreign holdings which took place at the fall of Batista was not a happy one. The regime of Fulgencio Batista was notorious for its poverty. Throughout the 1920s and 1930s, Cuba had become owned not by its people but by a business mafia of United States interests which squeezed the wealth out of it like juice out of an orange. The Platt Amendment was doing its work most effectively.

It was in this environment that Ernest Hemingway's lifestyle fitted; his social milieu merging imperceptibly with those who did the squeezing. Nonetheless, Hemingway gave as much as he took. The days with rich female friends being photographed carousing in the Bodeguita El Florida and scribbling '*My mojito in la Bodeguita, my daiquri in El Floridita*' were also the days when he was painting the word picture of his unforgettable old fisherman scraping a living from the sea near the Havana of the 1940s and 1950s. A sketch of Cuban poverty at one level; a picture of the resilience and hopes of humanity at another. Most Cubans were proud of Hemingway's association with their island.

In those decades, as the poor trawled the Gulf Stream for the fish of their dreams or toiled in the sugar and tobacco fields, the rich were building the great mansions which – crumbling and peeling – still line the residential streets and suburbs of Havana. The capital of the island was a haven for the high rollers – a kind of pre-war Las Vegas shining out like a beacon for anyone wriggling under the moral dead-weight of Prohibition or making millions from bootlegged liquor. For the rich, the party went on and on – several decades after the domestic United States had become a more relaxed place following the Second World War.

It was still going when the Havana Libre had been built as the Havana Hilton, with little thought for political change or the overthrow of capitalism. Over one billion dollars of US money were invested in the country during the post war years. Cuba was the pliantly governed Caribbean playground of its northern neighbour – its economy so intertwined with that of the US that more than half Cuba's exports were heading northwards and seventy per cent of its imports were coming via Miami and the Gulf of Mexico ports.

With so many American fingers in so many Cuban pies it was not unsurprising that considerable annoyance greeted the news that Castro's small army had moved out of the hills and actually managed to topple the Batista government.

Castro nationalised without recompense and the American mafia wanted its investment in casinos back. The Bay of Pigs told the world that this task was not as easy as it had seemed because – surprise – most of the Cuban people did not want the mafia to return. Social security and improved health care were better than the occasional handout from the gaming tables even if the price to be paid was life in a bunker on the exposed front line of the Cold War.

★

The taxi driver suggested a bicycle. These – apparently – could be hired from the Havana Libre. Although it would clearly be hot work pedalling about under the midday sun, the fact that a slight breeze had sprung up began to make the possibility more attractive than pacing the pavements. And hiring a bicycle would be a more socially and ecologically acceptable thing to do. The taxi driver didn't actually say anything about social and ecological acceptability, but the subject seemed somehow in the air.

That was another odd thing about socialist countries – the curious way in which visitors picked up the atmosphere of implied moral virtuousness and started to react accordingly.

⋆

Back to the Havana Libre. Reception had a telephone number which – once phoned – would result in the machine arriving at the hotel available for use. But the vast foyer of the hotel seemed to have no public telephones.

'A telephone is in the corridor behind me,' said the woman at the desk who handed over the number. The corridor behind her was lined with panelled walls interspersed with locked doors! Closer inspection of these was obviously necessary. No telephone, and, by the time I returned to the desk, no longer a woman visible, either.

Persistence eventually allowed the call to be made. Another foray into the corridor led to one of the blank, locked doors yielding to a push. Inside was the hotel manager – a woman in her late thirties with several phones and a tangle of day-to-day problems that anybody running a 572 room luxury hotel in an energy-starved communist country during an austerity campaign must have to cope with.

I was embarrassed. All I wanted was a bike. She was so busy – keeping the Havana Libre afloat must have been like crossing the Atlantic in a sieve, although Fidel might have helped out from time to time with the odd plane-load of asparagus and Scotch.

Dollars was what it was all about, however, and although bicycles were at the thin end of the foreign-earnings wedge, instructions had clearly come down from the top to take in as many as possible. She gave a brief, tired smile and – continuing to double-check a thick wad of receipts and sign off a note hurried in from the restaurant – rang wherever the bicycles came from in Havana and ordered one over. Just as the call was finished and she began an explanation of where and when the cycle would arrive, the office door burst open and two chefs heaved their way in to demand an instant visit to the kitchens. Something catastrophic had happened down there.

'*Espero, por favor,*' called a desperate voice from their midst as the chefs crowded her out into the corridor, each gesticulating vigorously about what the incident was and how it might be solved.

A man would make contact with me in the foyer.

When? Where? The foyer was a big place and full of people – many of them men and more than one who could vaguely be considered a dispenser of bicycles. It was midday and the upholstered settees and iron chairs and tables of the palm court bar of the Havana Libre were all occupied.

I had a beer and waited and – by one of those curious quirks of socialist countries – only a few minutes had elapsed before a man did indeed emerge from behind a potted palm, walk straight over to where I was sitting and motion that we should go out on to the hot street near the taxis. There we could discuss business.

But why not in the foyer? Did the potted palms have ears? Why was he so furtive? I only wanted to hire a bike – not carry the plans of the latest Cuban experiments in building sugar-powered reactors across to Miami. It was all dissolving into that murky atmosphere of intrigue and espionage. As we exited through the foyer door, security men stared impassively into space. Would one of them be slipping off for a quick status report to the authorities? Was the ferret-faced man with the charming smile somewhere at the back of it all – flicking his naked electric light bulb on and off in some hidden interview room, getting ready to blow the curling smoke of a cheap cigarette into my face and to repeat endlessly from the green-painted darkness of a long night: 'And why did you wish to look at Havana on a bicycle, comrade? What is the real purpose of your visit?'

We reached a van piled high with cycles. New-looking Chinese bikes – about fifteen of them up-ended on the back of the vehicle. They must have been bartered in exchange for a container-ship full of cigars. Each had the words 'Flying Pigeon' painted in cursive letters on the crossbar.

After saddle and handlebar adjustments had been made on the one he selected, the cycle ride through Havana looked ready to start. The bike was exactly the same as all the others – *sans* pump, *sans* lock. The final stage of the transaction involved a form printed on rough grey paper which I signed and paid cash in advance. The form was comprehensive: times of start and finish of the rental and a list of fines – $1 for a puncture, $10 for a '*biela*' (damaged piston rod?) and a grand $60 for '*Perdida del Ciclo*' – the complete loss of the machine. How could anyone lose a bicycle in Havana?

★

Free-wheeling down the gentle incline through Vedado from the hotel to the sea-front was refreshingly cool after all this admin had been completed in the hot sun and the constant waft of taxi fumes. The broad expanse of the Malecon led eastwards towards the old port. Suddenly and surprisingly it began to rain, just as I started to pedal along its two mile length to the Rampart of the Indies – those venerable Spanish-colonial fortifications which still guarded the harbour of Havana. The rain intensified in the customary manner of a sub-tropical downpour and soon blotted out not only this destination but also much of the sea wall and the Straits of Florida beyond.

With such rain, it quickly became impossible to cycle and I was forced to find shelter under the colonnades of a long row of grand (but now very dilapidated) nineteenth-century buildings. The colonnade was undoubtedly better than the open sky but gusts of warm rain constantly swept in as the deluge reached its height. The only hope of dryness was to retreat as far as possible under the high roof and let the pillars break the force of the onslaught. There was not much else to do but wait.

Others on the Malecon seemed to be finding the storm immensely enjoyable. A small group of young lads spilled out of a stone stairway nearby and began to prance on and off the sea wall with great glee. They soon looked like soaked puppies and were so obviously enjoying every minute of this brief interruption to the usual torpor of a hot

Caribbean afternoon that they took no notice of the first sound of an angry whistle.

This was a mistake. It was the Law. Two blue-uniformed policemen whistled again and then beckoned the lads over and into their presence. As the gusts began to ease and visibility improved I could see a lecture being given and names being taken in the door of the next building. Poor lads – Big Brother had been watching even in the rain.

*

The storm abated, the sun came back with renewed vigour and steam rose from the puddles still gurgling away down the drains of the Malecon. The journey to the port resumed. Before long, an interesting network of narrow streets was visible leading off on the city side and into the hurly-burly of 'Old Havana'. Many more people were about in this part of town – most likely prematurely woken from their siestas to enjoy the unexpected freshness of the shower.

Groups chatted at street corners and several women shouted across to each other from first-floor balconies where they had begun re-stringing their washing over decrepit wrought-iron railings. Old Havana was greatly in need of repair. On every street, once-dignified buildings now stood paintless, peeling or only half-inhabited. Not all street corners held chatter either. On some, clusters of people with small cloth bags stood glumly in line as they waited beside unmarked doorways. They were on the Cuban equivalent of a trip to the supermarket.

*

But there were no supermarket avenues of global produce in these 'shops' which seemed to be dispensing the government's meagre rations of the austerity programme – the post-Soviet 'bread and bananas' regime. Anything other than minimal food allocations was out of the question in Old Havana. And not just food was limited; department stores closer to the Capitol building stood dusty and abandoned. Grimy plate-glass windows stared forlornly out over cracked pavements – their emptied shelves now hiding behind the faded posters and news-sheets which had accumulated on the glass. For the ordinary citizens of Havana, the cupboards had long been bare.

In fact, it was difficult to see how ordinary Cubans were able to buy anything other than an absolutely minimal ration of food. Standards of living seemed to have come down as fast as the Berlin Wall. Since 1988, men had been allocated only one pair of new trousers per year and women had long forgone tights and lipstick. Havana's shops were like a harvested field stripped down to the barest shavings of stubble. In them was no sign of underclothes, of hardware, of shoes, of schoolbooks, or of any of the hundreds of small mundane items necessary to keep a certain dignity. Needles, nails and nutcrackers had all been sacrificed on the alter of Cuban socialism.

But... life went on somehow. Cubans continued to maintain a certain dignity. It was both admirable and puzzling how they managed it.

*

Sprouting amongst the scythed grass of an ailing centrally planned economy, a few small shoots of private enterprise struggled to take root in the market-place of Old Havana.

Whether Cubatur lay in the background or whether the enterprise was another dollar-harvesting campaign remained unknown. Looking down on this rather forlorn series of booths was the façade of Havana cathedral – the very same cathedral which had temporarily housed the Columbus bones claimed as those of the great admiral – the 1795 bones, that is – not the ones found in 1877!

There was no chance of peering inside this cathedral. The afternoon sun had re-emerged after the shower and now shone down on great doors which were firmly closed and had remained that way ever since the Revolution. As a mark of the thirty years or so since Castro's Cuba had turned away from the old Spanish ways and towards the Soviet Union, a sizeable tree now flourished where a portico joined the eastern bell-tower.

The square was crowded nonetheless. This was the heart of Old Havana: Cubans, Canadians, Spanish and some Germans milled about together – the tourists mostly bussed-in from the holiday resorts along the coast and growing increasingly desperate to find something meaningful to take home. The stalls, although ranging down the colonnades of the eastern and western sides of the Plaza de la Catedral and blocking the entrance to the Museum of Colonial Art, had pitifully little to sell – even in the line of semi-junk. On expanses of empty table-top sat a few earrings here, a purse or two there, five or six brooches, some literature and twenty or thirty postcard views of the city. In fact, hardly enough souvenirs of Havana to meet demand. Had they been so minded, an avaricious party of five or six German or Canadian tourists could have mopped up everything in a few minutes.

*

But it was more than a market; it was an amble through the recent past. The posters did it, and there was one particular one which could be guaranteed to give (foreign) strollers reason to pause for a second or two and look contemplatively at the face staring back at them. The stall was outside the art museum but it was not a Spanish face of centuries past which they stopped at, but a face of decades past. A face still familiar across the world; that almost Christ-like image of an eternally young Argentinian surgeon and revolutionary. The face of Che Guevara.

The Plaza de la Catedral saw one of the high points of his insurrectionary career as the triumphant rebels arrived from their guerrilla years in the hills and set about mapping a new future for the people of Cuba. Was that late 1950s world gone now? Time had undoubtedly flowed on beyond the first socialist dreams and taken a more prosaic and less idealistic turn towards open democracy. Che – under the black beret and the Star of Lenin – continued to gaze ever upwards and outwards across the colourful vistas of the 1960s. His was surely the great photo-portrait of those times.

Its power remained still – but maybe it was only nostalgia. More than one now stolid tourist in Havana market stopped and looked contemplatively in the direction of Che. What were they seeing? A misguided Marxist revolutionary? Or their own past?

Perhaps, for a few brief moments, it was not sun umbrellas, bright colours and Castro's Cuba they were gazing at but a student room somewhere. A first love; earnest late-night discussions; images of a freewheelin' young Dylan in a slushy Manhattan street; air filled with sweet smoke; *The Complete Works of Chairman Mao*; Joan Baez; Regis Debray; Herbert Marcuse; A. S. Neil; Wilhelm

Reich and his 'orgone box'? The 'times they were a-changing' but, perhaps, not in the way Che had dreamed.

★

He was in the Museum of the Revolution as well – obviously so. A kind of diorama with life-sized models of Che and one other (not Fidel, but probably Raul). They were caught in wax as they crested a wooded ridge in the Sierra de Maestre and gazed, not as Bilboa had done over the Pacific Ocean, but over that revolutionary future which awaited them in the years ahead.

That revolutionary future: until recently it had done much for Cuba – the early vision of land reform and a more equitable distribution of the riches of the island. More idealistic than Marxist in the early years, perhaps – it was the *realpolitik* of an invasion from the United States that quickly pushed Castro towards the Soviet side of the Cold War. Once the decision had been taken, most of the middle class and all the wealthy glimpsed the drift leftwards and pulled out to Florida and elsewhere.

★

Although concluding with Raul and Che, the story of the Museum of the Revolution began with earlier battles for independence and the long years of the Platt Amendment times – times which culminated with '*My mojito in la Bodeguita, my daiquri in El Floridita*'.

The first battle for independence in 1868. The poet-revolutionary José Marti. The defeat of the Spanish colonial interests and the rise of the American colonial interests. The US occupations of 1899 and 1906. The turmoil of the early twentieth century and the Batista years. The plump, comic-opera policemen striking lean and weary protesters with batons and rifle-butts. The clean-shaven faces of the young middle-class lawyer brothers Fidel and Raul and the post-graduate medical student Che. The idealistic Castros setting off from nearby Mexico in 1952 in the ramshackle motor-yacht *Granma*. The Caesar-like statement before they ventured over the few miles of the Yucatan Channel that they felt was their Rubicon: 'If I set off, I arrive: if I arrive, I enter; if I enter, I win.'

He very nearly didn't. The engine of the *Granma* failed; Castro was late for the revolution; the uprising of the student Frank Pais was crushed; the troops of Batista had spent several days lying in wait. Instead of a round of applause, all that met the triumphant arrival of Fidel, Raul, Che and eighty or so other revolutionaries was a hail of bullets. By the time the party had reached the cover of the Sierra Maestre, they were reduced to a band of twelve.

For two years Castro kept up a running battle with the authorities using the cover of the rugged and thickly wooded hills. Although hopelessly outnumbered by the men and guns of the government, he slowly gained the valuable support of ordinary Cubans and their dislike for the corrupt US-dominated Batista. Nonetheless, until the final drive in mid-1958, it was pretty much touch-and-go.

Six months on and Batista had fled; Fidel Castro and associates (less than a thousand in all), had won control of their island.

★

There were many photographs of the glorious triumph of the Movement of 26th July – such was the purpose of the museum after all. The entry into Havana on the 8th January 1959; the grim settling of debts with Batista's men after the victory; the turn towards Communism and the USSR; the CIA sabotage; the Bay of Pigs; the solidarity handshakes with Nikita Khruschev. A Cuba acting out the role of Russia's place in the sun. Photos of Soviet advisors, preparations for intermediate-range ballistic missiles, the crisis that made the world hold its breath for a few hours in the last week of October 1962. The lean, handsome, idealistic faces of the victors of the Revolution growing fleshier and older as they swapped skirmish and ambush for nuclear warheads and five-year plans.

Then more of Cuban soldiers battling against the shadows of American imperialism in Angola and Ethiopia; endless marches past red flags, joint space missions with the Soviet Union.

Long before this (in the early 1960s), however, Che had become restless. He appeared less and less in the solidarity pictures and was yearning to return to where his heart lay. Amongst the trees with a rifle and the company of a few brothers-in-arms. Being a government minister had palled. So had being an emissary for socialist Cuba. At first, he was still occasionally to be seen in various places on the other side of the Iron Curtain or in Africa or parts of Asia. His verbal attacks on US imperial and foreign policy found ready listeners as the Johnson administration stepped up the Vietnam War and the Cold War. Then, in 1965, he was gone.

To North Vietnam? To Uruguay? Venezuela? Chile or Argentina? To the hot jungles of Amazonian Bolivia, certainly – because in October 1967, Che's small group of guerrillas was encircled by a special detachment of the Bolivian Army and almost annihilated.

Bolivians or CIA Americans in disguise? Nobody really knew. He was captured in the last battle and then shot almost immediately before the world had fully realised what was happening. It was a death which came only eight years after the triumphal march through the Plaza de la Catedral.

The posters were still selling. Che's death sparked off something. The year of 1968 and a time when the flags of revolt were suddenly waved high against the old order. The time when Vietnam was soaking up more and more young Americans, the time of the US civil rights battles. The flags were being waved not – as he assumed – by uprisings of workers and peasants but by uprisings of students.

It was curious – that time. How dissent spread everywhere like an epidemic. Moving quickly around the world to the accompaniment of Dylan and Baez. In the United States; in France; in Britain; in China and in many other places. The Sierra Maestre image was a constant theme in all of it; looking down everywhere on the student rooms, the arguments, the barricades. Those times – they did a-change after all.

*

I had left the Flying Pigeon propped up in the square outside the Museum of the Revolution. It was mid-afternoon and the rain had long since passed. Few people were in the vicinity of the ornate building that had served as Batista's presidential palace. The bike had been partially hidden by a tank which had last seen action in the Bay of Pigs.

An abrupt end was brought to the musing as to whether it was the only tank in the engagement or part of a fleet, by the discovery that the Flying Pigeon was no longer where I had left it. Someone had pinched my bike in the Socialist Republic of Cuba! This was impossible. Nonetheless, the space it had once occupied now looked as forlorn and empty as a dismantled missile launch-pad.

A two-mile walk back along the Malecon to Vedado, to explanations and to the grand fine of *Perdida del Ciclo* seemed a long journey. It was not only the fact that striding was somewhat slower than pedalling. It was the fact that on a bicycle – as in a car or even whilst jogging – there was a certain insulation from the surrounding environment; a sense of detachment and invulnerability. A Malecon which had seemed benign on the way down to Old Havana now began to seem less and less friendly.

Poverty was more visible on foot. The old and dilapidated buildings closest to the Museum of the Revolution were occupied by those in Havana who were even poorer than everyone else (although perhaps someone had recently acquired a bicycle to boost their finances). The windows of the upper levels in the buildings suddenly took on the threatening blankness of despair. Shabby people who hung around the stone staircases of the colonnades looked as if they might pounce on a few more dollars if they could do so without being seen. Those blue-uniformed policemen might be eager for an income supplement, too.

★

'*Perdida del Ciclo!*' exclaimed the bicycle man when he eventually turned up outside the hotel an hour late.

'*Donde?*' he questioned and then appeared to lose interest when I said it had been propped up close to a tank outside the Museum of the Revolution. He loaded some

Flying Pigeons on to the van and then occupied himself with tying down the machines and rummaging about for more of the grey paper forms.

At last he came over. '*Perdida del Ciclo est $60,*' he declared with some solemnity but still with that furtive air of midday.

'But I had nothing to lock it with,' I replied – hoping for some kind of discount for foul play.

'*$60.*' Was the response.

Perhaps it was a scam. The thief waited until the coast was clear, nipped off with the machine and returned it to some central pool of identical Flying Pigeons where he was given a dollar or two for his trouble and the bicycle firm kept the rest.

Or could the Havana Libre or even Fidel be in on it? A supplementary way of ratcheting up the foreign earnings a notch and filling one or two more tanks with petrol. There was no way of protesting – the grey paper had it clearly printed in black ink – 'complete loss of bicycle: $60'.

I handed over the money and went inside for another beer.

*

Early the next morning, instead of travelling directly to the airport, I asked one of the taxi drivers waiting outside the hotel to take me to Cojimar. It was not far away, the place was part of the suburbs of the city and Havana itself was not large. As we approached the village, modern apartment blocks became more frequently interspersed with the aged and peeling mansions of pre-Castro days. Finally, the small harbour came into view. Beyond lay the Straits of Florida.

'What is it that you want with Cojimar, *señor*?' asked the taxi driver, clearly puzzled.

'Ernest Hemingway – I want to see the village of Hemingway,' I replied. 'The Old Man and the Sea.'

'Ah, Ernest Hemingway,' he said – his face softening and losing the early morning blankness which it had held until then.

'Here is Hemingway,' and he pointed to a kind of mock temple in which stood a bust of the author on a plinth. We stopped – but only for a short time. The harbour wall on which the plinth stood curved round towards an old stone fort that protected the entrance and looked out northwards towards the distant horizon.

Looking southwards towards us, however, and quickly descending its outer staircase, was a heavily armed marine who was clearly growing increasingly unhappy as he bounded off the final few steps. I suddenly noticed that behind the grizzled, bearded face of the author in my camera viewfinder was the battlemented summit of the fort of Cojimar bristling with radio and radar antennae – the latter busily sweeping northwards for signs of another invasion force. From here, the arch-imperialist nation was little more than one hundred miles across the Gulf Stream. Other marines clattered out of a door at the top of the staircase and began their descent. Hemingway or no, it seemed time to go.

*

'I can take you to the house of Ernest Hemingway,' volunteered the taxi driver after we had safely put a mile between us and the marines. 'It is near.'

If getting out of Cuba was anything like getting in, I feared delays. With a shake of the head and a quick glance out of the back window for any signs of a pursuing jeep, I asked him to go straight to the airport.

'He wrote good stories, that Ernest Hemingway,' said the driver as we cruised along the Malecon and passed the Habana Libre, a man now much more communicative than on the outward journey. 'He understood the Cuban people.'

'Even though he was an American?' I replied, nodding back towards the sea we had just left.

The taxi driver gave a sad smile and said no more.

*

Knots of brightly clothed people clamoured at the Cuban side of the green immigration cubicles which also served the purpose of emigration. Inside one, the ferret-faced KGB man was back on duty and continuing to give his shrewd glances at all those desirous of leaving the country. For foreigners it was the relatively simple process of passing through another mirror scrutiny as well as presenting the correct slips of paper and a duly stamped passport. For exiting Cubans, there was the additional requirement of proving a certain number of labour months had been put in on a rural work collective. And a valid US immigration visa.

But the brightly clothed crowd seemed to be Cubans who could pass through the green cubicles without unduly disturbing the stare of ferret-face and who looked as if they had been nowhere near a spade for years. An Air Mexicana flight was about to leave for Miami.

Of course, there were more Cubans in the United States than in Cuba. These were US citizens visiting through the back-door of Mexico. Cuba must be quietly kept afloat by money and gifts sent back from hundreds of thousands of now affluent relatives who sat waiting for Castro to go. As those resident in the socialist republic tearfully waved the exiles goodbye and remained in the austerity of the green-painted shed, their paunchy cousins and brothers – men with gold crowns to their teeth and greedy eyes – passed through into the waiting room for the Free World. Their women promptly sat on the nearest seats and fumbled eagerly in handbags for mirrors, lipstick and mascara.

It was not the last of ferret face, however. Another check was necessary at the door of the departure lounge where each passenger was ticked off a list of all those who had passed through the cubicles. And yet one more check was made on the tarmac when the two armed soldiers who were discreetly positioned at the boarding steps of the plane held out their hands in request of the boarding pass stub.

It was a hard business – getting out of Cuba. It was even harder finding your seat if you had not taken the trouble to note its number.

*

A nasty business altogether. At the start of the year, Luis Perez and Rene Mendoza had tried leaving by sea – taking a boat from a recreational centre and heading out into the Gulf Stream like the Old Man had done in the 1940s. They failed to reach Florida; in a shoot-out, not far offshore, three policemen were killed, the would-be defectors were captured and brought back to Cuba and an execution by firing squad subsequently took place in mid-February 1992.

Two stubborn old men. Fidel Castro – struggling to hold his dream together but in a Cuba where rationing was reducing most people to a diet of bread, bananas and one pair of trousers a year. The Old Man – the Cuban fisherman of Ernest Hemingway – also struggling to hold his dream together but losing his hard-won marlin to the sharks of the Gulf Stream.

It was off Cojimar that the gun battle had taken place and it was off Cojimar that the great fish was lost.

> *When he sailed into the little harbour the lights of the Terrace were out and he knew everyone was in bed. The breeze had risen steadily and was blowing strongly now. It was quiet in the harbour though and he sailed up on to the little patch of shingle below the rocks. There was no one to help him so he pulled the boat up as far as he could. Then he stepped out and made her fast to a rock...*
>
> *...That afternoon there was a party of tourists at the Terrace and looking down in the water among the empty beer cans and dead barracudas a woman saw a great long white spine with a huge tail at the end that lifted and swung with the tide while the east wind blew a heavy steady sea outside the entrance to the harbour.*
>
> *'What's that?' she asked a waiter and pointed to the long backbone of the great fish that was now just garbage waiting to go out with the tide.*
>
> *'Tiburon,' the waiter said, 'Eshark.' He was meaning to explain what had happened.*
>
> *'I didn't know sharks had such handsome, beautifully formed tails.'*
>
> *'I didn't either,' her male companion said.*
>
> *Up the road, in his shack, the old man was sleeping again. He was still sleeping on his face and the boy was sitting by him watching him. The old man was dreaming about the lions.*

Chapter Three

Weekend in Venezuela

Venezuela, February 4th, 1992. *Residensia Panorama, Apartamento 11, Piso 11, Los Naranjos El Cafetal.* Beautiful name – the orange groves of Cafetal. Beautiful view, too, from the eleventh floor windows of the Panorama's apartment. Right over the city of Caracas. Over the offices and the military airfield in the valley floor and on up the steep green slopes of Avila to the summit line of the coast range. A shell fired from the window would go straight across the valley and hit the flank of Avila about halfway up. A shell fired a thousand or so feet higher would brush over the summit of the mountain and drop gracefully down into the blue waters of the Caribbean.

The view from *Apartamento 11* – grand though it was – fell slightly short of panoramic. The other blocks on the steeply rising southern flank of the valley saw to that: fifteen-story *Residencia Bonpland*; the eighteen-story *Bellavista,* the ten-story *Paradisio*; the twelve-story *Concepcion.*

That is not to say there wasn't plenty to watch amongst the terraces, balconies and windows of such residential high-rise buildings: pool-side parties; tennis parties, barbecue parties, disco parties; dinner parties; late-night parties. There was plenty to listen too as well: Caracas was rarely quiet. Not long after the last of the music faded away – with the shouts growing distant and the cars roaring off down the hill – the soft thud of early morning would begin; joggers taking advantage of the cool pre-dawn hour before the sun and the traffic grew stronger.

But there was nothing going on this morning. It was all deathly quiet – no music; no shouts; no cars and no joggers. Only the pale blue light of television screens flickering from almost every window in *Bonpland, Bellavista, Paradisio* and *Concepcion.*

Sections of the military were staging a *coup d'état.*

It was hardly a surprise – rumours had been circulating for weeks. First it was going to be in mid-December on the anniversary of Simon Bolivar's death. Then it was going to take place during the Christmas break. Then it was going to be deferred until the Independence Weekend in April. Nobody really believed these stories. Military coups were... well... rather old-fashioned. Those days of generals in sunglasses and tons of gold braid; of attacks on the radio station; of sudden shifts of allegiance in the body politic; of curfews and states of emergency. All that belonged to the South America of the past – things had moved on since then!

Or had they? Three hours before dawn on the night of February 4th, Lt Col. Hugo Chavez landed by helicopter on the biggest tee of the Caracas Golf Club and made straight for the television studios with a detachment of paratroopers and a pre-recorded video announcing an end to the unpopular rule of President Carlos Andreas Perez.

CAP was unpopular because of middle-class belt-tightening caused by low oil prices, and because it was widely suspected he had his hands in the national till. There was no question of any dictatorial iron-fisted grip on the minds of the country – although the press sometimes had to tread with a little circumspection. Venezuela was, after all, a freely elected democracy and had been for some years. But the bolivar was slowly sinking against the dollar; the oil revenues had dwindled; inflation was rising; expectations had been dashed; crime was up; the rich were mysteriously getting richer; the poor of the *ranchos* might soon be rampaging through the city in despair over rising bread prices and bus fares and – very significantly – saucepans had been banged. A *caceroleo* had been heard – that traditional voicing of South American urban dissatisfaction.

Venezuela was not an easy economy to rule despite its wealth of oil and other mineral resources. A rich and beautiful country but one cursed with politicians!

And now the army, too. A military coup put an embarrassingly large spanner in the workings of democracy.

*

As things turned out, CAP and Venezuelan democracy had a surprising amount of international support. And it seemed that Chavez had not really checked out whether the US were sympathetic to a military take-over in one of their 'secure supply' areas for crude oil.

Nonetheless, the briefly deposed president had a bit of a rough night – he was still jet-lagged by a flight in from Switzerland and the World Economic Forum.

The early morning television sets of the inhabitants of *Bonpland, Bellavista, Paradisio* and *Concepcion* therefore showed a rather grey-faced Carlos Andreas Perez giving a breakfast transmission. Order had been restored, he said – although it was an opinion which a glance out of the apartment window revealed to be premature. Down in the Caracas valley, Lt Col Chavez and most of his men were clearly still active. Gunfire and explosions continued unchecked. A pall of smoke hung over the military airport.

The *coup* – or was it a *putsch?* – occupied the television programming for the remainder of the morning. It was a distinct improvement on the usual frantic mixture of *novellas* (soap operas), commercial breaks and news items that were often difficult to disentangle from one another.

This was live television – an outside broadcast so close to the scene of events that the cameraman suddenly found himself filming a gun barrel poking out of the windows of the airfield building he was panning across. Apartment viewers watched breathless as the lens suddenly grovelled down around amongst tarmac and concrete for minutes on end as bullets screamed nearby. Only an occasional disorganised poke above the parapet was possible whilst reloading was taking place. Then the tarmac appeared once again. A sudden lurch into ten minutes of the sky left viewers worried that events had got really out of hand and a bullet had found an unprotected spot.

★

By lunchtime the drama was over. Order had been restored. The cameraman was alive and able to stand once more. Colonel Chavez emerged from the now-battered airfield building and was filmed surrendering to the press. He now looked as tired as CAP but nonetheless triumphant.

Chavez was also undoubtedly more photogenic than the president. Waving to every *caraqueño* with a television set and a saucepan, he announced that the attempted overthrow of the Venezuelan government by rebel factions of the José Chirinos paratrooper battalion was over *'for the time being'*.

Then, with the air and bearing of a public hero, the handsome army officer was bundled away into captivity. The cadaverous CAP resumed running the country. The muttering began again.

*

With the February *coup* finished on the day it began, the blood, bullets and the hundred so bodies of the hapless rebels or loyalists (it was mostly young conscripts who took the brunt of the bullets and shells) were cleared up by late afternoon. Repair work began on office windows and chipped concrete. A state of emergency lingered on for a week or so.

Despite the curfew, muffled shots were heard in the night: some close; some from distant parts of the valley. There was the occasional rapping of a sub-machine-gun. Perhaps a rebel or two was still on the run; perhaps the gunfire had less to do with insurrection and more to do with a settling of scores under its convenient cover. Assassination was not a practice which belonged to the political past of Caracas – it could happen in the social present. The aftermaths of South American *coups* were dangerous affairs for some.

Nonetheless the business held a faint trace of farce. It was clear that, in the matter of organising the overthrow of a government, no one really liked to get down to the hard and uninteresting parts of the job. The glory of guns, and mortars, and of emerging victorious or even defeated into the glare of the television cameras was one thing; the checking-up on whether your specially prepared 'victory video' could actually be transmitted from the television station you had just stormed was another. The rebels had a VHS cassette which could not be played on the station machines! Instead of Chavez giving a pre-breakfast message; CAP was able to speak to the nation.

Getting to Caracas had been fraught with problems for the lower echelons of the rebel faction, too. There was no dropping in on the golf course by chopper for them. The bulk of the José Chirinos paratrooper battalion had come by coach down the one hundred miles of *autopista* from Valencia. It was a journey for which no one had thoroughly double-checked the transportation; whether the army coaches were capable of carrying hundreds of fully-armed men to the capital at top speed. Some failed in their duty about halfway up the climb through the hills of the coast range. To get to the *coup* on time, other innocently passing long-distance buses had been commandeered. These less-than-photogenic old vehicles still had the baggage of their ousted passengers on the roof. It wasn't quite the usual Venezuelan sense of style.

⋆

Venezuela, April 22nd, 1992. The *coup* was in the past but not forgotten. Saucepans had stayed quiet but murmurings continued. The state of emergency had been lifted; the curfew was over; the nights were once more noisy but not with gunfire. The old buses continued to trundle in from Valencia but contained no troops. The José Chirinos paratrooper battalion was being renamed.

No government overthrow and yet a massive exodus of traffic was taking place from the capital. A nose-to-tail stream of buses, trucks, land cruisers and the huge and ancient cars of Venezuela was fuming slowly up and out of the valley on the route west. It was Independence Weekend and the hot morning sun had begun to fray tempers. Limply hanging arms of drivers occasionally jerked up in despair. The sixth Marlboro was lit with its tobacco smoke curling vertically into the still air. The beaches of the west beckoned and yet nothing was moving.

It was a curious obsession – the business of the beach. Beach lifestyle was promoted everywhere in Caracas: it sold clothes; it appeared on advertisements; in films; in newspapers; on television. The media made it all seem reasonable enough – even exciting. Girls, clothes, rum, parties, waving palms, white sand and the blue Caribbean. Ice-cool drinks and joyously free individuals splashing about at the water's edge. That was what everyone was trying to get to on this first day of the holiday weekend; *coups* in the capital were something for the working week. Going to the beach was universal: only a few civic authorities were left in the city to mark the close of Spanish rule by placing a garland of flowers on the statue of Simon Bolivar; anyone with wits and wheels was off to the beach.

But the beach never quite lived up to its media image. The Third World would insist on intruding on the First! And, in Caracas, all sorts of worlds lived cheek-by-jowl.

From the luxury hillside apartment blocks could be seen the one-roomed breeze-block, brick and corrugated shacks of the *ranchos*; from the carefully manicured poolside lawns and flower-beds could be seen deep ravines choked with sub-tropical vegetation; from the edge of a lawn a snake would sometimes emerge; on the wall of an apartment bathroom a giant moth would sometimes alight. All this was a reminder of the fact that only a short distance from the urban veneer of concert hall, taverna, shopping mall and cinema lived armadillos, sloths, skunks and the occasional puma. Brahms

Festival Academia might be performing in one part of the city; a daylight robbery might be taking place in another part.

The beach was part of this Venezuelan mosaic. City slickers confronting the sun-blanched poverty of the Caribbean coast – yes. But city slickers also confronting a grubby, litter-strewn urbanised strip of over-used sand. Somehow, the myth continually survived aloof from the reality – as if a 'proper beach' could be found by travelling a little further abroad than everybody else. Like those striving to get away westwards on the Independence Weekend. One Japanese family, newly arrived in Venezuela and eager for their first day by the Caribbean, had taken one look at the reality closer to the capital and headed straight back into town.

★

By 10 a.m., this trek to the beach had started to gain a little more momentum. The climb past the last and poorest of the *ranchos* on the steepest and most outlying of the slopes around the capital had been left behind and the Valencia-bound *autopista* was carrying its busy load through the wooded hills of the coast ranges and on northwards to the coastal strip and the small resort towns of the *Golfo de Triste*. I was travelling south-west.

★

For a time it seemed that the entire world had turned north. They were going the quick way to the beaches of the *Golfo*. None of the buses, the trucks, the land cruisers and the huge and ancient cars of Venezuela appeared to want to travel south-west and across the flat llanos, down the eastern edge of the Andes, around the western side of the Maracaibo basin and then back east to Caracas via the Paraguana peninsula. It was a way to reach the beaches of the *Golfo de Triste* but rather a long way: three days travel from Valencia instead of three hours. It was also a way which led uncomfortably near to the border with Colombia.

Colombia. To the *caraqueños,* Colombia was a little like Belgium to the French – except, of course, that the Belgians were not known for their clandestine arrival around the scruffier edges of Paris or Lyons, for their ability to slip an unauthorised wire or two into the national electrical and telephone systems and for walling-off yet another piece of steeply-sloping *rus et urbe* with breeze-blocks and corrugated iron.

True or false, for a neighbouring country (which could also celebrate its liberation from Spanish rule by the very same Simon Bolivar), Colombia bore the brunt of a bad press in Caracas. Brazil – that other neighbour of Venezuela but the one whose population areas were separated by 2,600 miles of equatorial jungle – might not have existed when the time came for pointing fingers at those responsible for poverty and crime. Colombians – yes; Brazilians – never. After all, distance and the razzmatazz of Rio impressed the Venezuelans who were fond of a bit of that sort of thing themselves. The six hundred miles to drug-scandals and something like armed anarchy in the streets of Bogotá, Medellin or Cali was too close to home.

Maintaining Colombia as a *bête noire* was also, of course, quite useful to the Venezuelan authorities. Below grand initiatives of closer Pan-Latin American co-operation on oil rights or commercial activities, those drug scandals and that armed anarchy made a marvellous danger-flag to wave whenever the saucepan-banging looked as if it might translate into serious insurrection. Better to have veiled corruption than exploding airliners and armoured personnel carriers at every intersection.

And then there were the day-to-day annoyances which continually nourished this undercurrent of unease about the neighbour to the west. The stolen vehicles of Caracas! Nobody knew where they vanished to – possibly into the hold of some rusty cargo ship and off to India or China. But the *caraqueños* were convinced that it was not the Far East that was receiving their vehicles but that 'near west'. A quick paint job, Colombian number plates and a new life out and about in Bogotá, Bucaramanga or Barranquilla – probably part and parcel of the narcotics trade. The fact that it could never be proved that the cars and land cruisers were all ending-up in Colombia just showed how many people in authority were being paid off in both countries for it to continue. And who would be the brave owner who complained to the police or tracked down his or her vehicle as it sat outside a house full of armed men?

Furthermore, there was that insidious creep of the narcotics trade into Venezuela. The rise in assassinations. The huge exportation of Colombian cocaine. Rumour had it that more and more was finding a way past the Venezuelan border guards and into busy places where a lot of commercial coming-and-going took place. Ports like Maracaibo.

But it was the big stuff which was coming eastwards, the press were delighted to note that the smaller stuff seemingly went south via the lesser-known route of the Catholic Church.

'Bad Habits' said the *Caracas Daily Journal* gleefully, under a photograph of four glum-looking Sisters of Mercy staring out of a photograph taken at Quito airport. They had been arrested in Ecuador *en route* for Spain and each was carrying ten kilos of cocaine under their clerical robes. The paper did add that they were lapsed nuns, but combined the news (in the same edition) with a note of the seventy-second attack on the thirteen inch oil pipeline which led from the interior to the country's major refinery. One of the insurrectionary groups had blown it up – yet again. It didn't really seem to matter whether it was the work of the National Liberation Army or the Colombian Revolutionary Armed Forces, the deed clearly proved how stable Venezuela was and how terrible Colombia was.

★

Venezuela Route 5 turned gradually due west from that oasis of tranquillity that was Valencia and began its journey towards the frontier town of San Cristóbal some two hundred and fifty miles away to the south-west. Before long, a distant wall of grey cloud hiding the edge of the Andes could be faintly seen. The road turned to follow it in the direction of San Cristóbal. To the east, the llanos – those flat interior plains of the country – stretched away to a level horizon: an inland sea of grassland broken only by the occasional bush or palm. Except that it looked more like a vanished sea – it was the dry season and everywhere was yellow and dusty and waiting for the reviving moisture of the wet season.

Clouds to the west; dry plains to the east. Several hours of the same topography stretching ahead with scarcely a bend in the route to provide diversion or demand conscious attention. That left only the National Guard!

With a failed *coup d'état* forming so recent a part of Venezuela's history, the National Guard was perhaps more rigorous in its watch over travellers on Independence Weekend than during periods without *coups*. There was, of course, the slight complexity of men in uniform having been responsible for the insurrection.

Perhaps previous experience of too much military power growing out of regional interests had led government, military and social policy to endorse a practice which deployed members of this conscript National Guard as far as possible from their origins. Most young soldiers therefore found themselves transferred from one end of the country to the other to serve their time. Big cities or even towns had no problem soaking up most of this cross-migration, but a surplus of National Guardsmen had led to their widespread deployment along the internal road system of the country.

The trouble was that army units deployed in the middle of nowhere had to be kept occupied. Mutiny or even attempts to overthrow the government might grow out of the boredom of watching traffic pass day after day for several years. Then someone hit on the brilliant idea of resurrecting the *alcabala* – originally a kind of 'town tax' on travellers or a 'province tax' on the movement of goods – as a roadside post just outside communities or straddling provincial boundaries where a levy could be made for wear and tear on the streets and buildings of that town and the money be funnelled back into regional funds for infrastructure development. The 'spot fine' theory. The National Guard had been deployed throughout the country to man *alcabalas*.

It was no longer a neat mechanism for gathering money, at least not in most cases. It was to keep young lads busy and to keep an eye on who was travelling where. A sort of *ad hoc* official surveillance which applied on a graduated scale of watchfulness.

Grade one of official surveillance was nothing more than a token nod in its direction – a statement to travellers that the National Guard was abroad in the land but had better things to do with its time than stand around at the roadside looking serious. A few greasy cones, a limpid flag and a steep-sided sleeping policeman did the job for them.

Grade two was a slightly more advanced state of affairs and involved a uniformed man with a gun, but a man whose face revealed a state of complete and utter boredom. He had obviously been told to look at passing cars for a year or so but not to stop them.

Grade three involved slightly more complex duties. Traffic was actually reduced to a crawl by a hazard in the road. Not that hazards were uncommon on the roads of the Venezuelan interior. Since the early 1980s when the price of oil had dropped down from $38 a barrel to less than $18 a barrel, the spare cash for repairs to out-of-the-way routes had dried up. A deceptively smooth highway could – without warning and for no apparent reason – suddenly lose its tarmac surface and a foot or two of its foundations. Usually a wet-season stream was responsible. National Guard hazards were artificial versions of the same thing and were usually put in the middle of a long straight stretch of road across what was otherwise a barren waste. There was no choice about stopping at a Grade three hazard – it was a case of doing so or hitting it and reeling off into the dust and broken bottles of the roadside.

Grade four was the big time, however. The sequence of *alcabalas* reached its apogee of seriousness at this grade, with the greasy cones, the limpid flag, the hazard, the conscript, the next-in-command and the next-in-command to him all housed under a kind of roof. These several layers of the National Guard hierarchy took up positions of maximum surveillance. At night, strong lights shone down on the traffic to allow inspection of papers, day and night trucks unloaded and were searched for contraband. Frequently, bus passengers were required to parade in front of the soldiers. But this was Venezuela and the National Guard rather than the Gestapo. Everyone enjoyed the break; little contraband was uncovered and no one left with hard feelings.

Nonetheless, coming across a Grade four in deserted countryside (they were interspersed illogically between Grades one to three) still required a serious face and a co-operative manner.

★

Somewhere near the town of Acarigua, a Grade four *alcabala* hove into distant view. As I grew closer, the National Guardsman in charge of arresting the flow of traffic swung his sub-machine-gun into a more usable position, stepped into the road with a stern, inquisitive look and motioned that the car was to pull off the highway. He looked serious. Was this a mopping-up operation at the tail end of the *coup*?

'*Pare! Alt por favor. Donde va?*' he said tersely.

I offered San Cristóbal and muttered something about it being a long drive but somewhere I hoped to reach before it got too late.

At the mention of San Cristóbal he seemed to stiffen as if he had stumbled on some Caracas-to-Bogotá car-smuggling operation. Or could it be drugs from Bogotá to Caracas? Somehow, my going in the wrong direction seemed immaterial – perhaps even more suspicious. The situation worsened as he signalled to the hut that always seemed to accompany Grade four *alcabalas*. More troops poured out. With that sinking feeling that always accompanies lone tangles with the authorities deep inside a foreign country, I waited for the order to get out of the car and spread-eagle over the bonnet at gunpoint whilst the vehicle was meticulously searched from bonnet to boot.

'*Tu viajando hacia San Cristóbal?*' said one of the soldiers as he ran up. He motioned for the boot to be opened. I began to take out my bag and open it for inspection.

'*No, no,*' said the guardsman. '*San Cristóbal, bien, bien. Queremos ir a San Cristóbal.*'

'*Mi nombre es Ceser,*' he added with a slight softening of his serious 'National Security' expression as – rather than probing through the contents of my bag – he dumped his own in the boot and settled into the front passenger seat.

'*Y mi nobre es Nelson,*' said another as he too dumped a bag in the boot, closed it and climbed into the rear seat. The soldier with the sub-machine-gun melted away.

'*Bien, bien,*' said both of them. It was clear that the car was meant to resume its journey and leave *alcabala* Grade four as soon as possible.

Puzzled, I pulled back on to Route 5 and continued across the landscape of interior Venezuela – the distant grey clouds of the Andes on one side and the dry llanos stretching away to the horizon on the other. It soon became clear that they wanted a lift into Acarigua and had been waiting for several hours for a smart-looking vehicle that would get them home as comfortably as possible.

*

It was a complex business – demurring with the National Guard. As we reached Acarigua it emerged that 'home' wasn't there at all – it was San Cristóbal. And San Cristóbal was still three hundred and fifty miles away. I had a military escort for the rest of the afternoon and a good part of the evening as well.

Ceser and Nelson. Both in their mid-twenties. Both conscripts. Both with close-cropped hair and with uniforms which had that curious characteristic of looking neatly pressed and yet having been worn day and night for some considerable time. Life must have been tough in that *alcabala* hut – an ironing board, some bunks, a stove and a supply of *arepas* and grilled goat-meat. Heroic names, too. They weren't the only ones – the country was full of Alexanders and Alexandras, of Napoleons, of Marie-Antoinettes, of Raphaels. There was even the occasional Jesus.

And at the next *alcabala* it soon became clear that travelling with a uniformed military escort through the interior of Venezuela was rather like passing with Jesus (or, perhaps, with a very small detachment of the Roman Army) through the back-roads of the Holy Land. Every obstacle melted away. Flags, bumps, kinks, roofs, bored soldiers – all became a kind of backdrop which required the merest nod before we were through to the open road. The power was with us.

⋆

The landscape of the llanos had completely taken over the eastern horizon. Palms only occasionally reared out of the yellow grassland. The horizon was level. That is, what was assumed to be the horizon – the land and its vegetation had somehow become indistinguishable from the pale sky of late afternoon. No sign of settlement or animal life was visible on its wide spaces. Cattle were supposed to roam on the llanos much as they had done during and since colonial times, but there was little evidence of their presence anywhere near Route 5. Of other forms of farming there was absolutely no trace, either: infertile soils and the fierce dry season of the early months of the year shrivelled the grass and shrubs to the dead tones of winter in more temperate climates. The northern plains of Latin America were not an easy place to live.

A vast dryness and yet – westwards – a totally different world took over. First came low hills just moist enough to be cultivated, but these quickly dissolved into the heavy cloud which marked the real rise of the Venezuelan Andes. The mountains were growing closer and closer to Route 5. A dense vapour hid the mountain wall – thickly forested in its lower parts but soaring out of the dry tropical grasslands until it reached snow-capped summits some 16,500 feet above. Geologically young mountains and curiously only thirty miles wide – this cold and rather mournful place dropped equally steeply on its western side into the Maracaibo basin. Both sides of the Venezuelan Andes often streamed with torrential rain whilst its summits were not infrequently bathed in a freezing mist. Across the wall was Lake Maracaibo – the shimmering sub-tropics again – and only half the distance westwards beyond those mountains as my destination, at San Cristóbal, was to the south. With this thought, the journey had begun to seem infinitely long. I had run out of conversation topics for the National Guard.

Venezuela had a speed limit of 50 mph but Ceser and Nelson seemed in no mood to play out the official line when none of the other road users paid any attention to it either. And where did they come from – all those elderly cruisers of Venezuela?

No other Latin American country seemed to have so many old tanks on the road: so many 1950s Chevrolets, Fords, Oldsmobiles, Pontiacs and Cadillacs – eight feet of bonnet and clattering pistons in front, an acre of moulded metal and billowing blue-grey exhaust behind. Had they all been shipped over in the early 1970s when the first oil crisis hit the United States and kept going in back-street workshops and on rock-bottom Venezuelan gasoline prices ever since? Whatever their history, few of them could manage to get up to the speed limit let alone exceed it.

Trucks and long-distance buses usually travelled much faster. They had a mission to fulfil: the way they roared backwards and forwards across the country suggested that passenger throughput and turnaround time was the economic motivation rather than any concept of a smooth, safe service. Indeed, not far from the town of Guanare, one of them needed most of the road simply to travel forwards. It hurtled past at 90 mph in a peculiar crab-wise fashion which indicated a severely twisted chassis and the end of the trail for all concerned should the driver ever be required to brake sharply.

*

Clouds to the west; dry plains to the east. No let-up; no change. An hour or so in a big country can make very little impact on the scenery. These llanos of the New World must have seemed endless as the first exploratory parties of conquistadores began to probe south from the coast.

There were signs for the town of Barinas to the west. The place where the precipitous road from the high Andean town of Merida came winding down the steep rain-soaked mountain wall to meet Route 5 – a twisting, plunging road frequently blocked by landslide or tangled masses of vegetation. A road almost impossible to relate to the flat level landscape which continued to expand eastwards until it merged with the sky. Still 175 miles to go before San Cristóbal.

Clouds to the west; dry plains to the east. A greasy fly-blown diner and three battered petrol pumps standing crookedly in the middle of a great expanse of oily-pitted tarmac. A few heavy trucks beached on its irregular surface. Crude toilets, lazy fans trying to brush back the late afternoon heat, pin-ball machines clanking and ringing, the gush of coffee percolating. All around rough grass stretching away to infinity. We stopped for fuel and a break.

Excellent stuff – Venezuelan coffee. There was a finesse in ordering the beverage and a finesse in drinking it. Even in a greasy fly-blown diner thirty miles from Barinas! The orderer had to be precise; like *alcabalas,* coffee came in grades. For the faint-hearted and weak of stomach *con leche claro* would suffice; for those of middling tastes – *marron grande;* for those who kicked in the door, spat accurately into any nearby receptacle and clinked menacingly to the bar chewing the end of a cigar, there could only be *negro fuerte.*

It has to be three *negro fuertes* when you enter a greasy fly-blown diner accompanied by two National Guardsmen. Not long after, I began to wish it didn't also have to be six or seven *arepas* as well. The little round cakes of fried maize had the digestive qualities of lead.

Back on Route 5, a full tank, nine *negro fuertes* and some fifteen *arepas* later and we seemed to have lost all the acceleration. The vehicle sluggishly crept up to its former speed. Every bump in the road felt as if it were testing the shock absorbers to their limits.

Perhaps it was rhythmic thumping of National Guard boots which created this impression. As the miles increased from their *alcabala* hut and decreased in the direction of home, Ceser and Nelson progressively unwound. They were only conscripts after all and a four-month stint at the side of the road with a *coup d'état* thrown in for good measure had brought them to a point where they were going to enjoy as much of their short leave as possible.

Enjoyment in Venezuela was synonymous with having a party. The partying had begun. Their boot-thumping was in tune with their tapes of *merengue* music; the beat grew progressively more exuberant until – where the climax of a tune coincided with a poorer patch of road and we jarringly clanked down to the absolute limits of the shock absorbers – I had to call a halt. It had begun to seem as if it was to be *merengue* or San Cristóbal – but not both. Since late afternoon had started to give way to the short dusk of the tropics, we settled for San Cristóbal.

⋆

Just before night fell, the country to the east became much less dry. Perhaps this was linked to the gradual narrowing of the gap between the route south and the cloudbank to the west. Increasingly green and well-watered territory started to come into view. Soon, patches of forest appeared and Route 5 rattled over several narrow steel girder bridges which spanned brown, sediment-laden rivers carrying away all that rain of the eastern Andean wall. Fleeting glimpses of the River Anaro, the Caparo, the Doradas as they were suddenly crossed in the failing light – each pouring its piranha-haunted waters through bleached gravel banks and amongst numerous bush-covered islets before being swallowed up in the vastness of the llanos to the east.

This vastness extended over an area the size of France. Somewhere several hundred miles beyond the darkening horizon lay the River Orinoco collecting these and other tributaries and carrying the Andean water and its silt eastwards until it spilled into the Atlantic.

★

Darkness. More girder bridges with the rivers they spanned hidden below in the shadows. A westwards turn in the highway and a beginning of its climb into the Andes – no longer the cloud-covered wall of forested rock in this southern part of the route but rugged hills and steep valleys.

Precipitation began in earnest; water began to stream across the now winding road; a treacherous veneer of mud, small stones and the occasional rock worsened driving conditions. San Cristóbal (2,700 feet to Merida's 5,300 feet) was still twenty-five miles further on through the wet, winding darkness and its lights took an eternity to come into view.

Ceser and Nelson were ready to commence the party. A joint family fiesta that would begin as soon as they crossed the threshold and which would no doubt carry through until dawn. I was invited, but the last few mountain miles of the six hundred had taken their toll – all that seemed important was to find a bed for the night, wash off a day of driving, drumming tyres, *negro fuertes* and *arepas* and get some sleep.

★

Confusion. A mountain town picked out solely in lights. A town which seemed to sprawl across a rugged landscape with no clear indication of centre and suburb. We drove into San Cristóbal's outer environs: low single-story houses, empty unsurfaced back-roads and intermittent industrial plant laced with wide roads. Wet tarmac surfaces threw back the orange glare of street lamps. At the junction of two thoroughfares there was a modern hotel. Ceser and Nelson climbed out, retrieved their bags and cassette tapes, said their farewells and clomped off into the night.

That Andean night was surprisingly balmy. I had been expecting it to be much colder. In fact, the tropics were still in evidence in sheltered spots in this mountain landscape. Banana fronds brushed against the railings of a long balcony which allowed access to the second-story bedrooms of the hotel. The bedrooms had been steadily cooled by the efforts of an air-conditioner which had been so long at the job that a local mist suddenly formed when I opened the door and entered.

Outside remained warmer than inside. The coldness refused to budge even when the door was left ajar during the night. There seemed to be no way of switching off the equipment without tracking down the hotel management and I was too tired to do that. Thieves and conmen were widely reported to operate in the Colombian border town of Cucuta only thirty-five miles away, but they seemed a lesser threat than frostbite or pneumonia. As I woke shivering under the light bed-coverings of the room in the early hours of the morning, I began to wish I'd gone to the National Guard party.

★

San Cristóbal had a colonial centre which had been laid out by the Spanish in 1561. I never found it. The long road to Maracaibo beckoned more seriously. It wasn't so much the three hundred miles – the previous day's journey from Caracas had been twice as far. No, it was the sparsely populated nature of the country that the route led through which had occupied my periods of awakeness in those cold early hours of the morning.

The Colombian border crept up the western side of the Maracaibo basin – in some places only twelve miles from the route north to Maracaibo. In these many miles of deserted swamp country, banditry was gleefully reported from time to time by the ever appreciative Caracas press. This was the route through which all the drug-smugglers, car-smugglers and illegal immigrants were reported to come into Venezuela. Colombia – beyond the frontier – was a land of the remote and inaccessible hills which made up the *Serrania de Perija*. Hill country so remote, in fact, that it still held indigenous peoples who – not more than thirty years earlier – had got into the habit of spearing missionaries.

Swamps, bandits, Motilone Indians, those dreadful Colombians: National Route 6 leading through all this was a new road; a road called the *Carretera Nueva* for much of its way and cutting across a waterlogged tropical country in which (until the late 1940s), malaria as well as spears had been a very effective guardian of its solitudes.

★

A warming sun lifted the dawn mist from the hills surrounding San Cristóbal and, with it, any worries about a long and lonely drive soon dissipated like its vapours. No sooner had the northwards climb left the last out-buildings of the town and begun the rise up into the Venezuelan Andes in earnest, an *alcabala* hove into view at the culmination of a series of steep hairpin bends. Uniformed figures jerked into action – hands raised, gun barrels pointing the car to the side of the road, reinforcements spilling out of a nearby shed. Was the route north banned to non-military traffic – the preserve of border patrols and armed detachments of the National Guard hunting down bandits and illegal immigrants?

In part it was – but that didn't stop the 'reinforcements' needing a lift north!

★

Horatio and Raul. Two more lads with short cropped hair, heavy boots, small holdalls and a burning desire on the part of the former to get to a place called La Fria and the latter to go all the way to Maracaibo. Raul in the front seat looked particularly young – little more than eighteen years of age. It was a pity he wasn't getting out at the closer destination of La Fria, however. He seemed to have gone through his whole tour of duty without washing his socks once; three hundred miles was a long way to go for a breath of fresh sea air.

Socks and a youthful appearance notwithstanding – having Raul aboard at the approach to the next *alcabala* soon revealed that our passage had acquired even more prestige than on the previous day. He seemed to have some kind of seniority. Not only did we slip through Grade fours with consummate ease but whenever the duty guardsman caught sight of his face he snapped to attention and gave a Ruritanian salute. Sneaking a quick glance across the car on the first occasion this happened, I failed to see any recognisable signs of authority – either on his upside-down cap (which looked rather like a khaki version of a French gendarme's headpiece) or on his face which maintained one of those curiously nerdish expressions adopted by under-age youths in uniform.

The road wound on and upwards into high mountain country hidden in near-perpetual mists. Then – almost unexpectedly quickly – it began to descend down the western side of the Venezuelan Andes. Vapours grew thicker but rocks and rough grassland were soon exchanged for green trees and shrubs which then became recognisably subtropical. Any view of a distant Lake Maracaibo or even the swamps spreading north from the foot of the mountains remained totally hidden; the mists refused to clear.

⋆

The air was growing appreciably hotter, however, as vegetation grew taller and became a steaming cloud-forest. The road plunged steeply downwards. Bright green foliage interspersed with the darker greens of the forest from which came the occasional brief brightly-coloured flash of equatorial birdlife and a damp humid smell of constant growth and constant decay. All this flooded in through side-windows which had not long before been tightly closed against the damp cold of the high Andes.

That smell of constant decay – it wasn't just the plants outside!

As the descent came to an end, so the mists cleared and the land opened out as a green landscape under a bright blue sky. Before long, the town of La Fria was visible and with it the junction of National Route 6 and the road leading up to Merida. Horatio climbed out and we sped north once more through the hot equatorial lowlands of the Maracaibo basin. The Colombia border was very close. It had become baking hot.

Once the Andes had fallen well behind, a flat landscape spread out to the horizon. But it was a very different place to the parched llanos which lay the other side of that mountain wall. The yellow dryness east of the Andes had been replaced by an intensely green and luxuriant cover of trees, shrubs and marsh grass. Reed-fringed pools reflected some of the brightness of the blue sky and sunlight. A great clarity was in the air. Bird and animal life abounded.

No sign of habitation or cultivation showed in this now beautiful and fertile-looking land which spread on either side of the road. There was no sign, either, of that great shimmering expanse of water which lay some sixty miles to the north-east – Lake Maracaibo.

★

It was the *alcabalas* which revealed the extremely close proximity of the border only a few miles to the west. They appeared with such increasing frequency that they were almost in sight of each other. In the intervening spaces, heavily-armed border troops slowly moved along the road in trucks – seemingly the only other traffic on a deserted Route 6.

Deserted in colonial times; deserted in post-colonial times and now deserted in modern times. The designation of this tropical paradise as a nature reserve had kept the oil industry of the eastern Maracaibo at bay but that didn't really explain the absence of people and of settlement. The La Fria we had left Horatio at was the closest the colonial Spanish got to the area; the fact that this hot tropical little place was called The Cold revealed the shivers which its townsfolk had notoriously suffered from and the malarial fever which had wracked their bodies. All that, however – and the fierce spears of the Motilone Indians – was of the past.

Spraying the swamps with DDT after World War II had finished off the malarial mosquitoes. The Capuchin missionaries who had – since the 1960s – penetrated the hearts and minds of the hitherto stone-age peoples of the swamps had unwittingly achieved the same result. In two of three decades, no less than seventy-five per cent of the indigenous people of this territory had disappeared. Indeed, by 1985, the country was emptier than it had been for the previous five hundred years. Some of the Motilones had retreated into the frontier wilderness of the *Serrania de Perija*; most had simply faded away as the stone-age generation failed to make the leap of several thousands of years into the modern age.

The isolation of the Motilones was not only broken by the missionaries. It did not help them much that to the east and extending out into the shallow waters of Lake Maracaibo was one of the biggest oilfield areas outside the Middle East and the former Soviet Union. The Coastal Bolivar accumulations contained more than ten billion barrels of recoverable hydrocarbons – crude oil which had been pumping out of the Tertiary sandstone reservoirs deep below the lake ever since Shell made its first discovery during the First World War. First the timber derricks began to form a water-borne forest as the discoveries grew and production activities extended further and further afield. Then camps, roads, pipelines, schools, hospitals, more roads and – after the Second World War – a steady stream of tankers beginning to pass out through the narrows at the head of the lake and out into the Gulf of Venezuela. From there, most went north through the Caribbean to the United States.

*

Carretera Nueva – the New Road – continued ever northwards through the park-like terrain of forest, tall grass and reed-lined pools. Occasionally, a huge tree would rear up above more modest neighbours with its dark crown silhouetted in the fresh, clear air against the blue of the sky. Parrots chattered harshly in the tropical foliage close to the road – sometimes flickering colourfully into view.

It seemed that some people gained a livelihood in the country of the New Road. From time to time small groups of black heifers could be seen munching the grass around a pool, or single animals would be busy at the roadside with the green fronds that were always trying to crowd across the open space of the tarmac and turn it back to wilderness. Clearly it was one of these heifers which had been hit earlier that morning by a military vehicle (or perhaps a night-time truck-load of illegal immigrants?). The corpse lay half in the road and half in the grass and foliage.

The cycle of nature had turned: it was no longer feeding; it was now fed-upon. Hacking away at the flesh of the swelling carcass were fifteen or twenty *zamuros* – the black vultures of northern Latin America. All but the most preoccupied briefly turned their wrinkled, gore-spattered heads to give a fierce stare in the direction of the passing car before lunging back to tear another strip off the lifeless victim. The heifer would be a pile of stinking red bones by midday.

It was still mid-morning, however, and the insidious stink of Raul's socks was not so easily ignored on the *Carretera Nueva.* The pervasive odour had begun to get on my nerves and yet there seemed to be no alternative but to settle down and endure the remaining two hundred miles or so to Maracaibo. The strengthening heat of the day did little to help.

The remaining two hundred miles! It was, in fact, somewhat of a problem deciding exactly where you were and how far you had travelled along the New Road. Presumably for strategic reasons, no one had thought to put up a series of useful signs pointing in the direction of Venezuela's second largest city and inviting travellers to head there. The Colombian border had swerved off a little to the west before streaking northwards along the axis of the *Serrania de Perija* and as a result even the *alcabalas* had thinned out. That only left the rivers to mark progress, although none of these seemed to have a name on my map.

More steel girder bridges spanning brown piranha-haunted waters – presumably marking the River Catatumbo, the Tarra, the Santa Ana, the Tokuko and the Negro. All passing through thick banks of dense foliage and all heading eastwards off the *Serrania* and westwards into Lake Maracaibo – rivers which kept salinities very low in what was really just a huge embayment of the sea. A few Motilone communities still survived by these rivers: I caught brief glimpses of two or three dug-out canoes pulled high up on the muddy bank; a reed-thatched top of a hut in the foliage; but no people.

⋆

Then the country started to change again. The foothills of the *Serrania* began to appear distantly to the west; the countryside became less green and less luxuriant; the swamps dried out; the trees died away; grassland took over; the first settlements appeared. The town of Machiques marked a beginning of open prairie. This was the main milk-producing region of Venezuela.

All of a sudden, the stone age gave way to the twentieth century again. Petrol stations, truck stops and huge Texan-style signs replaced the *alcabalas* of the *Nuevo Carretera*. The curious mosquito-and-spear frontier land of Venezuela had been left behind; barbed wire fences now enclosed the open range; a taste of the southern United States was creeping back down the road which led to the oil-boom city of Maracaibo.

Before Maracaibo, there was a much smaller place called Rosario. In the heat of the afternoon and in the middle of the wide prairie, a stop for fuel and coffee after long hours of steady driving. A background hum of tyre on tarmac briefly stilled; a deserted crossroads; high clouds in the sky; a profound silence settling over the landscape; the quiet sounds of nature gradually intruding after rush and noise; the sudden awareness of birdsong and the rustle of grass in a slight breeze.

Birdsong slowly intruding into the peace of the silence which comes after noise and movement. '*...And for that minute a blackbird sang.*' Where had I experienced these sensations before? '*...mistier – farther and farther – all the birds of Oxfordshire and Gloucester*'. That was it – this crossroads in the middle of nowhere west of Lake Maracaibo was Addlestrop! Edward Thomas' station – that bare platform where the steam hissed and no one came and no one left. It was here!

Another slight breeze swept away Addlestrop. It was no longer Oxfordshire but Zulia. A little dust-devil whirled grit and paper scraps into intimations of the one-ness of things. The tiny prairie tornado danced across the baking tarmac before veering off on its giddy journey across the grasslands. It vanished out of sight in the general direction of Maracaibo.

⋆

Maracaibo. I tracked down Raul finishing a quiet smoke amongst the bric-a-brac surrounding the petrol station and we once more set off on the final leg of the journey. More of the huge signs appeared at the roadside as the route grew closer and closer to Texas. Combinations of tree-break, farmhouse and wind pump began to multiply, the grass dried out and yellowed; long-horn cattle started to become very common and Zulia took on the characteristics of Marlboro Country.

Steers and oil, jeans and pick-up trucks, barbed wire and a sky which had become a much paler blue as if it too had dried out a little with every northward mile away from the land of the Motilones. Finally, as that pale blue was beginning to change into a harsher glare, the first signs of the city appeared on the horizon. White high-rise buildings looming mirage-like above suburban foliage. An increase in traffic.

It was not long before we were sweeping through the main part of the city and within sight of the waters of the Gulf of Venezuela. The long trip into the interior had brought us once more to the shores of the Caribbean.

★

Not always a comfortable place to inhabit – those shores of the Caribbean. The twentieth-century wealth of Maracaibo had attracted the oil men of North America and Europe; its sixteenth- and seventeenth-century wealth had attracted pirates like Henry Morgan who had devastated the settlement and then sailed on to take as much as he could from the Spanish colonial plantations of cocoa, sugar-cane, corn and cotton growing up around the south-eastern shores of the lake. At one time or another, most of the buccaneers who parasitically fed off the riches of the Spanish Main did the same.

There was no doubt in the city of Maracaibo that those cold, misty Andes had completely gone. Pirates and sugar-cane; parrots and pieces of eight; huge Indian women from the peninsula of Guajira padding slowly through the wide streets near the port – their brightly coloured tent-like cotton dresses ballooning out over mountainous breasts and buttocks. The hot mid-afternoon tropical sun burned down on the light-coloured buildings of the waterfront. I dropped Raul off.

★

There was little incentive to re-enter the heat of that sun once inside the air-conditioned coolness of the Maracaibo International. In fact, night had fallen by the time I woke from a doze and hunger pushed me into any further action. A relaxing gin and tonic or rum punch at the poolside bar seemed just the thing to set off a civilised meal in one of the hotel's restaurants.

Once outside, however, it immediately became obvious that the daytime torpor of the tropics had been replaced by a strong inshore breeze as the air temperatures of land and sea fought to readjust themselves. The incoming sea air caused the palm trees fringing the pool to twist and sway in the gusts. There was a strong possibility of being hit by a falling coconut. Any hope of a relaxing sundowner soon became totally out of the question as the wind strength mounted and bar equipment, sun umbrellas and even deckchairs were swept hither and thither in the near-deserted gardens of the International.

This air was not cold, of course, and its moist balmy freshness would have been enjoyable had it not carried with it the slight odour of the refinery. A mile or two away and across the whipped-up waters of the small bay called the *Boca de Tablazo* could be seen the gleam of orange fire where a neon-lit glitter of pipes and tanks culminated in the tall stacks and flaring gases of a petrochemical complex.

Inside, too, the oil industry was difficult to escape. Texan engineers moved heavily and ponderously from table to salad bar as the large steaks they had ordered were being precisely charred in the kitchens of the hotel. String ties, bulging bellies, baggy jeans: a kind of off-duty uniform and one which suggested that – although Houston was two thousand miles to the north-west and Venezuela's oil production was currently the responsibility of the National Oil Companies – no one could seriously interfere with the US of A's strategic crude supplies.

An early highlight of the annual marathon which was held in the city of Maracaibo was the crossing of the five-mile long Urdanata bridge. This modern structure soared over the narrow channel leading out of the lake: the channel through which Henry Morgan and others had passed to find the bright gold of the south-eastern settlements and the channel through which the tankers of the Coastal Bolivar fields took the black gold out.

Such bridges were a devil to cross on foot – they soaked up energy like hard sandy beaches, undermining all sense of propulsion and of forward momentum. Even crossing the bridge in the comfort of a car seemed tiring. The Urdanata bridge went on for ever.

There were, of course, compensations. You could look at the view for one thing. And on the Urdanata bridge, I could see that elusive expanse of water at last. The silvery-green waters of Lake Maracaibo bending southwards over the horizon until they vanished under a slightly hazy sky. A small green-decked tanker moved carefully through the shallow, buoyed waters below. From the heights of the central span of the bridge, abrupt colour changes on the water's surface marked out how cautious pilotage had to be in such confined spaces.

Thinking of confined spaces – it was a relief to be rid of the lads in uniform for a while!

★

Unfortunately, the ridding of the lads in lasted only as long as it took me to cross from one side of the Urdanata bridge to the other. Just as I had assumed that this part of Latin America was more Marlboro Country than *alcabala* country, a roadside security checkpoint appeared in view at the start of the road to Coro and – eventually – to Caracas.

Caracas lay four hundred and fifty miles to the east. Surely the soldier signalling the car to stop was not going to ask for a lift to the capital! The novelty of travelling around much of western Venezuela in the company of its armed forces was beginning to wear off.

It was at least a partial relief that the small lean figure clutching a holdall and standing at one end of the sleeping policeman was neither a lad nor in uniform. Nor did he want to go to Caracas. But he plainly wanted to go somewhere and clearly had an official relationship with the soldier with the sub-machine-gun who stood at the other end of the sleeping policeman.

'*No hay problema, no hay problema,*' said the man as I explained that I was going via a very circuitous route. '*Quero Coro.*' He was, it transpired, a plain-clothes policeman!

★

The journey to Coro began. A long straight road which bore away from the Maracaibo crossing and into the low coastal country of Zulia Oriental as if its route had been drawn on the landscape with a ruler. It could adopt such an uncompromising way of getting from A to B only because this landscape was almost flat and a near desert. Few signs of any habitation existed amongst the dry bushes; no one seemed to be able to scratch even the barest living from the stony soil. The only evidence of life was the few skinny goats rummaging about amongst thorns.

It was still fairly early in the day. The air had not become searingly hot and – as it rushed in through the open side-windows of the car – no longer carried the tang of petrochemicals but a very distinctive burnt dusty odour and the slight fragrance of crushed herbs – sage or thyme. It was the smell of a land of little moisture and of bush fires where only very infrequent rain fell to wash away the charcoal from amongst the grit and stones.

A roadside sign showed where we left the state of Zulia and passed into the state of Falcon. The countryside remained unmoved by the change; the straight road continuing to swoop across an empty and dry wilderness. In time, however, the flatness of the coast began to be intruded upon by low hills. Stands of cactus sent pale green, fleshy arms up through a tangle of low thorn bushes covering the gently rising land. They looked as if they were drowning in the parched soil and waving for help from passers-by.

Goats still appeared from time to time – rooting for shoots around the occasional crude shack which now appeared at the roadside. In these places, goat meat on the hoof was for sale – my passenger indicating that it was something of a delicacy in this part of the world. For those too timid or too tender-hearted to commission the on-the-hoof variety, long strips of sun-browned goat flesh hung from poles.

More cactus and thorn country but to the south, first edging closer and then falling back until they were just a distinct blue-grey profile, were rugged hills: the San Luis 'mountains'. Surprisingly, had they been closer, their valleys would have starkly contrasted with the dusty undergrowth all around – being moist enough to cultivate the colonial crops of sugar-cane, coffee and cacao beans.

My lean plain-clothes policeman indicated that he wanted to be dropped off before we reached the main part of the town of Coro. His conversation had not been great but a flow of chatter across one hundred and sixty miles of near desert wasn't everything. In fact, long spells of silence had much to recommend them. He was a straightforward sort of person, not glum, and his feet didn't smell. I liked him and was a little sorry when the first of the low colonial houses of the ancient city appeared at the side of the route and he motioned for a stop. Thanking me warmly for the lift, he lifted out his small bag and set off – not towards the houses but into a desert-like patch of country near the town which was so arid that even the bushes had found it too difficult to survive. Curiously, he vanished in a direction where nothing appeared to be able to grow and which no one appeared to want to inhabit!

*

Living at the margins of habitability had been Coro's plight right from the time of its earliest establishment in 1527. Salt-flats had been the attraction to the first Spanish colonists – both here and at Cumana, which occupied a similarly arid spot where sea-water evaporated in a shallow coastal inlet several hundred miles west of Caracas. Salt and not gold laid the unglamorous foundations of the Spanish Main. The tide of exploration soon pushed inland.

As far as Coro was concerned it might have been better for the early colonists if they had stuck to boring exports of basic commodities. It might even have been better if they had stayed under the rule of the King of Spain. That monarch, however, was heavily indebted to the German banking company of Welser and the increasing flow of stories exaggerating the immense potential wealth of the New World pointed towards a neat arrangement that might be concluded to offset this liability.

Charles V of Spain was persuaded to carve out a Province of Venezuela from the Spanish Main and lease it to his bankers. It was a kind of franchise. What the bankers had in mind was not twenty years of digging sodium chlorate out of the natural evaporation pans of the nearby peninsula of Paraguana but to send off several gold-seeking expeditions into the interior. It was hoped – and expected – that these would duly return to the southern shores of the Caribbean with something like the rewards that Cortés had recently gained from penetrating beyond its western shores.

Unfortunately for both the Welsers and for Coro – they picked the wrong spot. Peru and the gold and glory of the Inca civilisation were still to be discovered but it was the Pizarro brothers who reached it in 1533 and not a family of German bankers. Whilst the conquistadores sailed down the Pacific coast and climbed on the Inca roads to the heights of the central Andes, the Welser expeditions struggled over the parched llanos, through the malarial swamps of the equatorial lowlands or into the cold wet mountains of the north-east.

Rumours of *El Dorado* drove them on; starvation, thirst, disease and the arrow wounds of the Indians kept them back. For twenty years, a series of disastrous forays set out for the interior in search of golden cities, fabulous riches and great New World civilisations.

Then the German lease ran out. Coro returned to colonial rule. Unfortunately, in the space of two decades of failed adventuring, an earlier accommodation with the local peoples of the San Luis area had disintegrated into constant fighting, devastated villages and repeated Indian attacks on the small settlement by the salt pans. Nothing had been gained except a better idea of the inland geography of what was eventually to become northern Latin America.

*

It took a century or so for life in Coro to improve. The lure of wealth to the south had been shown to be false; the seas and islands stretching away across the Caribbean became the source of prosperity instead. In the 1630s, when the Dutch eased away the offshore islands of Curaçao, Aruba and Bonaire from the Spanish Crown and filled these small dry patches of land only several tens of miles off the coast of the mainland with Jewish and other settlers escaping the uncertain times of seventeenth-century Europe, a comfortable business quickly grew up.

Colonial Coro flourished quietly as a kind of back entrance to Spanish Latin America. Food, livestock and building materials were smuggled out to the nearby Caribbean islands; European luxuries and manufactures crept around the cumbrous taxes and tariff barriers of the colonial mainland and slipped inland. The city quietly 'watched the wall' and grew prosperous as the equivalent of 'baccy for the squire and brandy for the parson' crept in and out of the Spanish Main. A cross-trade even developed with those other colonial settlers north of the Caribbean who felt the heavy weight of Old World taxes – the American colonies of the British Crown.

★

At the close of the eighteenth century, however, revolutionary wars put an end to all the undercover activity and Coro's fortunes once more passed back to the salt. Only a cathedral, a *casa de Balcon* and a number of grand old colonial buildings preserved signs of its former prosperity.

And nearby, the peninsula of Paraguana looked as poor as a church mouse and as if it had never been anywhere near the rosy glow of a lucrative Dutch-Jewish entrepôt trade. Funny that – offshore Aruba and Curaçao still Dutch and still rich; less than twenty miles to the south, Paraguana just a scrub-covered piece of desert with the odd pimple-like hill in its centre.

The salt-flats stretched westwards from a narrow strip of dune-covered road which struggled to keep this piece of desert joined to Coro and the rest of the coastal plain of western Venezuela. It was an unstable situation; tongues of fine-grained sand continually nosed across the route to the peninsula like huge creatures poking their way cautiously into the affairs of humanity. The road led ultimately to an oil pipeline terminal, refinery and tanker-loading facility spreading over the south-western extremity of the near island so the sand was never allowed to win. But beyond the dunes was mostly dust, scrub, cactus and stones – as arid and barren as the outskirts of nearby Coro. Only goats appeared to inhabit the areas between two or three small communities which eked a living out of the rest of the place.

If Paraguana was a place which wealth had briefly brushed over and then abandoned, it was also a place where the hours of the day could skip by too readily. Caracas was still a long way off and the Independence Weekend was drawing to a close.

★

That late afternoon journey from Coro to Caracas proved to be considerably more than the three hundred miles suggested by the map, although it all started well enough. More emptiness stretched ahead as the route continued eastwards and then began a swing to the south-east – crossing the broad coastal plain of Falcon before gently climbing and falling as it passed through sixty miles of scrub thicket, stony soil and waving cactus arms. The distance to the *Golfo de Triste* gradually lessened.

Dry, empty country persisted for some time until one of those sudden changes occurred when the route slowly began its long descent to the resort areas and towards the sought-after beaches. First to be left behind were the waving arms of the cactus. Then the scrub quickly showed signs of changing from grey to light green and then to a deeper emerald green. Then trees appeared, then grass, then fields and cultivation.

And then all those elderly Chevrolets, Fords, Oldsmobiles, Pontiacs and Cadillacs – suddenly appearing ahead as well as the Japanese land-cruisers, the trucks and the battered buses. All the world was suddenly to be seen flooding back on the road towards the capital; everybody had thought to leave that little bit earlier to avoid the rush; everyone was locked in the same traffic jam; everyone was on the one road which led north to Valencia and then on to Caracas.

Everyone looked like being in the same jam for several hours.

*

The worst of it came somewhere south of the resort town of Tucacas. Thirty-six hours of partying on the beach had clearly taken its toll. The road was full of jaded faces, crumpled clothes, crying infants and over-heated cruisers. Independence Weekend was over; all wanted to get away from the grubby sand and back into the bright lights of the big city. Hooting, shouting, revving of huge six, eight or twelve cylinder engines, impatient slaps on enormous rusting door panels, arms repeatedly raised in disgust, shakes of the head, adjustment of driving mirrors and more hoots – the cycle repeated itself but the traffic remained motionless. Nothing moved and nothing looked like moving until well into the evening.

Observed at close quarters with little to do, the Venezuelans were a physically attractive people to watch even with all their Latin impatience. Particularly attractive were the cosmopolitan *caraquenas* of the capital with a touch of Spanish, a touch of Italian and a touch of the indigenous peoples of the Spanish Main before the Spanish had reached it. The touch of the Caribbean after the Africans had arrived improved matters still further. Beauty, style and a light-hearted approach to sex. '*We are a microcosm of the human race,*' wrote Simon Bolivar, '*...we are a world apart, confined within two oceans, young in arts and sciences but old as a human society. We are neither Indians nor Europeans, yet we are a part of each.*' It was no chance circumstance that Venezuelan women had sauntered elegantly off with the Miss World title more times than most other countries had.

Unfortunately, I was trapped behind the wrong vehicle. There were no Miss Worlds on the open back of the large pick-up pumping out diesel fumes as it waited to move on.

Instead, its passengers were working their way through a case of canned beer and steadily tossing the empties into the nearby bushes. All that lay in view was a truck-load of flabby, ugly boozers in dirty vests getting progressively more raucous as the jam continued to show no signs of movement.

*

Time passed agonisingly slowly. A few cars appeared travelling in the opposite direction. Not vehicles which had broken through from Valencia and were on their way to Coro, but drivers who had decided to fight the blockage and take a back-road into the countryside. I watched them bump off the road and meander westwards. A convoy seemed to be heading into distant farmland – their progress marked by a diminishing trail of dust. At least they were moving – even if it was in the opposite direction to Caracas.

From the pick-up truck in immediate view, more empty beer cans sailed into the bushes. One of the drinkers added a stream of urine along the same trajectory.

*

The ribbon of dusty ruts and stony potholes headed unceasingly westwards and ever further away from Caracas! The hope that it would somehow veer southwards and then join the Valencia road somewhere ahead of the traffic congestion had long since evaporated. Two hours had elapsed since starting out into the open country west of Tucacas; two hours in which the convoy of vehicles escaping from the jam had gradually dwindled as first one and then another vehicle slewed to the side and gave up.

Dust and huge water-filled holes were the world of those who remained. Darkness was falling after a half hour of sunset during which the fierce golden light of the sun had bored its way directly into the line of vision through the windscreen. Now it had finally dropped behind the dry hills of Falcon – or were we now in the state of Lara?

Interestingly, all those smart Japanese land-cruisers and metropolitan safari vehicles had been the first to go. It seemed that it wasn't the engine or the tyres that had taken the toughest beating on this Venezuelan back-road but the people inside. Lurching around on a hard suspension in a cloud of gritty, choking dust could be endured whilst there was still hope of an early re-entry on to hard metalled surfaces but the continuous westwards passage had triggered off several family rows. On each occasion, figures with scarves half-covering their faces and ruined hairstyles could be dimly glimpsed through dusty side windows gesticulating at each other in angry dispute.

Going back was out of the question; going forward could mean an even deeper penetration into increasingly dry and remote country. The hired car took it surprisingly well – grounding occasionally where the pits in the road came close to coalescing and where the small car jerked over steep walls of hard gravel. In these places, its wheels shrieked and spread dust, grit and muddy water into a kind of soup which blasted out behind and covered the windscreen of the truck which was following. But that was a fair exchange – the same brown soup had come flying backwards from the wheels of the vehicle slewing along in front.

In the end there were very few of us left: two high-wheelbase pick-ups and me. A kind of thumbs-up camaraderie had developed – for a while, the fact that we were all still heading west and continuously slithering and bumping ever further from Caracas, was forgotten.

⋆

The real world came back into focus not long after the track made a slow curve to the south-west and then suddenly debouched on to a metalled road. It seemed almost too good to be true and – for the first few miles – could only be treated with some circumspection in case of a sudden reversion back into a welter of dust and potholes.

But it continued to be a proper road and even began to show signs of heading out of the wilderness and back into civilisation. We approached the town of San Felipe – some consolation that the main route to Caracas could not be far away; less comfort from the fact that the 'short-cut' had added at least fifty miles to the journey towards the capital.

According to the guidebooks, San Felipe El Fuerte was approximately four hours drive from Caracas and – at one time – the world's chief source of chocolate. This useful historical fact palled beside the four hours drive.

More travelling and more of the rapid vegetation changes. In the dark, semi-desert had quickly changed to an unseen tropical lushness. Fertile country now spread out beyond the glare of the headlights; hot and damp places where cacao beans and sugar-cane flourished. Somewhere out there, hidden in its lushness – between the town of San Felipe and the main Maracaibo-Caracas highway, was said to be a mythical palace. Not a jewel-encrusted version of *El Dorado* this time, but a pre-colonial Garden of Eden where deer and tapir herds roamed beside plantations of maize and the gorgeous gold-bedecked halls of the goddess called Maria Lionza were located.

Maria Lionza would have won the Miss World contest – or, at least, the statue of her which graced the lanes of the *autopista* leading through Caracas from the west. Supposedly the daughter of an Indian princess and a Spanish conquistadore, she occupied a spiritual location somewhere between Amerindian pantheism, African voodooism and Roman Catholicism. Her grandest attributes, however, were flowing hair, majestic breasts, bulging thighs and a decidedly uncritical view of free love. Strongly disapproved of by Christian clergy, put down as *mestizo* superstition by the Spanish government of colonial days, and spurned as part of an outdated belief by the republican governments of post-colonial days, she was, nonetheless, more interesting to many than Simon Bolivar or the Virgin Mary. The Caracas *autopista* statue of her astride one of the tapirs of the mythical palace gardens had a frequently renewed garland of flowers adorning it.

★

Caracas. The guidebook was right. It did take a solid four hours of driving before the glittering lights of the capital appeared in the wooded hills of the coast range. Once more the familiar black loom of Mount Avila could be made out where it towered over the late-night city.

It was already the next day by the time I had sped past the statue of the garlanded Maria Lionza. Much of the final leg of the journey from Valencia had been behind an overnight bus from the interior – perhaps from San Cristóbal or San Felipe. It had *El Proyectil* painted in large, flowery letters on its rear.

The name meant The Rocket. A name which had a faint military ring to it. Just the sort of vehicle which might have been trundling through the night towards a Caracas about to be subjected to a forced change of government. Just the sort of vehicle which might have been flagged down by stranded members of a José Chirinos paratrooper battalion who were anxious to get to the *coup* on time.

Chapter Four

Weekend in Colombia

Colombia. The country of 'bad habits', of the seventy-second attack on the oil pipeline from the llanos, of the National Liberation Army, of the Colombian Revolutionary Armed Forces.

The country next to Venezuela where any car disappearing from the streets of Caracas was rumoured to reappear with new number-plates in the driveways of the drug-dealers of Coro, Bogotá or Medellin. The country whose frontier lay just to the west of all those heavily populated *alcabalas* on the road from San Cristóbal to Maracaibo. The country of origin of many of the poor *rancho* dwellers. The country where trouble came from.

Or might there be another Colombia?

*

Calm, tranquil – almost soporific. As long as a patch of turbulence did not cause the big machine to momentarily lurch or shudder, the descent from cruising height to lower levels could be one of the most pleasant stages of a flight. The plane gliding gently down towards its destination. Whatever was awaiting the traveller on the ground was still sealed off by twenty minutes or so of descending flight. The business of seat belts, synthetic food, adjustment of watches and heartening weather reports from the cockpit had largely been concluded. The cabin was quiet; the stewardesses somewhere else in the plane; the jet engines emitting a low, steady, reassuring hiss; the cloud-tops slowly coming closer and closer.

Towering vapour mountains – the sun touching their peaks, striking down into their puffy flanks and lighting the darkness of valleys leading nowhere in particular; valleys sometimes inexplicably altering into ridges. The descent continuing. Down into one of these valleys – one wing-tip brushing an overhanging wall and briefly disappearing. Then a gloomy shadow passing across the sun; then grey moisture closing around the cabin window. Then the valley floor again and – through its swirling undulations – a brief vision of more valleys and more hills. Then grey moisture and then those same valleys and hills but this time patterned with forest and farmland, roads and the tiny specks of buildings.

An indistinct map which gradually became real. Roads took on more purpose, streaking like thin veins across the landscape – easily connecting those specks with long loops and yet crossing any change in relief with what seemed like unnecessary tortuosity. Roads twisting and turning through a cool green countryside where patches of water begin to glint like pewter. The plane altered course for the final stage of the descent. The sunlight high above became a fast-fading dream; a now unattainable heaven; a paradise lost. A grim dampness took over; the moistness of a wet day in a cool climate rising inexorably skywards from the place that lay below.

Avianca flight 068 from Caracas to Bogotá was about to land at El Dorado airport and would we please fasten our seat-belts and extinguish all cigarettes.

Flight 068 droned heavily down towards the last few minutes of the approach. A year or two earlier one of Avianca's planes had been blown up. The scene below showed no sign of internecine devastation. It was a calm, fertile-looking landscape which could be observed now at quite close quarters. Craggy, half-forested hills, a checkerboard of fields, the *Sabana de Bogotá*. Interestingly, we were still at an altitude of 8,000 feet.

*

One shower had just passed. Another seemed to be chasing the plane. The undercarriage whirred comfortably into place and the cabin crew were requested to take up their positions for landing. Below, rooftops and the surfaces of many low sheds slid rapidly into view. As they did, a brief shaft of pale sunlight struck down through the cloud cover and lit their reflective surfaces – showing it to be polythene sheeting which had been stretched tight across the metal framework of what were obviously commercial greenhouses. In each shed, under such protection, stood row after row of budding flowers.

Colombia produced a very lucrative crop of flowers up here in this moist *Sabana de Bogotá* not far north of the Equator. Most of it went out of the country by the means that we were arriving – plane-loads being regularly dispatched to the United States and Canada and allowing carnations, roses, lilies and tulips to be enjoyed throughout the cold winter of the temperate zone and to brighten up the foyers, table-tops, weddings and funerals of North America.

Unfortunately, it wasn't only the flowers that took this northern export route. Other crops were being assiduously cultivated in that same moist atmosphere not far from the equator: marijuana and cocaine did very well with year-round sunlight and a fair bit of rain. So well, in fact, that such narcotic harvests often (it was rumoured) found their way in amongst the carnations, roses, lilies and tulips. This was a trade which turned a bigger profit than blooms; an income so great that it encouraged the contorted, twisting fingers of corruption to slip around the throat of the body politic in Colombia and to hold it wriggling and squirming for air. Recently, other hands had gripped the same throat in an attempt to loosen those fingers. There was no small danger that the patient could expire from its cure.

⋆

A dose of the cure was applied immediately on landing. Heavily armed surveillance troops watched disembarking passengers with a professional gaze whilst their dogs tugged at the leash – clearly desperate to nosedive into hand-baggage from Caracas and come out with something of interest. Drugs were a terrible affliction – there was no doubt about that. But who in their right mind would bring marijuana to Bogotá; actually take cocaine into Colombia!

Nonetheless, the dogs were ready. Once the rest of the luggage had been collected, the inspection began. Nothing dramatic, of course. They didn't all rush towards one scruffy suitcase – legs slipping and sliding on the polished floor of the terminal building – and begin tearing at it with bared teeth. Their handlers had no cause to click the safety catches on their sub-machine-guns and stand around in a half-circle asking the owner to raise his or her hands. There was no wild fleeing down long corridors; no bullets in the woodwork; no innocent parties scattering for cover in a welter of tea and sandwiches. It was more subtle than that.

As we assembled in a file to present passports, the dogs strolled casually by us. No fuss, no sudden excitements. But you never quite knew where you were with a dog. The tension was palpable as each slouch-hatted soldier and each alert Alsatian came abreast and then moved on slowly past. Dogs can take a shine to a lot more than drugs. The luggage stacked beside us started to look as worried as those who owned it.

There were no coals-to-Newcastle; no oranges-to-Spain. Human, vegetable and mineral suspects from Caracas to Bogotá were all acquitted. They stamped our passports and let us in. Nothing seemed to interest the dogs who pattered softly off to survey some other part of the building. Colombia from the air had seemed unexpectedly green and surprisingly well-ordered. Now it was time to encounter Colombia on the ground.

*

A smart place – El Dorado airport. Red-jacketed, grey-flannelled porters waited discreetly for custom; obliging young ladies in tartan kilts slowly pushed refreshments about on wheeled trolleys and were able to rustle up anything from herb tea to gin and tonic. A smell of fresh coffee and newly baked croissants hung in the air. Illuminated advertisements offered information about car-hire, hotels, restaurants, leatherware. It wasn't hot and it wasn't noisy. (It wasn't Colombia, either – but more of that later.) For a brief few minutes – suddenly noticing the heavier clothes of the people all around: the dark suits and ties on men; the chic appearance of women; woollen skirts and cardigans; the several hats and raincoats – this was not Bogotá, this was Geneva. What had happened to the Wild West of South America?

It all looked fairly expensive and I needed money. Leaving Caracas had been a bit of a rush and I'd come away still clutching a thick wad of bolivares which were meant to be changed into the more universally acceptable US dollars. It was in counting up this Venezuelan money whilst standing in a queue at the airport bank that I noticed my sleeve was being gently tugged.

'*Buenos tardes, señor,*' said a voice which turned out not to be owned by another dog-handler slipping quietly up from astern but a small man in a slightly scruffy suit. '*Como esta?*'

That was a bad start. Trusting any complete stranger who was concerned about your heath and wearing a slightly scruffy suit was not a good idea in Latin America. The other members of the queue looked on dispassionately.

'*Bien, bien. Gracias.*' I didn't feel close enough to ask how he was and anyway he soon filled a brief embarrassed silence by shifting attention to the clutch of notes in my hand.

'*Por favor,*' he said, nodding at them. '*Hay un problema. No est posible aqui. I will change for you.*'

I declined. The queue was shifting closer towards the rather beautiful head and shoulders of a woman behind a glass window who looked like Joan Collins. The bank seemed a more attractive place for an exchange of money.

Unfortunately, Joan Collins wasn't very helpful. Although this was the very country in which Simon Bolivar spent a great deal of his revolutionary time, the moment she glimpsed the notes that had been named after him, a look of extreme contempt passed across her lovely face.

'*Solamente dolares,*' she intoned. '*Solamente dolares,*' and peered around for the next person in the queue as if I had been offering her some rotten fruit for cash. Or trying to exchange a pile of roubles in an eastern European country that was supposed to be a fraternal satellite. I shifted position to block off the next person and began again. She waved me aside and leaned sideways in a renewed attempt to catch the attention of her intended customer. She had a nice figure, too.

'*Otros dineros a las lunes – y en el centro.*' So that was it. Changing bolivares was something any right-minded person did in the centre of town – and not until the working week began on Monday. I started to explain that I had only US$50 in cash and needed the Colombian currency now rather than in two days' time but it was to little avail. The woman behind had got through; she had plenty of dollars and Joan Collins was already scooping up notes and tapping into the bank's calculator.

The man with my well-being on his mind. Where was he? As I searched down the length of the queue, a dog and handler were working their way slowly up towards the window. Not unsurprisingly, he'd gone.

*

Colombia on plastic and a shoe-string. It was possible, of course. Cars could be hired on credit card. If you picked a big enough hotel, accommodation could be dealt with that way. And meals, too – either in the hotel of choice or in an expensive restaurant. Food and lodging and transportation – they were not the problem.

Neither were the toilets and tips which sometimes drew down on ready cash. Nor the bit needed here and there for beggars, postcard-sellers and bag-carriers. These were all optional expenditures. What was rarely optional – if you were unlucky to fall into their path – were the official claimants. The men in Latin America who, with or without a uniform, supplemented their meagre incomes with 'spot fines'.

Not every official required such a supplement, of course. In fact, relatively few. Nonetheless, if the pointing finger of the next-door neighbour was to be believed, the one country where a bit of spare cash could usefully smooth the waters of any local difficulty was Colombia. And, in Colombia, $50 probably wouldn't be enough. I hired a car, nonetheless, and set off for downtown Bogotá.

As the clothes had indicated, the temperature was noticeably cool outside the terminal building. Not cold, of course, but that kind of wet coolness where people glance up to see if more rain is on the way and carry umbrellas.

The umbrellas soon faded as I drove away from the precincts of El Dorado. So did the elegantly tailored men and the women in stylish tweed skirts. Downtown Bogotá was a very different kettle of fish from downtown Geneva.

Municipal elections were in progress in the capital – political posters dominating the first three or four miles of highway leading east from the airport and towards the edge of the *Sabana.* The road headed towards a city which could been seen spreading along the foot of steeply rising ground. A distant white cross looked out over Bogotá from this range of hills, as did the tiny buildings of the convent of Monserrate which glowed in brief spells of sunlight – the sun also catching glass in some of the taller office blocks and making them sparkle and flash with a golden aura. It was as if the real El Dorado had come to life in this part of the Andes and lay only a mile or two ahead.

What was also ahead was a gallery of very large and very sincere faces. These now lined both sides of the road.

Some countries always projected very good photographic portraits of their politicos. France was one; Brazil another. Colombia was clearly a third. It was not just people who were gazing out at road-users. 'Integrity' was. And 'Fraternity'. And 'Resolution'. And 'Capability'. Such qualities oozed from the posters: eyes, mouths and chins were up to two feet across from hair to tie. It was impossible not to look into them and start wondering who would be the best man for Bogotá.

Could the six-foot head and shoulders of Alberto Puyano be right for the city? He certainly came across with a warm, relaxed manner although his image was so clear and sharp that a surprisingly wrinkled skin seemed to have been dusted over with some kind of face-powder. His poster sported a thumbs-up over the words 'VOTE FOR ME' and the motto 'the best of mayors'. He was already in place, then.

Was re-election a good idea? It might be better to have somebody new and 'turn the soil' every so often in somewhere like Bogotá. What about 'Victor G Ricardo'? His concerned but rather magisterial expression suggested that he not only knew a thing or two about the public sector but that he could soon clear up any mess that Alberto Puyano might be leaving behind. His poster said that Bogotá needed a 'new man; clear ideas'. Yes, Ricardo looked the man.

Although there was Andreas Pastrana to consider.

But that was a funny thing. Sometimes Andreas Pastrana was on Alberto Puyano's poster and, when this was the case, both had donned those rather heavy spectacle frames favoured by solicitors and clergymen. Perhaps Andreas Pastrana did need glasses but we had already been shown Puyano without them. And the latter's frames seemed suspiciously empty of lenses! Also, Pastrana had the motto 'I know the city, Bogotá knows me.' Fair enough – but sitting in the same seat as 'the best of mayors'! That seemed a bit too good to be true. For a passing motorist from Caracas it was a linkage which needed a bit of mulling over.

Widen the choice a bit? Was the kindly Rafael Forero up to it? He looked more of an eco-mayor and was for 'a dignified life'. I liked that. But then the outskirts of the city began to replace the fields and glasshouses and the road narrowed. As the inbound traffic shuffled from two lanes to one, José Blackburn came out with a strong play for the floating vote and the undecided. Clever play – coming in at the end. And he had both posters and banners, was a 'Force for Change' and sported a black beard. Quite a youthful man, too – no powdered wrinkles there. A bluff face which could easily have melted into a contingent of bagpipe players or caber-tossers. Did he really fit the mode of Colombian politician, though? How would a bagpipe player cope with the smoke-filled back-rooms and the deals? Image could be quite important. And that – I suppose – was Claudia's problem as well; a Claudia on whom it was difficult to form a clear judgement since she was always draped from lamppost to lamppost with a message about 'clean politics'. It was all very difficult to pick and choose between them – no sooner had you settled on a favourite than someone new was tied across the road or papered on to the side of a building.

Paper or cloth; poster or banner; smile or frown; new or 'known to the city' – they all had quite a struggle with the burden of Colombian history. Ever since Simon Bolivar was forced to leave Bogotá in a desperate hurry, the reality of political life in the capital was all-too-frequently interrupted by a sudden explosion or a hail of bullets. There were more strongly held views in Colombia than there were varieties of flowers: the acronyms in the hills like ELN and FARC; the Conservative Party; the Liberal Party; the Christian Union Movements; the Democratic Alliance; the United Movements; the National Salvation Movement; the Socialist Workers; the Patriotic Union; the Movement for a New Country; the...

Like present; like past. After the death of Bolivar in 1830 came the Epoch of Civil Wars – 1863 to 1880. Then the War of a Thousand Days – 1899-1903. Then, a welcome break on the sidelines of violence whilst the rest of the world fought it out in World Wars I and II. Then back again for '*La Violencia*' – 1948–1962. Then another break for the Cold War to almost run its course before a wave of assassinations in the early 1980s, a gun battle at the Palace of Justice in 1985 which killed a Supreme Court Judge and one hundred others and then the progressive murder of almost anyone who peered above the political parapet on behalf of the Far Left.

Somewhere in the middle of this hurricane of activism was a hidden core wherein the real power of Colombia was said to lie: some claimed it was the Far Right – that the Conservatives wielded it; some said it was the Catholic Church. Then, in the elections of 1990, when three of the presidential candidates were cut down by bullets and the Avianca jet was blown-up in mid-air, another candidate appeared. The Medellin drug cartel (it was asserted) lay at the real centre of power – a claim soon challenged by the Coro drug cartel. Tough job ahead – whoever won.

★

The equatorial dusk had settled on Bogotá; the golden offices suddenly gone; the cross of Guadeloupe and the convent of Monserrate only a dim reddish glow on the hill-top. The traffic had slowed appreciably from its bold departure amongst the posters near the airport. Intersections, red lights and a heavy cross-flow of vehicles from adjacent streets led to much waiting amongst houses and factories.

With the going down of the sun came the cold night of the Andes; the first signs of its diminutive people and the first evidence of its terrible poverty. Beggar children began to scratch at the windows of the car with plaintive, rheumy eyes; figures moved wearily amongst dim illumination at the roadside in hats and woollen shawls; old men and women patiently stood or crouched beside little heaps of produce. Impassive brown faces, wrinkled skin and high cheekbones waited to sell three peaches on a cloth; a few lottery tickets; a small pile of potatoes; two or three newspapers. The fourteenth century watched the twentieth century drive slowly past and held out its hand for a coin or two.

I suddenly noticed that – as well as becoming slower – the traffic had become poorer. Hunched on a rubber-tyred horse-drawn cart were three gnome-like figures in ponchos. The cart interleaved itself amongst the slow-moving stream of cars, buses and trucks and added to the braking effect. At a crossing, another of these carts brought vehicles to a complete halt as it moved slowly across the traffic stream piled high with heavy stones and listing badly to one side. The driver leaned precariously to the other in the hope of providing some sort of counter-balance.

And those cars and buses had become poorer, too. It was clear that this busy road in from the airport had no fences; it was not here that the stolen goods of Venezuela were received. Nowhere was there any evidence of re-sprayed Japanese four-wheel drives with new number-plates. Somebody else was taking the property. The ageing Renaults and Volkswagens all around were clearly indigenous to Colombia and were cars which no neighbour would dream of claiming back. The buses were the oldest yet in Latin America.

A stream of such vehicles crowded in close as we entered the central part of the city. Perhaps no bad thing – meeting downtown Bogotá behind a smokescreen of bus diesel. A certain amount of protection against the protectors looked useful.

Through the yellow haze, a number of roadside security posts had appeared which were presumably sited at strategic spots to keep drug and terrorist insurgents from taking the city by storm. No expense had been spared in terms of fire-power. Rambo-like soldiers swept their barrels over the traffic stream as if word had spread about ancient buses now being part of the elite strike-force of any *coup*. Machine-guns were levelled from their nests built into the roof of armoured personnel carriers and swung this way and that as they covered the progress of fierce little patrols of soldiers and heavily armed policemen who made random sorties into the traffic stopped at lights. It wasn't the place to run out of petrol or to break someone's rear-lamp, and it wasn't the place to stop and check for directions to a good hotel.

The Hotel Tequendama loomed up amongst the heaviest troop concentrations like a Stalinist pile. Reputedly the best hotel in town, it was the very place that the

Venezuelans claimed was regularly searched in the small hours of the morning for 'signs' of drug-trafficking. Foreigners, of course, were the ones who were checked – such 'signs' could include being in possession of two or three hundred US dollars of which most could be confiscated in the public interest in case it was a down-payment on a sack or two of marijuana or cocaine. Apocryphal or not, I felt I could not afford the Tequendama – $50 dollars might not be enough to get them out of the room.

The buses were all on their last legs in more ways than the obvious. One after another, they pulled to the roadside along a Carrera 7 and discharged their passengers and a lot more diesel smoke. High above this smoky mêlée of an impromptu bus terminus, a hotel sign glowed hospitably.

*

It was, perhaps, a hotel which stood a little too close to all the coming and going of the buses. It was also, perhaps, a hotel which was a little too far away from the five-star comforts of the Tequendama. However convenient for municipal transport, it was not really sited in the smartest part of town. The reception grudgingly allocated a room, mentioned that there was a panic bell beside every bed and insisted that my (hired) Renault 21 would be stripped bare if I left it in a nearby side-street. They had a piece of fortified rough ground at the back – a *vigilante* was to stand guard all night.

All night. It wasn't a night of pitched battles in the streets, of the *vigilante* blowing the smoke off his automatic pistol and saluting as – surrounded by bodies – he held out his other hand for a tip. Much more mundane but also much more wearying, it was a night of growling engines, hissing air-brakes; of the occasional shout or cry and of the progressive replacement of oxygen with carbon monoxide. A long and uncomfortable night. I would have got more sleep in a torture chamber.

It was also a night of toothache. As soon as I had closed the door in the room, the altitude seemed to have brought on a strange kind of nagging pain – flaring up as quickly as it then receded a few minutes later. Accompanied by this, the night hours began to pass inexorably slowly. I had no pain killers and was reluctant to activate the panic bell. Buses came and went – sometimes coinciding with the onset of pain and sometimes departing with its relief. It was when they had brought on the intense ache for a third time and – coincidentally – provided the signal for its passing as they roared off, that I began to get suspicious. Could it be...?

No, the fourth bus broke the cycle and with it a budding theory of the effects of certain patterns of throbbing engine noise on the human dental system.

In a painless interlude longer than most, I switched on a television set in the room. Colombian late-night fare was not greatly different from Venezuelan late-night fare – although (perhaps, understandably) bull-fighting occupied more of the news than drug and terrorist-fighting. It was quite an enthralling bull-fight, however, with the matador in a very close embrace with the bull's left horn. Then the pain exploded again.

When it had once more receded, a commercial break had replaced the contest. The usual sort of stuff. Soaps, cars, toothpaste and floor cleaners. That was odd – considering the apparent grip which the Church had over the political and public life of the country. A troupe of dancing nuns suddenly appeared – each armed with a mop which they swung in unison as they brushed a kind of wonder liquid vigorously over their convent floor. It was nothing short of a miracle how they brought the old stone flags to a brilliant shine.

I wondered what sort of floors they had up on the hill at Monserrate and whether anyone had tipped-off the Vatican.

⋆

The TV was still on when a grey Andean morning began to seep through the fifth floor window. The toothache had gone and the carbon monoxide must have put me to sleep. I now had a headache and felt a little sick. Buses started to come and go again as the city wound itself up for another day. The chatter of early workers drifted up. I had to get out; walk around in fresher air; shake out the dregs of the night.

It was a gloomy Saturday morning that had dawned over this valley high in the mountains. Carrera 7 marched off southwards towards a faint and misty distance with its office blocks and commercial buildings seeming to follow the broad thoroughfare for many miles. Conversely, streets crossing it soon faded into the green blur of the *Sabana de Bogotá* or ran up against the rising ground of the convent of Monserrate. There were few pedestrians, few cars and many buses. Some of the buildings looked a little faded and worn.

Walking briskly southwards, it took no more than five or six blocks before the headache had lifted. But what had replaced it was a growing sense of unease. The hour was approaching 8 a.m. and trucks were beginning to add to the bus traffic. There were still few pedestrians about, however, since most of those disembarking at the frequent bus-stops soon melted into side streets. Carrera 7 remained empty. It wasn't a question of guns and patrols and armoured cars, though; quite the reverse, in fact. The unease came from a palpable drop in the standard of living which appeared to grow with every step southwards. Buildings which had been simply faded and worn in the vicinity of the hotel had now become downright dilapidated. People had gone downhill, too. The occasional poncho-clad person selling newspapers was now replaced by dishevelled old men who slumped amongst the litter of abandoned doorways clutching unlabelled bottles. A body in rags curled against the barricaded entrance to an empty building – dirt-covered brown ankles and dusty boots protruding from scraps of coarse cloth. These were mean streets all around and yet the Tecquendama could still be made out in the distant mist – hazy, monolithic and very expensive.

Absolute poverty. It was a sad fact that twenty-five percent of the population existed in a state of absolute poverty. Colombia was not a poor country – quite apart from the illegal profits of drugs there were, like the flowers, many legitimate exports to a ready consumer market in the United States. The country had seaboards on both the Caribbean and the Pacific and it lay astride the land route from North America to South America (even if the swamps of the north-west and the forests of Darien had so far combined to prevent any real Pan-American highway sweeping trade and tourists down from one end of the New World to the other).

It was a poverty which was largely borne by the Andean Indian population – the people of the fourteenth century. Somehow, these highlanders had not managed to slip into the orbit of a minimal level of comfort; not even when they came to the city looking for it.

Perhaps particularly when they came to the city. It traversed a grim place – this southwards-heading Carrera 7 – and yet La Candelaria (the historic section of old Bogotá) still lay somewhere beyond. I decided travelling by car was wiser than on foot and returned to the hotel and the buses.

*

Absolute poverty as seen from the window of a car showed no better face. I returned along Carrera 7. As it passed southwards, the cue of a red traffic light pulled groups of ragged and filthy children into action – stumbling their way amongst the few cars and feebly scratching at the side-windows for coins. Faces with matted hair and beggars eyes loomed in through the glass and from their close presence came the rancid smell of unwashed bodies. On the pavements beyond, old men with leathery faces and bent bodies moved about amongst the rubble and rubbish of doorways where more huddled figures lay motionless. Two tattered youths limped away down a side-street – one trying to catch the other up but hampered by the fact that he had only a single shoe and that was several sizes too large.

But this poverty came and went down the broad sweep of Carrera 7 as it did down the avenues of Manhattan. La Candelaria was further south and, in the vicinity of its public buildings, the ragged and the foetid had been swept away like dust under a carpet. No broom-like programme of civic aid had done this; rifles were the persuaders and had efficiently cleared an island around the Presidential Palace. Soldiers again tracked the movement of each passing vehicle with their gun barrels; potential assassination was again in the air. Perhaps the security cordon was understandable, it was the very same building where (in 1828) Simon Bolivar had needed to flee from the same problem – narrowly escaping the bullets whilst being pushed out of a window by his mistress Manuela. In 1992, there was little opportunity to try and identify which window – traffic was not encouraged to linger and even less welcome to stop and park on the streets surrounding the Presidential Palace.

Difficulty in parking put me once more back on the streets. Bogotá was a disappointing place if none of its monuments could be reached without fear that a return to the car would see only the security forces sweeping up the wreckage left behind by a controlled explosion. The old cathedral looked a less hazardous place than the Presidential Palace and the famous Gold Museum was not far from it.

★

On foot and on Carrera 7 again. Half-naked beggars spilling out of the doorway of a sixteenth-century Franciscan church – entreating arms outstretched; some dragging themselves along the pavement with wild, imploring eyes. It was some relief that the street was a little more crowded than in the early morning. Despite the cluster of matted hair and ragged bodies that most pedestrians had to circumnavigate at they passed the church, Bogotá was about its normal business. Paramilitary police and armoured personnel carriers were nowhere in sight.

The pavement was quite crowded and it seemed difficult not to brush against those striding in the opposite direction. One man was noticeable as he stood in the hurly-burly like an islet in a fast-flowing stream; stationary, peering intently at a map and occasionally looking up and trying to catch the attention of one or other passer-by. He caught my eye.

'Por favor. El Museo Archeologico?'

We tried to find it on the map. An archaeological museum clearly wasn't the same kind of establishment as the Gold Museum. It was somewhere else in the city. The map didn't seem to list it amongst the tourist sites, which was curious. Just as he was on the point of thanking me and turning to the next passer-by, an older man – in suit and tie – joined us and asked courteously if there was anything he could do to help. He clearly assumed we were two tourists who were visiting the monuments and museums of Bogotá together. He studied the map for some moments and then looked up.

'*Señors,*' he said almost apologetically. '*Soy policia.*'

The directions to the archaeological museum seemed to have slipped his mind completely. Drawing a hand out of a thin document case, he quickly proved the point by means of a plastic identity card which had 'BOGOTA POLICE DEPARTMENT' printed in clear bold letters across a rather blurred head-and-shoulders photograph. A series of questions followed. You are together? How long are you likely to stay in the city? What were your plans for the remainder of the day? Could he make a note of passport numbers?

All this suddenly seemed a long stride from the map and a simple walk down Carrera 7 in the direction of the cathedral. I thought of shrugging off the questions as no concern of his but there were those posters all over the place. 'STATE OF SIEGE LEGISLATION', 'FOUR HUNDRED SUSPECTS ELIMINATED'.

He was there already. It wasn't usual for the police to ask this of visitors but the current situation made things difficult for everybody. The police were, of course, doing everything they could to protect the public and a recent drive had been set in motion to improve efficiency. Only that morning, he had been briefed by his superiors to keep more in touch with the flow of tourists to Colombia and to help prevent any unfortunate incidents.

The flow of people along the pavement momentarily increased and we were jostled apart. A bus fumigated all and sundry with diesel exhaust. In the choking air, the man with the map briefly explained that he was from Panama and that all this business was typical of Bogotá and nothing to worry about.

'These checks are common here – it's something everybody learns to live with.'

The older man rejoined us with two small notepads and two cheap pens. He would be most grateful if our passport numbers could be written on the pads as well as our country of origin and present addresses in Bogotá. It was a necessary part of helping Colombia's fight against crime and the narcotics problem. The Panamanian readily agreed and had now established that I had travelled from Venezuela.

'More efficient than the police in Caracas, eh,' he said laughingly. 'Out on the streets and not just sitting and dozing in their jeeps at traffic junctions.'

His information complete, the plain-clothes policeman thanked us both and asked if we would kindly wait just a few minutes whilst he telephoned into the station from a call-box across the road. He disappeared and the man from Panama began talking about how, only the previous day, some more suspects had been eliminated. He readily agreed that the heavy security as traffic came in from the airport could have something to do with this emergency. Nearly all the police were armed these days – even the plain-clothes branch. Under the present laws, they could all shoot on sight. Apprehending a narcotics suspect was no cosy business. You drew first or you were mown down.

The plain-clothes policeman returned. I casually looked for any unusual bulges under his jacket but the document case seemed the most likely home.

They wanted a little more information – the superiors. The mode grew tense although the Panamanian still seemed light-hearted about the matter.

'I will be happy to cooperate with anything they need,' he said – a little too readily, I thought. 'What do you want to know, *señor*?'

'*Señors,*' said the policeman with a serious air, taking out a thick black notebook from the document case. 'I have been requested to obtain and pass back to headquarters the full address of your hotels, your room numbers, the name of a person who can vouch for you in those places, the address of your place of residence in the country of your origin and the serial numbers of any foreign currency you might be carrying.' Whilst we were digesting all this, the notepads and pens were handed back with a clear indication that we were to begin jotting down the information immediately.

We began writing but were immediately interrupted by another request.

'*Por favor.* Do you have any United States dollars?' he said – as if their possession would prove beyond doubt that there had been some drug trafficking going on.

Under the circumstances, neither of us claimed to have any whilst each trying to concentrate on the difficult business of remembering hotel addresses and room numbers and all the rest.

'*Por favor.* Any other foreign currency, then?'

The Panamanian – who seemed to be ahead in the task of information provision – brought out a wallet stuffed with notes. It proved to be Panamanian money but the policeman wanted to see every note and enter its number in his black book. He took charge of the notes and turned to me for more serial numbers.

The thick wad of bolivares was difficult to hide – what with all the searching around for hotel addresses and passport numbers. My equivalent of $300 dollars was held together by a stout elastic band. With a severe look, the plain-clothes policeman signalled for its transfer to the black book. There were too many serial numbers to be written down so he would now have to read them out to his superiors over the phone. Meanwhile, we were to continue with the other questions. Pads and pens would be collected when he returned with the notes. The call would be made from the box across the road. We were not to move from where he left us.

There was little chance that we would move – after all he had all our money. I turned to the Panamanian to remark on this but he was not there! I turned to the call-box across the road and it was empty!

It was useless chasing after a plain-clothes policeman in the back-streets of Bogotá.

★

I turned to one of the pillars in the dusky interior of the cathedral and kicked it. What a fool. The old serial number trick – it was in every guidebook. The faint reverberation amongst the pillars as three white-robed priests at the far end of the church offered communion to a very small morning congregation did nothing to dispel the affair. What a fool. Over the centuries, the locals had made an art of extracting a fortune from the fortune-hunters of *El Dorado.* Unwitting Spaniards had been led on and on by trickery and deceit. And it wasn't just the Spanish, either. The Germans, the English and the North Americans had all been tricked.

The lure of the 'Golden One' had suffered no diminishment by the failure of the Welsers to find gold beyond their dreams. Probably aided by the Indians, the legend shifted like a mirage on the horizon: at one time it was a man sheathed in gold; at another, a fabulous city of great wealth which stood high in the mountains; at another, towers and temples of precious metals and gems glimmering at the end of tortuous jungle trails, beyond fearsome rapids and behind poisoned arrows. The legend probably did much to encourage the exploration of the interior of the South American continent. Felipe de Utre searched for his El Dorado in 1542 and failed. Diego de Serpa looked for his to the south of the Caribbean coastal region in the dry season and never returned. Pedro de Silva set off for his in 1569. Sir Walter Raleigh – somewhat desperate for a quick reversal of his sagging fortunes after the death of Queen Elizabeth – began his ill-fated expedition south of the Orinoco in 1617. Only the executioners were waiting at the end of the rainbow in 1618 when he returned to England empty-handed.

And then there was Colonel Fawcett and his son setting off into the Amazon rainforest in the 1920s and completely disappearing. Tall tales of giant snakes and impossible hardships and no sign of the golden man, the fabulous city or the gem-encrusted towers and temples.

But there really was an *El Dorado.* The Golden Man did exist – had existed. Echoes of him were displayed in the Golden Museum of Bogotá. A little model of the gilded raft which took him out on to the *Laguna de Guatavita* that lay less than fifty miles to the north of the city. The sacred pool where, in pre-colonial times, the Chibcha Indians (who inhabited this green *Sabana de Bogotá*) had placated the gods – first by coating their king in resin and then by dusting him thickly with powdered gold. A Golden Man emerged – a god on earth – who was then taken with due ceremony to the *Laguna* and slipped carefully into its cool waters. After a few minutes (when the gold and resin had washed off) the god had gone and the king had returned. He was retrieved – presumably for another year. Many people were of the opinion that a lot of gold dust must have accumulated at the bottom of the *Laguna de Guatavita* in the course of time but no one had ever managed to retrieve it. In the same way, no one had ever managed to return whence they came bearing the spoils of *El Dorado*. Indeed, they usually ended up with considerably less than they had started with!

*

I really didn't have the time or the money to see the pool where the Chibchas washed away their wealth – much of which was derived from salt. Those low wooded hills north of the city which the plane had passed over before the final approach to another El Dorado – the airport – were the site of extensive subterranean salt mines. In pre-colonial times, the Chibchas traded this salt extensively up and down the Andes and the Spanish continued to exploit the essential commodity. There were salt-pans down on the coast, of course, but they were a long way away from the *Sabana de Bogotá*.

The mines under the hills had grown extensive – enlarged and deepened over the centuries and still producing the stuff in the early 1990s. Although earlier workings had largely been abandoned, access was still possible. In fact, an adit-type entrance on the hillside above the small town of Zipaquira led not to dark and empty underground caverns but to the cathedral of Our Lady of the Rosary.

It didn't really work – the idea of turning a large man-made underground cavern into a church. It was the natural smell for one thing. The smell of fire-and-brimstone; the stink of sulphur was the very opposite to the odour of sanctity – whatever that was!

Salt (halite) was, after all, a product of past aeons of evaporation – building up to form substantial layers in the earth's crust and often containing within it organic material and sulphur and other rather caustic minerals. Frequently, those substantial layers would then flow and extrude into overlying strata as the overburden pressure began to increase with burial. It was a process called diapirism. Our Lady of the Rosary smelt strongly of bad eggs.

⋆

An elderly man guarded the entrance to a near-horizontal passage into the cathedral. The sides of the passage were heavily supported by massive bulks of timber. Diapirism was at work all the time and it would have been nature's preference to have squashed the narrow excavation flat in a few score years. The man sold tickets but no sooner were they proffered than he nipped to the far side of a rusty turnstile and took them back again. Time was short and the timber might not last as long as the tickets.

The way into the House of God proved ill-lit. A sort of Siberian gloom descended as soon as the last ray of daylight was blocked out by a downwards turn to the right. From this point on, the way forward was lit solely by widely spaced electric bulbs of very low wattage. Dimly reflecting from walls and ceiling was salt-encrusted wood under great strain. Below, an uneven floor of halite rose slowly inwards and upwards. The pressure on maintaining the *status quo* was almost audible.

What was also very clearly perceptible was that strong odour of sulphuretted hydrogen. It was a no-hoper – this idea of a cathedral. How could anyone pray alongside unremitting bad eggs. They should have opted for devil-worship instead.

⋆

Deeper and deeper. We seemed to be on our way to hell. Finally, somewhere far inside the grey halite, the roof soared away into darkness and the cathedral of Our Lady opened out as a huge dark chamber supported by massive pillars. Again, the strain was palpable as those pillars sagged under what seemed to be an Atlas-like weight. To help in their task, thick steel cables had been clamped around their bodies but these were taut and cut deeply into each vertical mass. All around, the floor heaved where stone slabs had once lain flat but now rose in response to the underlying pressure. The thought of inspecting the roof was dismissed as soon as it arose.

I was alone in there – or at least I could see no others. Deep recesses held black hollows where light bulbs had failed. Shadows seemed occasionally to flit between the far columns close to the altar and strange, muffled echoes came and went amongst the grey walls of salt. The stench of rotten eggs was everywhere.

*

A hopeless choice as a cathedral. Or could this be a different perspective on God? Why should He be always worshipped in bright light, coloured glass and sweet-scented air? Might not this, in fact, be closer to a celestial reality than all the rest: the art; the soaring naves; the bare simplicity; the gold; the candles; the incense; the spires, minarets and the domes. Might not all these just be an aberration? Something which suited the human race but which bore little resemblance to the Great Beyond?

Those pictures, for instance, returned from the Voyager space probe as it swung through the back-end of the solar system. There was not much in the way of celestial bright light and heavenly colours out there. What about that little moon called Amalthea which looked like a small red potato complete with discolorations? What about Io – the Galilean satellite with the complexion of a diseased apple? What about that great red spot on Jupiter? What about Triton, Neptune's largest satellite, where photospectural analysis suggested a moon suffering from a bad case of petrochemical smog? How were these newer images to be accommodated in the man-centred spiritual and artistic visions of Bernini or Michelangelo?

Perhaps, after creation, it had all become muddled up somehow and we humans had got totally the wrong end of the stick. Perhaps it was the devil who was supposed to be up on top amongst all the light and incense and God was actually meant to be down here and out amongst the lesser moons. Perhaps it was God whose natural inclination was to move around through the whiff of sulphuretted hydrogen and severe cases of planetary pollution. Maybe the rest of the universe was less like St Peter's and more like Our Lady of the Rosary than we cared to imagine.

The smell got to you after a time. It began to seem as if every scrap of clothing was becoming hopelessly impregnated with the odour of bad eggs. I had another plane to catch.

*

It was a terrible rush from the salt mine to the terminal of El Dorado. I just had time to fling the keys of the car at a man from Hertz and weave a passage through all the Alsatians and their handlers before the flight to Cartagena was closed. The cabin door was just on the point of being secured, too, when there was a sudden flurry of activity and two heavily armed soldiers pushed their way down the aisle and stopped at a seat several rows behind the one of which I had just taken breathless possession.

A powerfully built man was asked to vacate the seat and leave the aircraft. Close-cropped hair, well-cut suit – he was marched down the aisle with a soldier in front and a soldier behind. The soldier in front triumphantly carried a small hand-gun. Ten minutes later the plane taxied to the main runway. The man was back on board and – from the look of his suit – so was his hand-gun!

Perhaps he was being checked out for non-payment of airport tax. The Avianca flight from Bogotá to Cartagena surged forwards and we rose once more above the green-houses of the *Sabana de Bogotá*.

★

Down, down, down – from the cool Andean Highlands to the hot Caribbean coast. Down away from ponchos, grey poverty and salt-mines. Down to the noisy rustle of the cicadas, the trace of sea air in the warm evening breeze; the familiar silhouette of palm trees curving and exploding into black masses of fronds as they swayed near the terminal building. Suits, jackets, ties and heavy sweaters had come off; shorts, tee-shirts and flip-flops had returned. Instead of sulphuretted hydrogen, there was a strong smell of after-shave. The Colombians who had come to Cartagena had come for a holiday amongst the casinos and nightclubs. And who could blame them?

A sizeable disbursement of the $50 was necessary to get from this coastal runway and into the main part of town. We bumped past the floodlit outer ramparts of Old Cartagena and headed for the distant brightly coloured neon strip that was New Cartagena.

Although well-preserved, those ramparts were much lower than I had imagined. This was, after all, the place which had successfully held off the attacks of pirates and privateers; the place where – out in the now-dark and now-empty Caribbean Sea – those twice-yearly consignments of treasure had been shipped aboard the flotilla of galleons which then set off for Spain. As time went on (and more and more people got to hear of this), there was, of course, the gauntlet of those eager to extract a share or two of the booty of the Americas to run before it sailed away through the islands of the West Indies. Nowadays, the casinos were most efficient at extracting such booty.

It was full – was Cartagena. There was clearly a lot of money about. Luxury apartments hid behind more palms, all the big hotels were apparently over-booked and the prices of any odd suites or honeymoon apartments which remained unoccupied were astronomical.

The 'Raffles' hotel teemed with Canadians. It wasn't really called the Raffles Hotel but the impressive frontage of majestic old palms set amid lawns would have been to the satisfaction of someone like Somerset Maugham. Breakfast was being served amongst the chatter of tropical birdsong and the occasional splash and ripple as somebody took an early morning dip in the blue-tinted pool.

The Canadians had not ventured to the poolside yet and – pale and disorientated – were still tucking into bacon and eggs at tables well shaded from the morning sun.

'Sure goin' be a scorcher later today,' said one, who must have been muffled against minus thirty the previous day. A mobile telephone rang across the pool and a German wearing sub-aqua tanks fished out a receiver and dealt with the call. Preparations were being made for a diving lesson. This seemed a very far and distant world from that of Carrera 7.

Yet it wasn't so very far, really. The other Colombia was still there a few miles away in Old Cartagena.

*

Those massive floodlit walls which had looked out over the dark and empty Caribbean of the previous evening seemed to be squashed low under the brilliant glare of a day that had already become a scorcher. They encompassed an almost completely preserved colonial city. Narrow streets of two and three-story buildings led in from the stone gateways. It wasn't as busy or as affluent as New Cartagena. The heat soon made the need for shade desperate.

Sunday morning and most of the Old Cartagenians had come to the same conclusion. A few heads popped out of windows to water plants. One or two sheets were shaken from upper balconies. The congregation of the Jesuit church of San Pedro Claver filed into its morning service. The rest seemed to be still a-bed.

It was not long before a guide appeared – one of those endlessly persistent 'guides' who refuse to be thwarted and who rely on a gradual breakdown of their victims' will to achieve results.

The 'results' appeared to be at the top end of the range – a price which would have cut deep into the remainder of the $50 and left an unpleasant feeling that there would be insufficient left to deal with an airport departure tax payable on the return flights via Bogotá. Anyway, it was too hot for a conducted tour.

San Pedro Claver offered sanctuary from both the heat and the avaricious. A cool and serene interior with most of those attending the service far down at the end of the nave and kneeling in front of the altar and the glass coffin of the saint. A priest began a curious high-pitched singing and I wondered if he might be a eunuch. The noise rose uncomfortably and echoed around the stone pillars and walls of the ancient church. It was enough to make anyone turn in their grave and might even have evoked some response from the mummified body of St Pedro himself – had he not been such a kindly and considerate man.

San Pedro was a monk in the early 1600s. He lived in the days when the colonies of the Spanish Empire were building up to their heyday and the exploitation of the natural and mineral wealth of the New World was reaching its climax. Indians and Africans toiled in the plantations and mines of the coast and interior. Life was cheap and labour was endlessly renewable. Whips, fierce dogs, chains and near-starvation kept the holds of the flotillas full; mule-train after mule-train carried the flow of gold, silver and goods down to the departure point at Cartagena. Compassion took a rear-seat whilst all this was going on, but Pedro Claver did what he could to ease the burden of the toilers at the port – devoting his life to collecting money and using it to remove a little of the hardship and misery from the lives of the Negroes who mostly carried the cargoes, cut the cane and died in their thousands of exhaustion and the fevers of the coastal Caribbean. And for all the whip-lashing and striving of the Spanish to extract their new-found wealth, as the flotillas continued their twice-yearly passages into the late sixteenth century and throughout the seventeenth century, there were more and more of those envious other Europeans struggling to grab a share of it before it reached the open waters of the Atlantic and the home run to Spain.

Queen Elizabeth's envy of the towering wealth and ambition of this new Spain – pushing out the last of its Moors and now bloated with the riches of its New World – was such that she sent Sir Francis Drake to Cartagena with instructions to cause as much damage as possible. He did as she wished. In fact, he almost destroyed the credit balance of Philip II. The sack of the city in 1586, coupled with his rampages through Santo Domingo on Hispaniola and St Augustine on the North American mainland sent ripples of panic back to Europe. Fast growing empires needed credit, capital, cash flow and confidence. Drake struck at the latter with his 1,300 man attack and his breakthrough into impregnable Cartagena. The bank of Spain collapsed, money houses in Venice were seriously threatened and the financiers of Augsburg refused to extend any more funds to the Spanish Crown. And then, a year later in 1587, when the galleons of the flotilla were directed not from Seville to Cartagena but from Seville to the British Isles, there was Drake again with his fire-ships and Protestant Wind scattering the mighty vessels of Philip's ill-fated Armada.

The guide had scattered, too. It was indeed a real scorcher outside and the sunlight blasted down from above and glanced off the light-coloured walls with a vengeance. Those few who had been about earlier had now totally retreated. As I walked from one patch of meagre shade to another, the heat began to bear down until it was almost impossible to see through the sweat pouring off my forehead.

Indeed, salty perspiration reduced vision so much that it was difficult to make out what had suddenly swung into view down the road with any clarity – or sense. Approaching along the brightness of the street seemed to be a kind of whirling dervish – a wild-looking female figure leaping about and waving a long stick. The dance grew wilder as she approached – black matted hair shaking vigorously and the stick swooping from side to side. Close-up, she was virtually naked except for the shreds of a blanket draped over her shoulders and a ragged skirt. Face, breasts, torso and legs were caked in filth – not only dust and dirt but a kind of tarry substance which was also smeared over the blanket and the skirt. She blocked the way uttering something unintelligible but which sounded as if it might be a demand for money. I fished out a coin but it obviously wasn't enough. Lunging forward and grabbing an arm she struggled to hold on. The stench was powerful and, as tried to I break free, she reeled into the shadows and disappeared into an abandoned building.

It was all over in what seemed like seconds but the legacy lingered on for several hours. In the brief encounter not only had one sleeve become covered in that foetid tarry substance but some of it had obviously transferred from the stick to much of the rest of me. Ten more minutes in the powerful heat, with nothing to wipe it off and with an uncertainty of where the smears actually were, caused a gradual spreading over a much greater surface area. The stuff had begun to behave like an oil-slick. Dabs of an evil-smelling black goo were everywhere.

A battered taxi rattled down the road and I got out of Old Cartagena as quickly as I could. The driver seemed oblivious to the smell but I sensed Avianca at the airport were a little reluctant to take it on board. A few spare clothes helped to dampen things down a bit but not entirely. Scrubbing with water made absolutely no impact on it. The odour accompanied the entire flight from Cartagena to Bogotá and then travelled on from Bogotá to Caracas.

*

With cents to spare (the remains of the $50 had just covered the airport tax on departure at Bogotá), there was nothing at all for the taxi drivers in the Arrivals terminal at Simon Bolivar airport and no way of achieving the late-night climb from the coast to the city of Caracas in the hills above.

A deal was worked out. One of this normally rapacious band agreed to carry me to the downtown area and collect his fare once a bank-dispensing machine had been located. It was past midnight but we patiently drove around the city streets until one was found which worked.

'It was kind of you to wait for your money,' I told him as we arrived outside the entrance to Edificio Panorama in Los Naranjos. 'I've just come back from Colombia. My cash all disappeared there.'

'*Muy interesante,*' he said. '*Es mi pais – soy colombiano.*'

Chapter Five

Weekend in Ecuador

London, 1973. The executive dining room of Burmah Oil – sometime corporate parent of Anglo-Ecuadorian Oil Company. One of the Ninian partner lunches. A good oil flow from the third appraisal well on Block 3/3. The wine had turned turtle and someone suggested cognac all round. The old South American hands were at it again! The same old story!

...and then we'd hit the cloud cover. Quito's 10,000 feet up, you see... a trip to Head Office in the late '50s meant coming in and out under all sorts of conditions... and those Air Ecuatoriana kites were so ancient that their idea of maintenance was to repaint the cabin interiors once a year... used to be done out in a sort of beige gloss. They'd paint the seat backs and the cabin roof... you could see the brush marks

...lovely place Quito... up in the Andes... go back there tomorrow. Coming in with a clear sky and long row of snow-capped peaks lined up for you. Not just on one side of the valley... both sides

...the pilot, of course, had a bit of a job in that narrow valley. No time to enjoy the view. And when we'd hit the cloud cover, he was really busy. Not the sort of thing for a beginner, either... putting a sizeable aircraft down on to the

floor of a sloping trench coming up at you as you tried to keep her dead level at 10,000 feet. Lots of side-wind shifting you about. Hundred feet too high and you were over the top... Cotopaxi, Antizana and Cayambe... all 5,000 or so feet above you. Turn to starboard and you were into some very solid volcanic rock... Pichincha, Atacazo, Corazon, Iliniza... none of those'd move to one side and let you through. Turn to port, and you rammed into Puntas, Pasochoa or Ruminahui. Couldn't see them in the cloud but they were all out there just the same

...no – if that Ecuatoriana pilot hit zero visibility on the approach to Quito, you could hear a pin drop in that aircraft. We all knew the chap up front had started counting... turn into the valley... level off at 10,000 feet then fly straight into the mist for twelve minutes. One, two, three, four, five, six... by six you'd be glued to the cabin window, of course... seven, eight, nine, ten, eleven... Jesus! There it was... a light or two, a few rooftops... just below... twelve... thump. There was a big round of applause at that point. The wheels were down on the runway and not on grass and rocks.

⋆

Quito. The final glide path on a damp evening in 1992. The Air Ecuadoriana Boeing 727, with seat backs and ceiling repainted in a kind of beige gloss which showed up the brush marks, drifting slowly down through an opaque darkness and wheeling into the central Andean trench. At 11,000 feet, a glimmer of lights appeared, rising up to meet the aircraft, taking shape as the last wisps of cloud drifted aside to reveal a pattern of residential streets. In patches of darkness, car headlamps twisted and flashed as vehicles below climbed a land surface that was clearly rising steeply upwards and towards the lowered undercarriage of the lumbering plane. A few seconds later came rooftops and street lamps which had suddenly jumped into the air and were now only a few hundred feet below the cabin windows. A few seconds more and an ordered arrangement of a strip of runway lights filled the fast-closing gap between plane and ground and we were down.

It was 10.30 p.m. and an almost imperceptible landing at Aeropuerto Mariscal Sucre. An old plane but an experienced pilot. Perhaps a gadget or two extra. No one seemed to bother with counting any more, but a thin clapping broke out as the aircraft finally rolled to a halt.

Quito. Not an imposing airport but one well-organised for late evening arrivals. A money change was still open for business; a tourist office was eager to advise on accommodation; taxis waited outside in the night air of the Andes. No Alsatians, no soldiers, no money-changers; no tropical heat (although the equator was only a few miles away) – no hassle, seemingly, in the second smallest republic in South America.

⋆

No hassle, either, in dropping in on Ecuador and finding a room for the night. A taxi driver showed me a seven-story hotel close to the airport which revealed itself to have a calm and welcoming atmosphere, plenty of space and with very reasonable prices. The fact that it stood close to the far edge of the runway and may well have been the first obstacle encountered by any late-night Air Ecuadoriana flight coming across a misty Quito that was 100 feet lower than expected did not seem quite so important once you were on the ground. And the altitude was playing its usual tricks again. The few short steps into the foyer revealed that the place was not at sea-level but one third of the way up the side of Mount Everest! Breathlessness and a slight dizziness – *soroche* compounding the weariness of a day's work in Caracas; a rush for the plane and six hours of flying. It would be good to get some shut-eye in this deserted place.

Suddenly – as if the catch on Pandora's Box had come loose – the doors of the hotel crashed open and two large suitcases slid rapidly across the polished stone floor until they collided with the reception desk. More cases slid up behind them – their checked velocity causing one of the original pair to ricochet sideways until it hit the metal doors of an elevator with an echoing thud.

> *...Yale... worse than Harvard... terrible stuff... not even pigs would eat it... Milken must have stashed something away somewhere... all of them hacked down... it's got to be stopped before the hole gets any bigger... shit... my watch says seven-thirty... hey guys... what time is it here?*

Tranquillity was shattered by the Peace Corps. Fifty or sixty of them – pouring into the hotel from a coach that was still unloading the heavier of the suitcases and sliding them into a growing mêlée of tall male and female North Americans. An interpreter with a clipboard took up a marginal position and tried to count bare heads, heads with floppy hats, be-shorted backsides, chatting tee-shirts, seriously discussing short-sleeved jumpers, people who had quickly sat down on the floor and people who were unpacking hand-baggage to look for a pen.

'*James Littlep—*' shouted the interpreter who was suddenly drowned out by a shriek of laughter as the five men and three suitcases which were already packed into the narrow elevator were joined at the last minute by two women.

'No, no! El ascensor es delicado!' she screamed. *'Es fragil.'*

It was too late. The door had already been pummelled by the severe blow from the suitcase; five men were already a strain; their three bags added to its burden and two extra women were simply impossible. The equipment was designed for Ecuadorians of modest height carrying normal amounts of luggage. The door closed; an attempt was made to rise two or three feet; the motor stalled and the lift jammed. A view of the outer pair of fourteen legs could be seen pressed tightly against the window. The chattering amongst the remainder of the Peace Corps in the foyer continued unabated. The interpreter brushed back her hair, threw down her clipboard and stormed off into the nether regions of the hotel – muttering angrily in Spanish.

★

A fifth-floor room. Occasional gales of laughter from the fourth floor – or was it the sixth floor. An hour of heavy breathing as a hundred or so suitcases came via the nearby stairs – hauled slowly by people who suddenly realised they were the equivalent of a third of the way up Everest as they reached the second floor. And – at intervals – a steady banging. Hammer on steel. The lift remained stuck for thirty minutes and so did the seven Peace Corps and three bags inside it. Slowly, the former tranquillity of the Ecuadorian night slipped back over the building. By 1 a.m., the last shriek had subsided, the last scuffle taken place and the last goodnights had been hoarsely whispered in the corridor outside.

Poor Otavalo Indians! Poor Third World about to receive assistance from the First. Poor villagers with shallow cesspits which the world health authorities thought should be deeper and unrelated to their drinking water supply. Dysentery or a good night's sleep – after about a week of it, the choice could be quite difficult.

Tranquillity did not necessarily bring sleep to my fifth floor room, either. The silence of the hotel was matched by the silence of the city outside. No sound of cars could be heard, no late-night buses trundled up and away, no footsteps echoed on the pavements. It was a very clear night and, beyond the orange glow of nearby street lamps, the ground began to rise towards a black velvet sky crowded with brilliant stars. Quite where the earth stopped and the stars began was difficult to make out. Pinpoints of brilliance curving skywards could have been Ursa Major seen from an unusually low angle near the horizon or could equally have been a distant housing estate clinging to the valley side.

Nothing was familiar in this lofty place. The altitude had turned things inside out. The equator which straddled the country (and which formed the basis for its name) was only fifteen miles to the north and yet the same few miles to the east brought you to the perpetual snows of Cotopaxi. Snow on the equator – and a thick eiderdown on the bed. The equatorial night air was decidedly chilly.

★

The Peace Corps were sleeping off jet lag, altitude sickness, jammed elevators, the terrible food at Yale, the problems in the rainforests, the problems of Michael Milken...

Unoccupied table settings for fifty or sixty people in the restaurant of the hotel gave a bit of room to spread out the map of Ecuador and establish with the waiter (who, I had also observed, looked very much like the hotel's lift maintenance man) how feasible it was to drive down the steep rim of the Western Cordillera and reach the Pacific shores at Salinas.

And what a view that must be. Perched up at 9,000 feet on the edge of the Andes and looking out over the ocean. That would be as good as Keats had imagined for the first of the conquistadores. Those who '*...with eagle eyes... star'd at the Pacific.*' Those who '*...Look'd at each other with wild surmise – Silent, upon a peak in Darien.*'

That would be worth the hours of driving. To reach the edge of the South American continent from this high place and – on the way – suddenly be brought to a stunned halt by a first glimpse of a vast glittering expanse stretching westwards to the far horizon. The waiter said it was a reasonable road along the valley and down to the coastal city of Guayaquil – it was the route all the long-distance buses and petrol tankers took. Nothing was mentioned on either side about peaks in Darien, looks of wild surmise and long views over the ocean. It seemed too poetic for a pragmatic conversation about getting from A (here) to B (there). Anyway, there was something about the way he tackled a map which suggested it might just as well have been unfolded upside down. Guayaquil was the way the long-distance buses and the petrol tankers went. Going south here, veering west there, then turning south again there and then west through here were all ideas he readily agreed to. The way was clear – all that was required was a vehicle, a full tank of petrol and a start as soon as possible that morning.

The way wasn't quite so clear. It was the business of being on the equator that messed things up. The first part of the route from Quito to Riobamba was south along the Pan-American Highway. Casting an appreciative eye at the sun, I set off in this direction and began to wind down the long incline which car headlights had suggested from the previous evening's landing. The surface of the highway was reasonably good, the traffic moderately busy, the sun high in the sky and the bright Andean landscape of the central valley began to unfold ahead of me – a somewhat stark scenery but intensively cultivated, nonetheless.

Indians began to appear in view: walking alone at the roadside or out in the fields harvesting some sort of crop. As I was wondering whether it was potatoes, the first road signs for Ibarra and Tulcan appeared.

Ibarra and Tulcan! But the map said they were north of Quito. Tulcan, in fact, was on the border with Colombia. And here I was heading south! I knew it was south – the sun was clearly in view above me.

However, when you are on the equator, the sun can be clearly in view above you whether travelling south or north. And one line of snow-capped volcanic peaks belonging to a Western Cordillera can look very much like a line of snow-capped volcanic peaks belonging to an Eastern Cordillera. And Ibarra and Tulcan were unlikely to be places which could be uprooted and transplanted a similar distance south of Quito as their position to the north of it. It just wouldn't be worthwhile – uneconomic! Even if the Peace Corps helped the Ecuadorians out with the task.

⋆

It wasn't very economic (on fuel) to return crest-fallen to Quito as Eastern and Western Cordillera changed places without a murmur and the sun obligingly slipped around and remained clearly in view above me. Even the airport gathered up its runways and shifted from the southern to the northern edge of the city.

And it wasn't very economic on time, either – changing a faulty south for the real one meant becoming entangled in a complex traffic flow around some vast fossilised earthworks which were supposed to aid road communication through the central part of Quito. The old highway had been dug up and totally destroyed but whoever was responsible seemed to have run off with the men, equipment and possibly the money to build a new one. A stream of vehicles vaguely attempting to exit the capital city of Ecuador was left to make what it could of heaps of soft topsoil, piles of rounded stones and pools of choking dust. Fortunately, it hadn't rained for a while. False trails led through grubby outskirts until they either faltered at other huge piles of earth or led aimlessly into expansive rubbish tips seeded with shreds of thin polythene.

Nobody seemed to know anything – the Pan-American, the road to Guayaquil or even the way back into central Quito. Time passed and yet time stood still – the unreliable sun remained stupidly static whichever way I turned.

In the end, the only way out was to identify what looked like a long-distance bus, tuck in behind its dusty exhaust and stay in that grim spot until the buildings fell behind and the open road began. There was only one slight snag with this practice: it was impossible to tell whether the vehicle was heading in the direction of Guayaquil or had the small towns of Ibarra and Tulcan in mind for its first port of call.

★

Latacunga and Riobamba – it was going south, but the sun still shone stupidly above. The central valley was divided into a series of huge intermontane basins and a slow climb began across one of the intervening areas of high ground. The heat of the equatorial midday sun bore down on the car but the snow-capped volcanoes of the Eastern Cordillera were in full view as they marched off southwards – those of the Western Cordillera being hidden by rising land. Despite volcanic soils having a reputation for fertility, this land close to the road looked dry and unpromising. Only on lower slopes did tiny fields begin to patch its surface – then reaching across the wide valley floor to where, in distant view, toy villages appeared as a lateral spread of red-tiled roofs. Through these, the twin-towers of a Spanish-colonial church sometimes poked and a few poplar trees mimicked the plaza and the cathedral of the conquistadore cities.

There was no doubt that this road was the route long-distance buses and petrol tankers took to get to the coast. The waiter was right. As soon as the climb started to get more serious, a coalescing stream of such vehicles could be seen – all beginning to find the way long and the going tough. Thick clouds of yellowish-grey exhaust poured out as they laboured slowly up the inclines – a pall of petrol and diesel fumes hung motionless over the road as the entire traffic stream became enveloped in gloomy vapours.

Ecuador started to appear as if through a glass – darkly: surrounding countryside losing its bright, high-altitude clarity; the hillsides acquiring the burnished tones of a sepia print; the snow-capped peak of Cotopaxi turning a sickly brown. If this business continued up to the summit and the crossing of the Western Cordillera, the Pacific, too, was hardly going to look the stuff of poetic inspiration.

As the twentieth century struggled through the rugged landscape of the Andes, earlier centuries walked along at the roadside or worked in nearby fields – diminutive Indians who seemed to have little time to stand and stare. In Ecuador, such small, hardworking people made up forty per cent of the population. Men – sharp reddish-brown faces with the upper part obscured by a rammed-down hat – all wore near-identical woollen ponchos, thick trousers and rubber boots. Women – black hair tied in a long single plait and under a bowler hat – were dressed similarly with either a bright red or green shawl, a thick blue skirt and the ubiquitous rubber boots. Tiny children's faces peered from some of the brightly coloured wrappings of the women, a passive reddish-brown face looking exactly like a little model of its mother or father. In fields, workers often added dusty over-clothes and sacking aprons to their costumes. Seen through the petroliferous haze, every stooping row of potato-pickers which I passed slowly formed itself into a vignette of a Van Gogh – albeit a heavily varnished one. The fumes were still with us.

⋆

Peasants or peons? Were these people still bound by inherited obligations or enslaved as a result of their grandparents, or parents, debts – debts frequently not the result of money mis-management but deliberately created by the Andean equivalent of the 'King's shilling'; a lifetime commitment hidden in the haze of cheap alcohol or confused amongst the small print of a contract or loan agreement. It looked a hard life. Out in the fields until you could dig and stoop no more – then more work.

As the road took a sharp bend in one place, an ancient man (or was he only in his fifties?) lifted his work-twisted, arthritic body from one farm building to another using crude brushwood crutches to wave off birds. At another place, two similarly ancient-looking women scurried along in a kind of breathless hobble towards a dilapidated shed – breathless because they were pressed almost double by the long baulks of timber which they carried between them. The virtual slavery of peonage – the debt-overprinted employment of estate labour in a theoretically free wage-earning relationship, had not evaporated with the demise of colonialism. Large twentieth-century peon-worked estates existed in parts of the Andean countries as much as large twentieth-century slave-worked estates existed in parts of Brazil.

The Pan-American highway reached the top of its long climb over the intermontane hump and began winding down into the basin to the south. Traffic spread out on the descent, the exhaust fumes clearing and Cotopaxi falling behind. Perhaps the toil in the fields was nothing new in the lives of the people of the roadsides and the fields – this rooting of their labour and their lives in the service of a large *hacienda*. The Incas demanded a very similar commitment for their empire.

⋆

The town of Latacunga came into view and there were signs for Ambato and Riobamba further south. These were towns which had also lain on the Inca route to its one-time second capital at Quito and which – then and now – lived a precarious existence built around hot springs and in the shadow of active volcanoes. Most of those snow-capped peaks of the Eastern and Western Cordillera had burst vigorously into life at one time or another since the last days of Atahualpa. Pinchincho had showed signs of erupting in 1981, Sangay frequently spewed out dust and ash, the eruption of Cotopaxi had been a favourite topic of eighteenth-century landscape painters. In fact, Latacunga had been completely destroyed by Cotopaxi in 1797 and Riobamba severely damaged. Ambato was nearly obliterated in 1949.

In between times of disaster, however, the curative and relaxing properties of the hot springs had drawn patrons in Inca times as much as later. It was in the hot spring town of Cajamarca (now in northern Peru), that Atahualpa had rested and repaired his army after the victorious battle with his elder brother at Riobamba in the year 1532.

Unfortunately for the Incas, while the troops recovered their energies in the mountains, history was on the move from the coast. A small party of horsemen and soldiers was disembarking and was about to begin the slow ascent up the steep Pacific-facing side of the Western Cordillera and into the high Andean interior. It was late summer. Before long, the one hundred and eighty men of Fernando Pizarro would make contact with Atahualpa and his thousands. At Cajamarca, the days of the 13th emperor of the Kingdom of the Sun were already numbered; the light of treasure was already beginning to shine in the eyes of the Spanish conquistadores and the first creamings of the wealth of the Inca state would soon be expressed as the twenty-four tons of gold and silver ingots which formed the Inca king's 'ransom'.

*

The one hundred miles from Quito to Riobamba down this volatile central valley seemed to take most of the afternoon. The heat began to seep out of the day as the road began yet another part-ascent of the Western Cordillera. I passed the small town of Cajabamba: a significant junction on the Pan-American highway where one fork started its real climb up and over the cordillera before making a precipitous descent on the Pacific-facing side down to Guayaquil. The other fork stayed in the mountains, continued south and headed towards the border with Peru. I took the fork for Guayaquil and began the climb up from Cajabamba.

As one hour became two on this road, however, the crossing of the Western Cordillera started to seem more and more elusive. The point where a summit should be reached and a descent could be started became long overdue. My route – tossing aside notions of a twenty mile ascent and then a sharply dropping downhill run – insisted on staying aloft. I should have been enjoying the growing warmth of a hot equatorial evening and yet here I was still stuck in the coolness of an Andean dusk.

Another half an hour passed and still the route insisted on bracing itself for sterner conditions. For some inexplicable reason, it continued to mount higher and higher and into ever more inhospitable countryside. The map, of course, insisted that a descent was taking place.

*

Many miles of slow upward winding: too tedious to return to Cajabamba; a great uncertainty over where the ascent would lead; some comfort in the fact that it couldn't go on for ever.

Or could it? The light of day began to fade – prematurely. Traffic dwindled until one or two labouring petrol tankers were the only travelling companions. There were long impatient waits as they slowly climbed what had become a tightly-winding mountain road. Thick exhaust-charged air. Rear lights in banks of mist. The word *PELIGROSO* appearing and disappearing as they vanished, braked and then were found again grinding up another steep incline as visibility was restored. Small stones beginning to litter the road surface. Curiously, far up in what was now beginning to feel like the infrequently visited attic of the world, a rusty railway track crossed the road.

The Western Cordillera was not festooned with railway tracks. Only one snaked its way along the central valley from Quito, climbed over the cordillera and then somehow made its way down the other side to terminate at Guayaquil. This was Ecuador's famous railway – built by the British (like most of the South American rail system) and now a rusty reminder of nineteenth-century enterprise and the capture of transportation by the internal combustion engine and the jet engine. Often washed out by landslides, the tracks did not always offer a through route from the highland capital of Ecuador to its main lowland city. However, they did offer a navigational fix. I was way off course; too far south; on a deteriorating road heading towards a place called Chunchi and with the prospect of an extremely steep descent down to the coastal plain. The only course seemed to be one of continuing until an intersection with a minor road allowed what appeared to be a drop of ten thousand feet in ten miles!

It grew darker and darker as the ascent pushed into heavy cloud cover. The mountain landscape became vague and insubstantial – what could be seen of it. On either side of the route lay desolation. The rough grass was uncultivated. The petrol tankers had gone. No traffic came out of the mist from the opposite direction. Small rocks joined the stones that had tumbled from outcrops which increasingly loomed over the route. These rocks sometimes became boulders.

The sense of gloom and foreboding was only partially alleviated by a faint illumination which began to light the mist to the west. The road curved around the lip of what was evidently a broad valley which showed signs of dropping away in that direction. The glow grew stronger. A vast space was suggested; a space still brightly lit by the sunshine of early evening.

The coastal plain? Could it be that, from this lofty vantage point, the mist would suddenly clear to reveal the entire plain which must now lie below the summit of the Western Cordillera? Could it be that, at the next bend, this desolate road would suddenly cease its climb, poise momentarily on the crest of the Andes and then begin a sharp descent to the tropics? Could it be that a grand view of the Pacific was just about to reveal itself – a view of the greatest ocean in the world which, from this high western rim of the Andes, was only to be met with awe; with Keats' sense of 'wild surmise'?

*

Quite possibly. Unfortunately, the climb continued, the glow to the west faded and the mist drew the road ever more closely into its cold damp bosom. Visibility dropped to a few feet, the bends tightened and became steeper. Boulders became more frequent. Fuel began to run low.

It was a lonely place and the forces of darkness really did seem to have the upper hand. The air was unpleasantly damp and chilly. Beyond tightly closed windows, vapours drifted over faintly perceived roadside edges: in some places tumbling off as bare rocky slopes; in others rising into that ubiquitous coarse grassland which, in turn, dissolved upwards into nothingness. Long stretches of the route were devoid of any sign of human activity. Only occasionally would the dripping stone wall of a single-story building loom up, or a rough track appear and bring gravel and pebbles to the road.

Of the inhabitants of this Andean upland there were only rare glimpses: once a shadowy man in rubber boots half-seen on a sharp turn; once the inexplicable figure of a sad little woman in a bowler hat standing motionless in a rocky field.

A subsistence life in what must be a land of near-perpetual cloud and rain. A place where the hot moisture-laden air of the coastal plain was forced skywards by the sharp wall of the Andes to create endless mist. I felt uncomfortable in what looked to be the misery of life lived out in this dripping world. The rocks scattering the surface of the road grew larger and appeared more frequently. Had another wrong turn been taken after that brief bump over the tracks of the Quito to Guayaquil railway? What if this route was winding its way along the cordillera and the route down to the west had somehow been missed? What if it was actually leading into the high southern sierra of Ecuador and growing closer and closer to a Peruvian border which was now less than two hundred miles away across bare and chilly highlands?

Growing closer to a country which – in 1992 – was becoming increasingly violent and increasingly xenophobic. Growing closer, in fact, to the Andean heartland of the *Sendero Luminoso!*

★

Fuel was very low and, in such situations, the last thing a traveller expects to encounter is a convenient petrol station in the middle of nowhere. But that was exactly what loomed out of the mist just as the fuel gauge needle had reached the end of its remorseless passage towards empty. A ramshackle old place: a couple of rusty pumps – one diesel, one petrol – sticking up drunkenly in a forecourt of cracked concrete slabs and pools of oil-blackened water.

Nonetheless, a petrol station. Unfortunately, no one seemed to be about and, in the silence of the mist, the place quickly took on a disappointing air of dereliction. The solution to the fuel problem began to become as insubstantial as the clammy air enveloping the location. Then, something moved behind the vague outline of a shed and two Indians emerged on to the forecourt. Grim-faced and unsmiling, they came slowly towards where I waited and set about operating the petrol pump.

Or – more precisely – one of them set about operating the petrol pump. The other stood a short distance away and began to stare fixedly at the scene. It was a very hostile stare.

Staring was rare in South America. People, if curious, tended to politely disguise their interest or – if not – would quickly exchange a serious or sullen glance for a sudden brief smile after their eyes were met. Life was hard for many but the response invariably said: 'go on your way stranger, I mean no harm.'

This stare did not break into a brief smile and for a complete stranger to be intently and continuously observed with a certain hostility spelt danger. It spelt danger in a lonely place and it particularly spelt danger for an isolated foreigner less than two hundred miles from the operational territory of the *Sendero Luminoso*.

The other Indian, who had been hunched over the nozzle of the pump as he filled the tank, slowly returned the hose to its position. The tank had been filled. I gave him a large denomination note and waited for change. The familiar note trick began.

However, a sleight of hand concerning the change for the fuel had been overshadowed by a feeling that something much more serious might be about to happen. The hostile starer had started to edge around to a position behind me. It was becoming difficult to watch the returning notes as well as keep an eye on the starer.

The man at the pump moved into the usual routine: first low denomination notes from a wad in one pocket; then a slightly higher note handed over with a gesture which implied payment in full had been made and the transaction was over. Then – noting that had not had the desired effect – more slow fumbling in back pockets for another higher denomination note. Then, after another longer pause, the final notes of change emerging. These, of course, would be the highest denomination of all and, perhaps, count for seventy or eighty per cent of the value of the change. The unsuspecting victim usually drove off after the first stage.

I wanted to drive off as soon as possible – and particularly before the Indian who was behind me had brought whatever he held behind him to the fore. It looked as if it might be a knife.

For a foreigner in a lonely place in a tight spot the situation was not only dangerous – it could also be very complicated. If he made a lunge for me with the knife – that was one thing. If he attacked me and then got injured in the ensuing scuffle, that could be another. Like all Indians of the highlands, they were of small build but wiry. The man who operated the pump seemed less hostile and it was possible that he might not have joined in any fight. It was impossible to tell whether they were acting together or whether the grim starer was trying something opportunistic and unplanned. Might this be straightforward robbery or a political act? Or the usual combination?

Was it *Sendero Luminoso*? Delivering a car and money could be seen as quite an entrance fee if the Shining Path were moving up into this part of Ecuador.

Events began to unroll in slow motion. Still with his hostile look and still with his hand clutching something behind his back, the starer moved to insert himself closer. Split seconds became minutes. He was reaching for the space between where I stood and the open door of the hired Fiat Uno. He would have to be pushed aside if I were to be able to drive off. There seemed little alternative. I stepped forward and tried to keep both Indians in view.

Suddenly, a truck loomed out of the mist and rattled over to the diesel pump. Its cab was tightly packed with men and women all squeezed together and trying to give enough room for the driver to operate steering wheel and gears. Clammy with mist, three or four other Indian passengers had taken an outside ride – their faces peering over the dented roof of the cab as they stood on the flat-bed rear of the vehicle and braced against its bumpy approach. The new arrival stopped a few feet away. The scene being played out on the forecourt now had an interested audience.

The mood instantly changed. The hostile Indian returned whatever he held behind him to a hiding place and quickly backed away out of view. He disappeared into the mist behind the shed. The petrol pump man switched to a diesel hose and began refilling operations on the truck. The audience continued impassively staring but there was no hostility in their looks – only curiosity.

I started the car and drove off. I'd been in the deserted highlands too long.

*

Fortunately, it was only another ten miles or so before a change to the vegetation began to occur. Despite the mist continuing to reduce visibility to little more than a car-length, and despite the road remaining deserted, the landscape started showing an amazing transformation. With every minute that passed, bare rocks and clumps of stiff highland grasses which seemed to have such a hard time in the stony mountain soil were being replaced by a more prolific vegetation cover. Thick green bushes soon lined the road; lush meadows appeared dimly in view behind them.

Several miles of an increasingly profuse vegetation cover was accompanied by a return of that brightening of the mist to the west. The feeling of a vast empty space in that direction grew increasingly strong until – as the road dropped a few hundred feet – the land could be seen to begin to fall sharply away. As it did so, moreover, it joined a wide and well-surfaced highway which also plunged sharply downwards and into the lightening mist.

I had – at last – arrived at the 'minor' road which swooped down ten thousand feet in ten miles. It was a highway which was clearly better than the 'major' road I was on. Like a magnet, the modern and fast-growing coastal city of Guayaquil must be re-drawing the lines of north-south Andean communication in the direction of its busyness. The main traffic streams of Ecuador now seemingly preferred to bypass the world of mist and danger from which I had just escaped. Who could blame them?

But there was no long view of the Pacific to the west as the precipitous descent began. A world of cloud forest enveloped the route as it began to zigzag down a steep valley. Forested slopes gradually became more and more visible as the mist started to drift apart into long white stringers of vapour curling just above the top of dense tree growth. As light improved, the intensity of this green world became ever stronger. Thick mosses and lichens colonised the few rock surfaces that were visible – even clothing the walls and floor of a deep concrete channel which now lined either side of the road. Several vertically-layered climatic zones were passed through. A hundred shades of the colour green were to be seen amongst the growing luxuriance of the vegetation. The air grew noticeably warmer at every bend.

It seemed that no time at all had passed before the tropics were reached and the bright foliage of coffee and cacao trees was all around.

★

Those moss-coated concrete channels were not for decoration, however. Further down – wherever the route crossed or re-crossed one of the deep and narrow ravines which characterised this luxuriant western face of the Andes – great tumbled masses of freshly torn branches, foliage, tufts of scoured-up grass, soil-stained boulders and thick mud sheets revealed the chaos which the high volumes of rainwater cascading down through this landscape brought with them.

Nearly down but – like the Pacific – the coastal plain of a thousand feet or so below remained invisible. It was not until the moist balmy air of the last few hundred feet was reached that a westwards view opened.

What it showed, however, was certainly not the stuff of Keats' poetic imaginings. A dark haziness seemed to lie above the now-hot and now-flat landscape – a haziness which appeared to be closing with the very spot at the base of the Andean wall that I was about to arrive at.

★

It was rain. At first, a light patter began as I passed through the scruffy looking town of San Antonio. Then a shower rapidly strengthened to become steady rain as the road began its sixty miles to Guayaquil. Then a full-blown tropical downpour.

The storm brought with it the night.

From cold mists to hot darkness, streaming with water. All in an interval of less than two hours. And water also booming with the powerful resonance of thunder; teeming rainfall brightly lit and constantly crackling in the brief flares of lightning. White flashes of electricity spiked into nearby vegetation; the car rocked and slewed in the sheets of water which poured over the road. Heat and humidity quickly steamed up the interior, whilst any attempt to improve vision was quickly met by a blast of warm rain forcing its way into any crack opened in a side-window.

With the rain came the distinctive aroma of a hot, wet landscape. A landscape where palms and bananas had replaced potatoes and sheep; a landscape in which ponchos and the mountain people were gone.

*

The highland Indians might have been left behind, but there was no shortage of people in the lowlands. Small towns along the route were crowded with cars, buses and bystanders and – even as the rainstorm intensified – business continued unabated in shops below colonnaded frontages of main-street buildings. In the town of El Troncal, hundreds of Saturday evening pedestrians milled about seeking whatever shelter they could find.

Completely dry spots seemed very rare, however, unless they had managed to be the first of those crowding into the dimly lit inner sanctums of shops or had inserted themselves around the tables seen vaguely through the streaming condensation of cafe windows. In such towns – ignoring the downpour – tricyclists continued to ferry passengers from one end of the main street to the other or to zigzag dangerously backwards and forwards across its uneven concrete surface. Street maintenance was clearly as difficult to achieve in the small provincial communities of Ecuador as it was to achieve in the high-altitude capital. Water-filled potholes and heaps of rubble waited to receive the axle or sump case of unsuspecting motorists. High and sharp concrete sleeping-policemen had been put in place but did less to slow the traffic than to seriously damage it. In El Troncal, one nasty rib of masonry jutted out of the road surface so fiercely that it was surrounded by several feet of sump oil and soot.

Many an exhaust system must have been arrested by that chunk of concrete as car, bus or truck accelerated out of town and straight into its unyielding presence.

The world of the long-distance buses had also returned. Several of these dilapidated warriors stood waiting to continue their journey across the coastal plain and into the bright lights of Guayaquil. As they loaded up, rain cascaded from the lightly-clad bodies of men securing baggage to their roofs. It was certainly turning out to be a wet old night.

★

Beyond El Troncal's sleeping policemen and westwards to Guayaquil were many miles across a hot, flat country hidden in darkness and rain. Headlights fleetingly brought into view more of the banana plantations and palm trees. The road continued towards its destination. Traffic began to intensify where a distant orange glow in the night sky to the north-west seemed to imply street lights and a dense population.

Regrettably, it was a glow which never seemed to creep any closer. The journeying through the incessant storm required intense concentration and the distance began to feel never-ending. It was 8 p.m. and – after another two hours of streaming glass, thumping windscreen wipers and frequent wallowing splashes through large puddles – an eternity before those elusive city lights at last came into view. The largest metropolis in Ecuador (larger than Quito by nearly half a million people) had at last been reached.

The rain was undaunted by the largest metropolis in Ecuador. It continued to pour unceasingly out of the darkness above, to spill endlessly over an already soaked road surface and then to run vigorously off into the blackness of the confluence of the River Guayas with the broader expanse of the *Golfo de Guayaquil*. Water now stretched away on either side.

The route was crossing a long causeway leading towards the main part of the city. Once over the bridge, a dual carriageway then boldly took the incoming traveller past modern apartment blocks and towards what appeared – in the shadows of night – to be the most exclusive residential area of the city. Dim lights were scattered amongst trees growing over a low hill – trees whose crowns were profiled against the lights of the downtown area which lay somewhere beyond.

Closer too, white surfaces glistened with moisture; high walls kept out intruders; lanterns suggested a man-made environment of ease and pleasure. It looked just the kind of place where a modern hotel might be set amongst spacious gardens and shady foliage – a hotel that might even sport a softly lit swimming pool. Blow the cost.

This brief vision of washing away the long day with a pre-dinner gin and tonic and a dip was rudely shattered by the realisation that the exclusive residential area was a little too quiet and restful. The long-dead of Guayaquil had commandeered the higher ground of the city; it was a cemetery. The still-living had to make do with marshier and more pestilent surrounding areas where modern office blocks, banks, cinemas shops and garages had sprung up to service the needs of the twentieth century. Taxis, cars and pedestrians in this downtown centre of Guayaquil all streamed with rain now coloured by the gaudy tones of its neon advertising.

I eventually found a place for the night in Guayaquil – noisier than the cemetery and in too close a proximity to the living, but perhaps jollier. A cheap hotel like all cheap hotels: cash in advance; room halfway up an indeterminate number of identical floors overlooking fire-escapes and dirty brickwork; bare walls; dim light bulb; painfully hoarse air-conditioner; and a man who was being violently sick half the night in a room across the interior well.

The pestilent lower ground of Guayaquil. I hoped it wasn't the bubonic plague which had once stalked these tropical lowlands or the dysentery, dengue fever or typhoid which still lurked here and there in coastal Ecuador.

⋆

Morning – although it was difficult to tell from the amount of daylight filtering down the same interior well. The rain had stopped. Guayaquil might have been on the coast but it was far from the open sea. The road to the small town of Salinas led to the edge of the South American continent – and to that view over the Pacific Ocean. Apart from a bulge to the south and in the northernmost part of Peru, Salinas was one of the most westerly extensions of the continent.

There were no sleeping policemen on the westbound route to the coast. They were clearly all awake. For some reason, a complete dearth of uniformed figures in the (much greater) part of Ecuador which lay to the east of Guayaquil was being compensated for by their representation in the (much smaller) part of Ecuador which lay to the west of that city. Sitting in patrol cars, flashing past on motorcycles, busily setting up radar traps and warnings – there were officers everywhere. The entire policing capacity of the country seemed focussed on this sixty mile stretch of highway leading seawards to the Santa Elena peninsula. Perhaps the quality of the road drew them out in force: a good road which swept in long curves across a gently rolling country; no potholes; no rubble; no piles of earth or stones; no dilapidated buses loading suitcases.

Before long it became confusing and difficult to place this Ecuador in relation to the rest of the country – the hairpin bends, the exhaust fumes, the high mists seemed somehow totally different. Even the rain-sodden banana plantations and tropical palms felt as if they were part of another world. In fact, this part of the small but evidently varied country had changed so much that a completely new landscape was taking over.

Between Guayaquil and Salinas, the level of rainfall had dropped from an average of forty inches to a miserly four inches. The tropical vegetation which had surrounded the metropolis had quickly dried up over the space of thirty miles and had been replaced by grassland, then scrub and then – thirty miles further on – by nothing but dry grey dust and a few cactus plants. The last few miles of the journey to the shores of the Pacific were through the northern tip of that desert which began on the Santa Elena peninsula and did not release its arid grip until central Chile – nearly two thousand miles to the south. The road was entering the rain-shadow of the western edge of the South American continent, moving into one of the driest places in the world.

Sand – or sandy dust – but where was the view of the Pacific? At the crest of every slight rise, a promise of the sea was replaced by the reality of parched land, stunted thorns and an absence of any sign of human impact on the landscape. Even the distant view of the towers of a church at the town of Santa Elena failed to suggest that the desert did not dominate every aspect of life in the surrounding area.

It was when the buildings of the town gradually came into closer view, that the coastal environment showed itself as one where even gold probably took second place to water – fresh water. Twenty or thirty tankers stood clustered in the dusty main street of Santa Elena surrounded by a clientele who had brought every conceivable receptacle that would hold supplies of the stuff: cans; bottles; buckets, barrels. Guarding the tankers was a detachment of the Ecuadorian army and it was clear that feelings were running high on this Sunday morning. Soldiers deflected passing traffic out of the row and on through a back-street diversion which then twisted and bumped its way around the fracas and back into the surrounding desert.

Clearly – despite the massive volumes of rainfall which had cascaded over the coastal plain only one hundred miles to the east as yesterday's storm moved inland to the Andean wall – little had run back to fill the tanks of Santa Elena. The whole place looked as if it was on the brink of drying out almost completely – a small parched community shrivelling up from lack of water and virtually surrounded by the sea. It was odd to know that the moist, dense foliage of the wet tropics was only an hour's drive down the road. It was odd to realise that the equator was so close to here, too.

Salinas was at the end of the desert road. Much more recent in age than Santa Elena – it was a town of modern residential blocks. A resort town and one seemingly without a water shortage. Luxury apartments lined outer streets shaded by palms. Large dark fronds took the glare of the mid-morning equatorial sun from the pavements. The deep purple-red of bougainvillaea tumbling out of gardens glowed intensely wherever it was set off by a whitewashed wall.

Yet another Ecuador and one seemingly fed by a different water source than that tapped by poor old Santa Elena. Or, perhaps it was the same water? Salinas might have taken over a limited supply in the interests of national tourism! Perhaps the angry scenes just a few miles inland were about garden hoses for some and cans and tankers for others!

*

The Pacific. Its swell came into view from the apartment balconies of Salinas after a near uninterrupted passage from the island of New Guinea to the shores of mainland Ecuador. Only the Galapagos Islands were out there to briefly obstruct the ocean rollers.

But, after nine thousand miles, why was there was no surf crashing boldly against the western edge of the Americas; no glimpse of the awesome size of the world's greatest expanse of water? This Pacific Ocean lapped meekly up to a beach on which lay a few people grilling on brightly coloured towels. A family sat eating ice-cream cornets under a sun umbrella. A man plied up and down on the sand clutching a handful of balloon strings. Someone collected shells. And, on the far side of the road, an almost complete wall of new holiday apartments swept off towards the very tip of the peninsula. From all about – instead of the thump and rush of water on shingle – the all-too-familiar ringing of steel on concrete and the staccato rattle of pneumatic drills could be heard. It was Sunday but developers were still competing with each other to block off the last few glimpses of the sea.

This wasn't the ocean I'd come across the Andes to see. This wasn't the Pacific of Keats. This wasn't a place where a traveller '*...star'd at the Pacific*'. This wasn't a place where anyone '*Look'd... with wild surmise*' at anything. True, Salinas wasn't a peak in Darien. But neither did it seem like a town on the westernmost coast of Ecuador. This was a beach in Benidorm!

★

The Pacific would have to be seen elsewhere. I turned my back on it in disappointment. The long, hot return journey towards the mountains and to the flight out of Quito began.

First desert became scrubby forest and the scrubby forest became rainforest. In the rain forest, it started to rain. Then came Guayaquil under shrouded skies as the good road from the coast became another pitted, litter-strewn thoroughfare where it touched on the grubby edge of the city. Then it improved and set off northwards through the fertile green lowlands of the River Guayas.

It was another way back to the capital: a route substituting the long passage down the central valley for a long passage up the coastal plain – a swap of the best part of a day's drive through highland mists for the best part of a day's drive through tropical cattle-lands, banana plantations, dark groves of African oil palms and the occasional rice paddy.

In this country, horsemen in stetson hats herded small groups of longhorn steers along the grassy edge of the highway. Then cattle country became banana country – a tropical 'bread-basket' in earnest. Not bread as such – but a wide variety of more valuable export crops. Ecuador is the world's largest exporter of bananas.

An agricultural heaven. Rich soils. Abundant rainfall. No doubt two or three harvests a year. A paradise. Why then did its towns all look like organisational disaster areas? Daule, Santa Lucia, Palestina, Balzar – each a version of El Troncal. All grubby little places full of reeling tricyclists; peeling plaster; pitted main streets; and cratered pavements. There was something seriously wrong with the infrastructure of Ecuador. The money just wasn't getting through; the place was falling apart.

But – out of the disorder of these small places and in its stride across the broad stretches of open countryside which separated them – the highway usually improved and it was possible to travel at some speed. Traffic seemed light and the lowlands did not appear to be fuelled by the convoys of petrol tankers which plied up and down the Andean highlands. Only the long-distance buses continued to rattle past – each one spraying out stones and fumes as they overtook at speed, and each one continuing down the highway in a cloud of dust and flapping tarpaulins. The men who did the tying of baggage on to the roofs frequently seemed to have skimped on the task.

Most Ecuadorian buses did not leave the overtaken traffic without a brief inspirational message. Pithy mottoes, decorously painted below a travel-stained rear window would be: '*Christ y Consuela*' or '*Ayer, hoy y siempre*' (Yesterday, today and always). And, at times, one bus would be in the process of overtaking another: '*Señor del los milagros*' would be desperately trying to get ahead of '*Nina Narcisa*'.

In fact, 'He of the miracles' tried so hard on one blind corner to get the best of 'Nina Narcisa' that He lost half a silencer and most of His exhaust pipe through too much acceleration and not enough circumspection.

Such speediness – but not noise – was clearly beyond the capability of the dilapidated and heavily overcrowded old bruiser which I had passed in the dry country on the first few miles of the journey back from Salinas to Santa Elena. This elderly '*Tormento del deserto*' had no silencer at all. For a bus called 'Desert Storm' it sounded quite appropriate.

Yes – they were a playful crowd those drivers. Two of them were enjoying a game of tag as they hurtled past on the open road between Palestina and Balzar: one bus trying to nudge the offside rear light of the other with his front bumper as they simultaneously overtook me. Inside, rows of a closely packed captive audience tried to make the best of it – grinning nervously or looking anxiously at the roadside vegetation as they mentally appraised the possibility of the bus meeting it at speed. A dangerous game – and one best avoided. When another two began the simultaneous overtaking manoeuvre I decided it was time to accelerate out of harm's way.

Unfortunately, it soon became apparent that this acceleration and overtaking had also to encompass more buses. A column came into view ahead – a column moving fast but headed by what seemed to be a racing pig! The animal was travelling at some speed but veering wildly from one side of the road to the other as such pigs do.

The pig cleverly prevented anything from overtaking it. Furthermore, a narrowing of the road did not help matters. As the convoy coped with the turn of events, the two original overtaking buses now closed ranks with the three or four others – all behind the pig and temporarily shutting off any thought of my retreating back to the right-hand side of the road.

Such thoughts had suddenly become more pressing. In the distance, an oncoming vehicle had appeared – a bus travelling fast and seemingly completely oblivious to pigs, small cars or whatever temporary obstruction might lie in its way. As it thundered closer, I noticed that my impending fate was to be squashed flat under a vehicle whose message was clearly emblazoned across its front. '*Tia*' it said – 'Auntie' in Spanish!

Auntie somehow got past. The pig made a great leap into the roadside ditch, the column of buses eased over to the right, I managed to swerve and simultaneously balance on a roadside verge which was partially covered in drying rice grains and '*Tia*' flashed remorselessly past on her regular morning journey to Guayaquil.

★

Morning gave way to afternoon. And afternoon was becoming early evening before rising land took over from the lowlands and the town of Santo Domingo was reached. A Santo Domingo at the foot of the Andes. A large and ramshackle place of narrow streets choked with traffic and people. A place which showed – by the composition of its inhabitants and local visitors – that the mountains were close. The people of the highlands reappeared: familiar figures once more mixed and traded in the colourful hurly-burly of a street market; people in bowler hats over black, plaited hair; people in ponchos; people with reddish-brown faces; people whose squat heavily clothed forms were in strong contrast to taller and slimmer inhabitants of the coastal plain clad in vests and shorts or light cotton dresses.

Rising land, but the Andean wall to the east remained hidden in thick cloud as the route began its steep climb up to Quito. Precipitation fell once these clouds had been entered: mist and coolness quickly returned; dense vegetation crowded ever more closely over the upward winding road. The world turned to water again – sheets of it streaming across the tarmac as rain increased in intensity and used the highway as a short cut to the lowland streams now far below. Visibility shrank to a few feet beyond the sweep of the windscreen wipers and the pre-twentieth-century world of the Indians returned amongst the mist and moisture.

But an old world overlapping with the new. A file of mountain-dwellers leading steaming pack-horses up a trail towards some hidden hamlet or small-holding; the horses laden not with produce or woven textiles but with butane gas canisters. Little huddles of ponchos and shawls stood at the roadside as the highway crept ever higher and higher up the steep wall of the mountains and on to the heights of the Western Cordillera. Thick green leaves and fronds dripping with moisture gave way to the rough grassland of the highlands.

★

The climb still seemed to have some way to go through mist rapidly darkening with the approach of night, when the road unexpectedly levelled out and slipped away from the clouds. Set out below was the central valley. A patchwork of fields and cultivation still palely illuminated by the last golden rays of a setting sun. The Western Cordillera had been crossed and the land of the snow-capped volcanic peaks and potato harvesting had returned. From here, the capital of Ecuador was only twelve miles or so to the north.

Equatorial nights fall fast whether in the lowlands or the highlands. It was very dark when the route entered the earthworks obstructing the passage of the Pan-American in the southern outskirts of Quito. Not unsurprisingly, confusion took over even more under the darkness of night than in the exhaust-tainted atmosphere of day. A few flaming markers were the only guide though the chaos of soil and stones. It was as easy to get lost going into Quito as it was trying to leave it. Somehow, a detour led not to a reunion with the main thoroughfares of the modern city but to narrow passageways and the gridiron of dark streets first laid out in 1534 by one of Pizarro's lieutenants. I had arrived back in the very heart of the capital – in the densely built-up centre of the old Spanish colonial Quito but regretfully passing amongst its venerable *plaza grande, case del gobierno, casa episcopal and cathedral* at the very time when a power failure seemed to have blacked out every available lamp.

Little could be seen beyond the brief sweep of car headlights except flickering shadows. Small groups of Indians clustered at street corners – shawls and headgear casting looming silhouettes against the red glow of fires whose flames were fuelled by empty boxes, cartons, old newspapers, scraps of wood and other rubbish gathered from around the ancient buildings. Some newly restored buildings gleamed fresh blue and pristine white against the car lights; others stood shakily buttressed against collapse. Keeping Old Quito in one piece looked a never-ending task – Pichincha loomed above and the last tremors of its great volcanic bulk had been felt as recently as 1987!

Although Pichincha overshadowed the *Palacio de Gobierno* and formed a backdrop to the city of the sixteenth century, its disruptive influence seemed somehow to lessen only a short distance away. And so – curiously – did the power failure. The main downtown area was brightly illuminated. There was no shortage of light as late nineteenth-century and early twentieth-century buildings took over – none of which seemed to need buttressing. Neo-classical banks, offices and public buildings came and went as the main thoroughfare was regained – thence to be replaced northwards by late twentieth-century Quito: modern glass offices; well-kept boulevards; open parks; residential suburbs and the airport.

★

It was an early plane which left for Bogotá and on to Caracas the next morning – a plane lifting off from the runway just before dawn. On the short journey between the Peace Corps hotel and the terminal building, the route had briefly wandered behind some of those neat residential areas close to the airport and past a wide open expanse of bare hillside. Here, the rotting waste of the city was regularly dumped. At 4.30 a.m. – in the cold blackness of an Andean night dimly lit by street lamps – people slowly moved about on discarded rubbish: picking here and there amongst the stones and scraps of polythene; sifting through boxes or turning over decaying leaves and stalks with short sticks. They were gathering edible scraps. Some of them were children.

Chapter Six

Weekend in Peru

Sssssssssssssssssssssssssh THUMP! The floor underneath vibrated; the plane lurched; the starboard wing dipped sharply down; a grey hillside rose up to meet the cabin window and there was a sudden sensation of falling. Bloody hell! He's lost it!

An aeon passed – or was it a split second. A heartbeat or two – or no heartbeats at all. For that long/short time it looked as if we were going to end up as lifeless as old Pizarro down there – or whoever once owned the wizened body which now lay mummified and in a glass coffin near the door of Lima cathedral.

But the Fawcett pilot bought the plane back under control, gingerly lowered the undercarriage and prepared for landing at Cuzco. There must have been something loose in the cargo hold. As wheels touched tarmac, the round of applause was well-earned. It might even have been a standing ovation had the experience not weakened us at the knees and doubly-fastened our seat-belts.

*

That battered but good friend, the sixty-seventh edition of *The South American Handbook* was something which told a person more about how a country was run than any list of principal exports, indices of wages and prices, percentage of the population with drinking water or the budgeted government expenditures on roads and railways.

For some countries, the Handbook had a tongue-in-cheek feel about it. Argentina, for instance. Telling the reader to watch out for dangerous animals in the country – the worst of these being a species called *homo sapiens*. Ha, ha. Brazil, too – in order to avoid a big shock in Brazil 'treat electrically-operated showers with some circumspection' when away from the big cities. Chile: watch out for that hole in the ozone layer – some Patagonian fish were having trouble with cancerous growths. No mention about having trouble with the general and his men. Bolivia: don't wear shorts in town centres. Good advice – particularly if it happened to be an altiplano evening and the town in question was above ten thousand feet.

There was a slightly less jokey category of countries. Ecuador – a problem with thieving and pick-pocketing. Very true – but also a problem with north and south and of getting a decent view of the Pacific. Colombia. The same – but nothing extra about serial numbers or four hundred eliminations. One of the Handbook's biggest worries with regard to Colombia was what went into its bottles of imported spirits – not what came out at you from abandoned buildings waving a stick covered in foetid tar.

And then there was Peru!

In the 1991 edition of the Handbook, Peru wasn't funny at all. Warnings shouted from almost every page. Thieves in Chimbote, Trujillo and Atequipa! Pickpockets at Cajamarca! Terrorists in Huaraz! Bombings by the *Movimiento Revolucionario Tupac Amaru*! Explosions in the Miraflores suburb of Lima! Intermittent murders and shootings of tourists and highland bus passengers by the *Sendero Luminoso*.

It wasn't just the Shining Path – half the population seemed to be turning anti-social in one way or another. Not everyone, of course – this was an exaggeration. The death toll in the troubles of the 1980s amounted to 22,500 persons – sadly, most were innocent bystanders in the conflict.

Whilst some happenings had made a big enough bang to reach the ears of the global village; others were simply routine harassment. And routine harassment in such an unsettled country had a habit of spawning other difficulties for the ordinary traveller. Difficulties like the drug-planting endemic in Lima – $500 being a common demand from the police for release.

It was no better in the countryside. Indeed, for every potential hazard presented by the capital; there seemed to be five or six more in the provinces. The Handbook gave a series of terse advisory notes on moving around in the interior in the early 1990s.

> *Don't travel alone... Avoid remote villages... Under no circumstances get involved in any political demonstrations... Avoid confrontations with the military... Remain silent and unobtrusive... Post guards to avoid armed robbery on the Inca Trail.*

The Inca Trail. Poor old Peru. It hadn't been like that in 1979 when the early morning train from Cuzco stopped briefly at 'Km 88' in a deep Andean gorge and a slender suspension bridge pointed the way across the River Urubamba to the start of 'The Royal Highway to Machu Picchu'.

*

It was only twenty miles long – the Inca Trail. A day's walk from the railway halt by the river crossing to its end at the ruins of Machu Picchu. There were only four snags to getting the business over and done with in the interval from sun-up to sundown. The first three were physical: a pass at 13,500 feet; a pass at 12,900 feet and a pass at 11,600 feet. The fourth was also physical but to do with supplies. Few people lived in the rugged mountain country. One day was too fast and too risky. Food, tent, sleeping bag, cooking equipment, high altitude clothing, rainwear and heavy boots were all part of the Trail: nights were bitterly cold; the passes high and close to the snowline; the valleys in sub-tropical jungle. In earlier years, hikers starting out without adequate precautions had perished from hypothermia on the heights, been plagued by biting insects on the hillsides and been attacked by poisonous snakes in the valleys. Others had suffered the indignity of 'Montezuma's Revenge' in a landscape devoid of flush toilets, running water or supplies of extra lavatory paper. There were no emergency services.

'Atahualpa's Answer' – the Peruvian contemporary of Montezuma struck hard on the first stage of the Trail. As the climb began through the eucalyptus trees and thick bamboo groves which had established themselves near the bottom of the Urubamba gorge, it turned south to follow a tributary valley (of the River Cusichaca) and then steepened into something more serious.

Unfortunately, at this point, so did the microbe-attack of a meal taken the previous evening in Cuzco. Preoccupied with climbing, the home team who normally dealt with suspect ceviche, elderly fish or murky mineral water were completely unprepared. A touch of *soroche* probably added to their preoccupation, but by the time the first mile was over, any defences had been completely overwhelmed. It was a complete rout! The Peruvians were winning! Atahualpa was returning with a vengeance. It quickly became uncomfortable pressing on in such an unsettled state and yet too complex to go back. 'The Royal Highway to Machu Picchu' had been declared a one-way route – walkers were forbidden to retrace their journey (although no one with a plastic helmet stood guard to prevent that being done in 1979).

As the path left the last bamboo grove and opened out into the brilliant sunshine of mid-morning, it became obvious that every hour of the four days' journey to the 'Lost City of the Incas' was going to be required if a 'bowel stop' had to be made every five minutes.

*

Slow progress has some compensations, however. What had first appeared to be tumbled rocks amongst the yellow mountain grass now began to assume more ordered shapes. The world of the Incas slowly came into focus: a ledge here, a slope there, a block in one place or an entire hillside revealed that nothing much in this Andean landscape was the work of untrammelled nature – the more one crouched and looked outwards; the more it became apparent that nearly everything in view had once been ordered, repositioned, carved, built or dug. Remnants of walls, terraces and the stonework of an old irrigation system – all of Inca or pre-Inca origin – became visible. Clearly, this quiet and now empty place – called Llactapata – had once been the site of intensive cultivation.

It was on the ascent of the Cusichaca valley that the microbes began a second offensive. All through a climb of nearly two thousand feet up from the 8,200 feet at Km 88, the battle raged on. The grassy hillsides closed in. Just after four rather unpleasant miles had been covered, another bifurcation was marked by the few grass-thatched buildings of a place called Huayllabama – at this point the Trail moved into the valley of the River Llulluchayoc but nonetheless continued its long ascent.

The battle of the River Llulluchayoc was where the big guns really opened up. As the climb grew serious and distant glimpses of the heights of the first pass were to be gained, a pitched 'tooth-and-nail' contest was in progress. The height rose slowly one thousand feet by one thousand feet. Dense woods gave way to bushes and then to stunted trees. Then the land opened out into bare rocky slopes clothed in the coarse yellow grass of this part of the Andes. The first pass was near but progress slowed as a point of surrender began to approach. Atahualpa had won outright – the tent had to be hastily pitched on a sloping hillside at nearly twelve thousand feet, gear pulled out of the pack between bouts of dysenteric distraction and the best made of a long high-altitude night with frequent opportunities for a brief glimpse at the southern hemisphere stars.

★

Things seemed much brighter in the morning – the battlefield of the night became calm and serene as the first rays of sunlight filtered through the green nylon of the lightweight tent. The long, cold and uncomfortable night had ended. A scanty breakfast of dried eggs and the last one and a half thousand feet to the summit of the first pass started the new day.

Bare rock outcrops and small patches of scree now began to intrude on the coarse grass: the grey and yellow colours of the mountain summit stood sharp and clear below a mid-morning sky which was intensely blue. Not an ordinary blue but a deep and almost purple-blue which took on the kind of semi-transparency of fine porcelain: a sky through which it seemed – if it were possible to see just a little bit further or climb just a little higher – the stars and the blackness of space might just be perceived in the full visibility of day.

But 13,500 feet was not high enough – even though the air had become noticeably thinner as the ground levelled off and the path strayed on to the crest of the pass.

⋆

The Inca Trail lay on the eastern side of the Andes and followed the foothills of the Vilcabamba heights which paralleled the Urubamba gorge. This was a part of the range that had been caught up in great plate tectonic movements. Quite recently in geological time, a westwards shear – the Fitzcarraldo Fault – had dislocated the generally north-west-south-east axis of the rising mountain belt and caused the Urubamba to flow north and not east before it entered the huge basin of the Amazon. The river tumbled down towards the tropical rainforest along a course which had etched its way deeply into the mountains.

Above Km 88, a drop of three thousand feet in twenty miles was made by its surging waters. It dropped another four thousand feet in the next fifty miles as it wound past Machu Picchu and on towards the small town of

Quillabamba where the railway from Cuzco ended at a football stadium and a Dominican mission.

Lower down, things were a little less frantic, the Urubamba valley opened out more and its fierce pace slowed. However, it continued to be framed by higher land until a place called Camisea. There the equatorial lowlands began – the Urubamba flow finally turned north past a cheerful-sounding settlement called *Colonia Penal del Sepia* and became one with the River Ucayali. The Ucayali rolled on into the Amazon system which eventually took these Andean waters to the Atlantic.

Remote country – except that a major gas-condensate accumulation at Camisea was likely to bring the world's oil and gas industry to the tropical lower reaches of the Urubamba as the twentieth century came to a close.

*

From high above, the views on the Inca trail showed nothing of the vast Amazon basin. They looked west, instead, to the Vilcabamba range and the twenty thousand foot peak of Mount Salcantay rearing up with its snows blazing out sharply white against the near-indigo blue of the morning sky.

That was the inaccessible country in which the last serious Inca resistance to Spanish domination had retreated. Manca Inca in the late 1500s – like Che Guevara in the late 1960s – attempting to continue a guerrilla action amongst the thick jungle cover of the eastern Andean foothills.

In fact, it was the gushing waters of the Urubamba that Francisco Pizarro used in 1539 to send a cruel message from the Spanish base at Cuzco to the Inca base at Vilcabamba. His men had captured the Inca's wife (who was also his sister) and sent her naked and flogged body spinning down the gorge to its presumed discovery by Manca in the jungles below. A Spanish adventurer was the next to hurtle downstream. In 1542, Francisco de Orellana took the same trip – inadvertently – and, after drifting two thousand miles through the rainforests of Amazonia, eventually found himself alive and amazed in the Atlantic Ocean.

There was a slight flavour of the Amazon in the thick sub-tropical vegetation which appeared to fill the steep incised valley of the River Pacaymayo. This small hanging valley curved southwards from the Urubamba gorge and divided the heights of the first pass from those of the second. The Trail led on and its steep course passed downwards through several ecological niches. Coarse grass and scree turned to yellow highland meadows; these quickly became stunted forest; these changed to bushy scrub then, with a final descent into the ravine-like floor of the Pacaymayo, the sky was closed off by the dense foliage of full-sized trees.

*

It was on the climb back out of the valley that the work of Inca engineers began to aid the labouring traveller. Stone steps prevented slippage in the moist forest, and then appeared at intervals until the 12,900 foot summit of the second pass was achieved. There, once more looking west over the Vilcabamba range, it became obvious that the best part of the day was over and the sun was beginning to set. Inca ruins stood nearby – a place called Runkuracay.

One whole day to traverse from the first pass to the second – a distance of three and a half miles! That was terrible, but the combination of a pack weighing forty pounds, lingering *soroche* and a stomach full of Peruvian microbes contributed to an excuse. Runkuracay made a good site for a second campsite.

Runkuracay was simple but built to last. Massive stone walls enclosed inner walls which looked as if they might once have been covered by a roof of grass thatch supported on a wooden framework. All was open to the glow of the sunset and no longer offered shelter against the onset of the cold Andean night. Coarse grass crept up to the masonry and colonised its interior spaces. What purpose did it serve?

Perhaps a fort or some kind of guarded entrance to the approaches to Machu Picchu. The view from Runkuracay was over the entire Pacaymayo valley: an enormous sweep which – in daylight – could have told the watchers by the stonework that friends or enemies were approaching and must be prepared for.

Or had it once been more of a 'hostel'? One of those *tambos* where authorised wayfarers could find overnight accommodation and sleep warmly under government-provided woven blankets and help themselves to government-provided freeze-dried meat, fish and tubers. Perhaps it had accommodated one of the teams of relay runners who were able to pass messages, orders, special foods or other material over distances which could be up to one hundred and fifty miles a day.

At the time of the arrival of Pizarro and his men in the 1530s (when the Inca empire was in its heyday), over fifteen thousand miles of paved highways crossed the rugged terrain of the central Andean cordillera – from Ecuador to Chile. The system of graded roads, bridges, tunnels and steps knitted communications together more effectively in the early sixteenth century than the Peruvian road and rail system did in the late twentieth. But, of course, the Incas had no wheel. Every part of their engineering was scaled to human or animal movement which needed water, food and fodder to keep it functioning over long distances. Runkuracay could well have been one of the thousands of resting places and storehouses fuelling the Inca system.

Or was it a customs post or police station? Some sort of Inca equivalent to one of those Venezuelan *alcabalas?* The Inca network was strictly controlled. Not everyone could move about on it. In fact, few in the empire were allowed the full freedom of its roads. Travel was restricted; special passes were required and endorsed; authorisations needed from local authorities. The Inca state was totalitarian. Inspection posts, toll-gates, retractable draw-bridges, watch-towers and a hundred-and-one other devices locked the social planning in place and ensured that the deliberate displacement and ethnic mixing required by the empire was maintained and – where necessary – harshly enforced. There was no little similarity with the Roman Empire and no little similarity with the Third Reich, either. If a member of an ethnic group or community who had been displaced to colonise a newly conquered part of the empire then wished to return to his or her former home without permission, the punishment was torture for a first offence and death for a second.

The roads were not for pleasure or pilgrimages through the Andean landscape: they were for armies of conquest; government business or the privileged few – everyone else was expected to stay at home and work. The state required a nine-day week on the terraces and pastures and a full day's work for a full day's pay in all its many ditch-digging, road-mending and bridge-building projects.

Fort? Hostel? Customs post? Police station? That was the problem with the Incas – nothing was ever obvious. Whatever purpose Runkuracay served in the empire of the sixteenth century, it offered only a bitterly cold night on the Inca Trail of the twentieth. It was good to see the dawn. A thin sleeping bag and another meal of dried eggs and powdered potatoes was probably worse fare than the board and lodging of earlier travellers on the Royal Highway – Third Reich or no.

★

On the Trail once more with bright sunlight and warmth filling the steep valley of the Pacaymayo; wisps of mist curling out of the hidden depths of the Urubamba gorge. Ahead lay another steep valley which curved west. Machu Picchu was still ten miles away. Runkuracay was exactly halfway between Km 88 and the 'Lost City'. Did that have any significance? Everything in these mountains now seemed impregnated with purpose.

From the campsite, it was a short but stiff climb of just under one thousand feet to the summit of the second pass at 12,900 feet. The route wound past small pools of black mountain water and then led on down a spine-like ridge before dropping sharply towards one of the headwater streams of the westbound river – the Yanaconcha. Inca engineers and road-gangs had put their forced labour into this section and stretches of paved highway began to speed-up progress from the three and a half miles a day of the earlier part of the trail to something a little more acceptable.

Atahualpa's Revenge had now abated, too: acclimatisation, the bright sunshine and the clear mountain air were beginning to make the second half of the Inca Trail look a much more interesting prospect than the first half.

More and more Inca ruins were appearing as Machu Picchu was approached. The stone walls, towers and staircases of a place called Sayacmarca came into view – looking out this time to the west and over any movements in the valley of the Yanaconcha.

What sort of place was Sayacmarca? The view and location suggested a military purpose or another police station, but it was only one mile from Runkuracay! A greater complexity in the ruins of the buildings indicated a small community – but who lived in it?

Was it a monastery? Some sort of religious halting place? The enigma of the Incas continued to puzzle. Nothing in these half-tumbled stone walls was quite straight; there were few right-angles; too many shelves which sloped; too many steps leading up to nowhere; too many tapering doorways; too little that could be grasped and placed in the context of the closing years of the second millennium AD. In fact, there was little which could be placed in the context of the opening years of the second millennium BC! The ruins were only five hundred years or so old but they showed less meaning than Stonehenge; less meaning than the pyramids of Teotihuacan; less meaning than the pyramids of Giza.

The ruins did have one strong characteristic which should have pointed towards a purpose – they all possessed a kind of huddled verticality; a maze-like assemblage of rooms connected by steep narrow stairways which usually clung to the side of a precipitous hillside. But – nearby – there were easier locations on which to site buildings or to access water. The Incas seemed deliberately to choose difficulty and complexity rather than ease and simplicity.

*

For a short distance, the Trail steeply descended the valley side of the River Yanaconcha using a section of Inca roadway – five or six feet in width and made up of rounded blocks. In this place it was almost perfectly preserved. No conquistadores or Spanish colonial troops had marched or ridden along this road – Machu Picchu had remained hidden in its eyrie above the Urubamba until very recently.

With the Yanaconcha remaining in view, a gentle climb then began along the flank of the valley and towards the third pass at 11,600 feet. This section of the Trail was almost entirely paved – even, at one place, passing through a sixty foot tunnel allowing access from one side of a rock buttress to the other. Was this the only way to Machu Picchu? Why did it all have to be so tortuous?

*

The third pass presented a stupendous view of the Urubamba. The incised gorge cut heavily into the surrounding uplands – the curving meanders of a once leisurely lowland river had become the channel of a fast-moving mountain river as the Andes rose. It twisted north, south, west or east across the landscape as it made its steep descent to the Amazon basin. The sudden and unexpected glimpse of this glittering ribbon of water trapped in its steep, dark-green walls took the breath away.

The Trail set off along a route high above the southern wall of the great bend. It was in this precipitous position that the Incas had decided to build another complexity of staircases and stonewalls which had been given the name

Puyupatamarca. The huddled verticality of the site (seven miles from Machu Picchu) allowed the passage of water from its higher parts to its lower through a series of five open stone baths. From the lowermost bath, the water rejoined what appeared to be an irrigation system feeding into a series of terraces. These crop-growing strips of soil were poised dangerously above an almost vertical drop to the river far below.

Why? Why did Puyupatamarca have terraces and Sayacmarca not have them? What was grown on the narrow strips? How many people could they feed?

⋆

Obviously, the Inca empire was adept at producing enough food for a dense population from an environment which ranged from tropical valley to snow-capped peak. The knowledge and enterprise which terraced and watered the mountainsides did not spring into place in the couple of hundred years before Pizarro appeared in the Andes – the Incas were inheritors and not creators. Earlier societies had slowly evolved these methods of farming. The cultivation of maize, potatoes, tomatoes and tobacco grew up over several thousand years. Puyupatamarca could be older than the Incas – so could Machu Picchu for that matter.

It seemed that with the huddled verticality came the obsession with self-sufficiency. Part of this self-sufficiency was probably necessary – there were no wheeled carts to carry bulk produce from one region with surplus to another region with shortage. The whole mountain range was the farm and the nine-day week of tilling and watering the produce of the narrow terraces of somewhere like Puyupatamarca merely the local expression of a highly productive food generating machine which spread the length and breadth of the Andes.

It was a machine which required careful maintenance to keep it functioning – an organisation which the Spanish overlooked and which disintegrated only a few short decades after the colonial period began. The once dense populations that the terraces supported throughout the Andes declined drastically as the break-up of traditional patterns by forced labour in the silver mines and elsewhere took their toll. Malnutrition increased rapidly in the decades after the conquest; Old World diseases had made their mark even as the Spanish were arriving. The inhabitants of Sayacmarca, Puyupatamarca and Machu Picchu could remain hidden from the Spanish in their lofty communities but smallpox or measles or influenza could still have found them out and destroyed their communities just as effectively.

Indeed, Old World pestilence was sweeping its way through the Inca empire from the jungles of the east in the years before Pizarro first landed on the desert coastline of the west. It was European viruses which killed Huayna Capac (the 11th Inca) and, by so doing, set off the war of succession; the civil war that Atahualpa had just won when he rested at the hot springs of Cajamarca and heard news of bearded men approaching from the sea.

⋆

In 1979, Puyupatamarca did not have a terrorist problem but it did suffer badly from litter. The Inca Trail was already growing popular and, although the one-way stipulation of the Peruvian authorities meant that walkers all travelled in the same direction and rarely met, traces of their passage had become very obvious. Cans, food-packaging, paper, old shoes, sometimes discarded clothing, lay alongside the path wherever it opened up sufficiently for people to gather. Despite the height and arduous nature of the trip, a surprising amount of unwanted material had found its way to the edge of the Urubamba gorge; material which a work party a year or two later found amounted to several tons.

Origins were analysed and would have proved as puzzling in meaning to an Inca farmer, priest or policeman as an Inca farmer, priest or policeman's buildings were to an intrigued passer-by. Fifty per cent of the rubbish originated in Peru; thirty-seven per cent had been carried from Germany, seven per cent from France and the remaining six per cent from a wide variety of countries ranging from Iceland to Australia!

⋆

From Puyupatamarca, the gentle traverse of the near vertical side of the Urubamba gorge continued westwards for a little over two miles. Far below, the glittering ribbon of water continued winding in its great southwards curve. Wisps of cloud drifted amongst the dark green of the vegetation. Care was necessary for the Trail had become increasingly narrow and clung much more precipitously to the steep rocky hillside. It became so narrow, in fact, that any stumble would be difficult to recover from. Once momentum had got under way there would have been no stopping a plunge into the gorge below.

The reason for the 'one-way' rule became clear. Any travellers approaching from the opposite direction would have caused a considerable problem. In Inca times, pack-horses could not have passed each other on this stretch and pack-horses were notoriously difficult animals to persuade to walk backwards. Perhaps some of the smaller rock shelters which now occurred every half-mile or so were designed to control the flow of traffic?

They seemed to have thought of everything. The world of the Incas which had slowly come into focus at the beginning of the Trail was still coming into focus – rock outcrops more and more took on the forms of a simple building; indentations and shadows on nearby boulders more and more became carved faces; steps would more and more leave the main route and disappear into dense undergrowth.

As the Urubamba gorge bent northwards – so did the Trail high above it. The ruins of a place called Winayhuayna hung above the sharpest part of the bend – facing north in the direction that the winding Urubamba was taking on its path into the Amazon basin. Flecks of mist still curled in the valley although the late afternoon sun had already turned one side into deep shadow. Beyond the gorge, the same afternoon sun had made a series of east-west trending ridge-tops into profiled shades: first green-grey; then grey-blue; then light grey; then only the faintest tint of grey in a light haze as this northern edge of the Andes plunged towards the equatorial rainforests.

★

Why did Winayhuayna have to perch in such an inaccessible spot so high above the river?

Admittedly the view was superb and it did catch the full light of the rising sun, but what made the Incas build and cultivate in these most difficult of places? Surely a society which had conquered the Andes did not need to hide away in defensive positions where the more primitive peoples of the tropical lowlands could not reach them. One or two expeditionary forces and several small forts could have sorted out such a threat.

Terraces showed that this vanished community was again self-sufficient. Another series of cascading stone baths showed that it was well-washed.

Or was that a completely facile interpretation? Was that merely an attempt to force the patterns and meaningful activities of one society on to those of another. A forced banging of the proverbial round peg into a square hole.

What would an Inca think the function of an oil-fired power station was if one was presented as a five hundred year old ruin? No trace of the fuel; no trace – probably – of the generators. Just the remains of an evidently large structure, some odd holes in the ground, a few heaps of brick or concrete, some congealed masses of rust. And – from his cultural framework – what interpretation would be placed on an abandoned crematorium? A railway embankment with no rails? An overgrown airport?

⋆

Perhaps Winayhuayna was not perched high above the Urubamba for defensive reasons but for religious ones. Perhaps the 'Royal Road to Machu Picchu' was not a road at all but a physical 'Pilgrims Progress'. Perhaps all these places with their cascading baths; stairways which led to nowhere; sloping niches which couldn't hold any object; strange knobs of stone and trapezoidal doorways were not meant to have a purely practical function. Perhaps the whole place held a more spiritual meaning. After all, Mecca was arranged around a meteorite; the basilica of Assisi grew out of one man's vision of God; and Orthodox priests still live in tiny monasteries perched high on humps of conglomerate in the Pindos Mountains of central Greece.

But spiritual or not – these Inca ruins still left too much in question, – even after applying the widest measure of lateral thinking. The world of the Inca Trail remained an enigma. What purpose did that tiny platform that perched over a one thousand foot sheer drop into the Urubamba gorge have at Winayhuayna? Did people volunteer to sacrifice themselves to the rising sun? Were prisoners or captives executed there? If so, where did they come from? Why choose such an isolated spot?

*

Beyond Winayhuayna, the Trail assumed its most hazardous form and took on some of the sinister aspects of the tiny platform over the one thousand foot drop. Barely fifteen inches wide, it clung to a near vertical hillside. A stumble would send any pack-bearing walker straight down to the ribbon of river in view below. There were no passing places. The hazardous traverse ended in an imposing flight of steps which led to the last ridge before the 'Lost City'.

Intipuncu was only one mile from Machu Picchu. The ruined masonry entrance structure or gateway had been given the name 'Gateway to the Sun'. It did indeed face west; its far side was lit by a sun which was now golden-red in colour and just about to set, but did the Incas see it that way?. Through the 'Gateway' another great bend of the Urubamba could be observed, although the depths of the gorge now lay in deep shadow. Ahead and below was Machu Picchu and towering one thousand feet above was the slender peak called Waynapichi. The scene formed itself into one of the best-known colour-plate pictures in the world. The Lost City of the Incas – the centre page of every book on South America.

★

Had the end of a 'Pilgrims Way' also been reached? All those steep climbs and descents, the high places and the places of danger. Was this Canterbury? Or Rome? Or Mecca? Or were the ruins below just those of a small out-of-the-way town which happened to be in a rather grand setting?

Did a monastic order live beyond the Gateway to the Sun, perhaps? Or astronomer-priests?

The buildings of Machu Picchu rose up the shoulder of the ridge below Waynapichi until they reached a small platform area in which stood a piece of carved and polished granite. A light grey sculpted form – beautiful and elegant in its own way and about the size of a man. It seemed to point upwards and outwards to somewhere beyond its own being. It also seemed to be dormant; unused; waiting – rather like a car or a grounded aircraft but more focussed somehow than those machines.

A granite telescope?

★

It was too late for a close inspection of Machu Picchu in the fading light of evening. A place to pitch the tent was found in meadowland close to the Gateway of the Sun (not allowed even in 1979!) Overnight the Peruvian custodians of the ruins took the tortuous road down into the gorge and to Machu Picchu station.

Another Andean morning followed the slightly less cold night: bright sunlight streamed across buildings which had been excavated, investigated, partially restored and generally spruced-up since Hiram Bingham first found the site in 1911. The remains of temples, baths, palaces and more humble homes spread over the ridge which fell away sharply on both eastern and western sides to the river below. Terraces sloped away from the city on the eastern flank of the ridge. Some terracing also sloped west. Incredibly, more utterly precipitous terraces could be made out on sheer slopes close to the peak of Waynapichi. Why? Why cultivate a rock pinnacle? Even the priests of the Pindos Mountains hauled their supplies up from below.

The morning sun did not change the focus of Machu Picchu. Everything still led up to that smooth curiously bevelled piece of polished granite. It was one of only two surviving 'Intihuantana' – the rest having been destroyed by order of the Spanish clergy who sensed a non-Christian power in their strangeness. Another more popular name was 'The Hitching Post of the Sun' – an appellation which suggested a complete ignorance of any purpose or function.

But what was the Intihuantana for? Somehow, it didn't seem to have a sacrificial element associated with it. There was nothing of the Chac Mool about the shape: none of the lingering grimness; no cups for throbbing hearts or channels for blood. In fact, there was nothing either human or animal about the Intihuantana at all. It was an abstract form – rather like a piece of modern sculpture. It did not look the kind of form that would be idolised.

★

Was it the kind of form which could be used? Not a stone telescope, obviously – such an object was a contradiction. But something like it – something which could be used? There was undoubted precision to the carefully smoothed surfaces – the same kind of precision which had been brought to bear on fitting those huge three hundred and sixty ton masonry blocks in the 'fort' of Sacsayhuaman above Cuzco; blocks which adjoined so tightly with their neighbours that it was impossible to insert a knife between any seams.

Had the Incas stretched their obvious engineering expertise in the direction of the stars like the Mayas? The functional symmetry of the Intihuantana; the angled orientation of one facet that was curious and satisfyingly picked up and echoed by the orientation of another. It was a characteristic which gave the form considerable aesthetic appeal. Was there a kind of 'Golden Mean' present in the summation of its angles?

From one direction, imaginary lines traced from its surfaces into the air above it all seemed to meet at an invisible focus point positioned not far beyond the top of the tooth-like rectangle which formed the most upstanding portion. From another direction, the imaginary lines carried away across the Urubamba gorge and into the blue of the sky.

Was that where the Intihuantana pointed? Into the blue of the sky. Like the 'windows' of the Mayan buildings; those 'windows' which have recently been found to point towards the rise and descent of sun and moon, towards the passage of Venus, the Pleides and others. Did the mystery of the Inca priests lie in how they used the orientations of the stone to make predictions of equinox and the movements of the planets? Was the Intihuantana not religious at all but a form of scientific instrument?

Or – if not science – then its forerunner. A tool used in astrological predictions. Did the surfaces help predictions of the dates of change in the agricultural and religious calendar?

A sextant was rather like a telescope. Was the Intihuantana a stone sextant? An instrument to join the Inca world with the stars above; to anchor life in the Andes to a point in space and time; to harmonise one with the other.

Maybe 'Hitching Post of the Sun' was right after all!

Chapter Seven

Weekend in Bolivia

When crows (or condors) fly from Caracas to the capital city of Bolivia, they fly almost due south for two thousand miles. When anyone else wants to spend a weekend in Bolivia, they fly north-west for one thousand five hundred miles and then south-east for three thousand five hundred miles!

There seemed to be no way around it. Northwest across the Caribbean to Miami first – and then back down the spine of the Andes to La Paz.

*

A lovely clear afternoon which laid the world out like an atlas. The coastline of Venezuela fading southwards and then returning once more as we crossed the *Golfo de Triste* and the pimple-like shape of the Santa Ana mountain came into view on Paraguana. Then a slow reel to starboard bringing dry Aruba below the wing-tip before it too fell behind. Then only the deep blue of the waters of the Caribbean spreading out in every direction. Its surface was lightly ruffled by the westward-moving Trade Wind.

Time passed and – with it – Hispaniola and a distant blur of Jamaica. Then, the deep blue was replaced by pale shallows and white fingers of coral where the treacherous reefs of the Great Bahama Bank began. Then the blue returned to join the white – a sharp line marking where the eastern shelf of the Caribbean dropped sharply away into the bathyal depths of the Atlantic. Then, a descent towards evening, smoky air and a flat expanse of southern Florida growing rapidly closer. The strings of lights, cars and a great busyness. Miami – the terminus of the Americas; the Crewe Junction of the New World.

Miami airport as the great meeting point of the Americas. An aviation crossroads – a place like Singapore airport. A place where north rushed past south and vice versa.

At Miami, the Latin world transferred to the Anglo-Saxon world and vice versa. Aircraft from every country in Central and South America set down and lifted off from its runways: Taca from El Salvador; Faucett from Peru; Avianca from Colombia; Mexicana; Lineas Aerolineas Paraguayas; Lan-Chile; Aerolineas Argentinas; Lloyd Aereo Boliviano. People too: stocky black-haired Mayan ladies wearing *huipiles*; beautiful Venezuelan and Brazilian women with mischievous, smiling eyes and huge padded shoulders; grizzled Japanese-Peruvians with plastic bags; worried Chileans in overcoats; fat Cuban-Americans in shorts.

Miami was the world of the late twentieth century. But it was to a very different century that I was heading, in a country where some of the rural inhabitants knew nothing of the city and very little of western civilisation.

*

La Paz, Bolivia. A frosty morning in a drab terminal building. A building seemingly isolated on the cold altiplano with no other signs of habitation or cultivation. A splitting headache and breathlessness – the *soroche* which accompanied sudden exposure to an altitude of thirteen thousand feet. The shock of transferring from high summer in the tropics to deep winter in the Andes.

Dawn had yet to reveal much of the cold, stark landscape of the early morning altiplano when the Lloyd Aereo Boliviano 747 first landed. It was 4.30 a.m. and still dark. A bare approach road led away from the car-parking area surrounding the terminal building – its route marked at intervals by a line of lampposts each illuminating a small circle of dust and stones. A chain-link fence followed the road and – in the dim outer glow of the lampposts – looked as if it was enclosing nothing more than clumps of rough, coarse grass and bare soil.

A terminal building with few seats, a closed restaurant, some small tourist shops (also closed) and a freezing draught of thin air which swept in every time the door to the car park was opened and shut. The occasional entry of squat Bolivians – presumed to be taxi drivers – marked the passage of time. There was a distinct and pungent odour every time one of them passed close. It wasn't the odour of unwashed clothes or bodies; I guessed it was the smell of chewed coca leaf.

It was too early to attempt to work out how to see the rest of Bolivia and – in any case – I felt like a punctured balloon.

The odour of chewed coca leaf grew suddenly strong.

'*La oficina para los cauchos es en el centro,*' said a voice through my aching head and half-closed eyes. One of the stocky taxi drivers stood blocking the draught from the door. He was wearing a cap with ear flaps and was clearly intimating that a cab would be needed to go to wherever the city of La Paz had hidden itself.

'*Abierto a las neuve,*' he added. Bolivia was slow to wake up in the morning and – with the frost and the cold – who could blame it.

I established the cost and we walked out to an elderly saloon car parked near that draughty door. There was no need to hurry. It was still well before 9 a.m. The growing light revealed a pale grey landscape which had the slightest tints of pink and orange in it. Not the warm pinks and oranges of sunset but the cold colours of a winter's dawn. The air made sharp needle-like stabs at the nose and quickly took face and hands in its cool grip. All around, more of the dusty, bare soil could now be seen. It stretched away from the terminal – scantily clothed with its coarse grasses – until it reached a distant huddle of dusty buildings. A rather sordid unpromising scene except for where, in the distance to the east, a line of majestic mountain tops stood cloaked in snow. The peaks of the Eastern Cordillera.

Of La Paz, there was absolutely no sign – although the land could be seen rolling away in all directions until it either met these mountains or was swallowed up in a kind of icy ground mist.

We bounced down the road and towards the mountains. Frost gleamed in tyre marks at the roadside. A group of Indians passed by – each wearing the same woollen hats with ear flaps as the taxi driver but also encased in thick, coarsely woven ponchos. More came into view; standing about in small groups as if waiting for transportation, and rubbing hands or blowing through ragged gloves as they tried to bring some bodily warmth into the coldness and dust of a working day.

The *soroche* began to ease a little. Perhaps it was the close association with coca leaf. Strong wafts from the driver's breath dissipated into a background of coca leaf odour which had obviously been impregnating the car's upholstery for some years. Evidence of light industry started to appear amongst groups of low buildings which had crept up to line the route. We joined a busier highway. There was still no sign of La Paz.

★

When the city did appear, it was a complete surprise. Under the steeply rising foothills of the Eastern Cordillera, a massive chasm began to open up. The highway swooped around its lip and started to descend sideways along steeply plunging flanks. Soon the surface of the altiplano had been left several hundred feet above as the route dropped down through a clutter of dusty buildings and curved past a grove of bare and peeling eucalyptus trees. Highland Bolivia was no country of moist greens and budding flowers. An overwhelming bleakness had invaded this attempt at afforestation and the trees looked wan and sickly.

Then thousands more buildings became visible – all clinging tightly to the sides of the chasm and becoming more and more densely packed as the road twisted and worked its way lower into an urban tumble of single-story pale-brown and grey *ranchos*. Then more substantial buildings showed themselves; three or four story apartment blocks, offices and more light industry. Then the towers of a great church. Then modern office blocks – their tops dropping away and marking the continued descent of the valley as it wound further and further away from an altiplano lip which was now several thousand feet above.

This was it. This was La Paz. A city sheltering from the coldness of those high-altitude grasslands by huddling itself into a huge defile which rapidly descended until it was three thousand feet below the airport. No wonder it had been invisible to new arrivals. The soaring snow-capped peak of Mount Illimani was the only pointer to where the founders of the capital of Bolivia had tried to escape the worst of the wind and cold.

Even down in the chasm, it was still cold – despite, in the course of the thirty minute taxi ride, the sun having risen properly. As its bright illumination flooded into the deepest shadows, there was little warmth in it. In such a landscape and at such a height, those rays had the harshness of a naked light bulb.

Neither the land nor its vegetation provided colour. Only humans. Bright splashes of intense purple, deep red, scarlet, flaming pink, bright green and blue were all about, but they clothed its people – particularly the crowds who filled the open plaza in front of that great church. It also came from their bared skin. Sharply and intensely defined in the cold air, the faces of the Quechua and Aymara Indians of Bolivia added a copper-red tint to the strong primary dyes in the fabrics – an animated kaleidoscope which spilled away from the massive wooden door and ancient wall of the *Basilica de San Francisco* and out across the town square and into adjacent side streets.

It was Saturday morning and the weekly market of La Paz had clearly been in progress since the dark hour of dawn. A large affair of clothes, food, furniture, pots, pans and plants. A market which looked as if it had taken place in much the same spot for centuries. A market which had probably gathered together since the church's foundation by the Spanish in the latter part of the sixteenth century. A market which, quite possibly, not only pre-dated colonial times but pre-dated the Inca times, too.

With the wheel, the Spanish were the first to bring a concept of money to the farming communities of this high plateau. But they had survived very well without it. The agriculturalists of the Quechua and the Aymara had been bartering and exchanging the products of their labours for more than five millennia. The Incas – like the Aztecs – were only 'johnnie-cum-latelys' on such a scene. Crops, seeds, fruits and vegetables, pots and pans had been changing hands for many centuries in markets like this – it was part of the stuff of altiplano life.

*

In the big square outside the church, too, it looked as if much more than the sale and exchange of produce was going on: match-making; information exchange; a time for a social drink; the transfer and hiring of men and machines all seemed to be in full swing.

To this mêlée was suddenly added many more people – a great crowd eagerly spilling out through the church doors and away from the seriousness of morning Mass. The already dense kaleidoscope of stalls and shawls, puffed-out skirts, bowler hats, potatoes and ponchos, caps with ear-flaps grew much more densely packed.

A stream of 'children' bursting out of Sunday School. That was what it looked like to the new arrival to the altiplano. This was no preserved remnant of a picturesque folk-history long since overtaken by the late twentieth century. This was real. And the brightly coloured 'children' were not youngsters but adults.

The huge size of the church doorway dwarfed them, of course. But it wasn't just that. The indigenous peoples of Bolivia were very short in stature. A genetic stream which had become totally adapted over thousands of years to living and working at altitudes above ten thousand feet. And there were so many of them. Andean Bolivia was less ethnically diluted thkgan any of the Latin American republics.

During the last millennium, the altiplano had supported a surprisingly dense indigenous population – despite the Inca state undertaking massive relocations and the Spanish colonists bringing a severe epidemic of smallpox which may have swept up to eighty per cent of the population away in the sixteenth century. In the twentieth century, however, Amerindian peoples remained the dominating statistic. Of Bolivia's six million inhabitants; seventy per cent were of Aymara or Quechua stock. Of the population of La Paz; less than half were Hispanic. I began to feel a little like Gulliver amongst the Lilliputians.

The smell of coca leaf, the two thousand foot drop in altitude to get down into the central part of the city, or the three hours or so of acclimatisation which had already taken place? Whichever it was, I began to feel much better. The headache had gone and the breathlessness was becoming familiar.

*

Clean up in a downtown hotel, some breakfast and the hire of a car to travel the three thousand miles along Bolivia's National Route One to visit the colonial town of Potosí. Potosí was the place built in the shadow of the 'silver mountain' from which came so much of those New World riches shipped out of Cartagena by the galleons of Seville. There was only one slight problem. The offices of the car-hire company were still shut and looked like being so for the remainder of the day.

I signalled to a man working in an adjacent office. It took several attempts before he was prepared to acknowledge that a figure trying to catch his attention from the road was important enough to warrant a break from his papers.

'*La oficina para los cauchos – es abierto?*' There was thick plate glass between us. Clearly, all he could see through it was a tall *gringo* mouthing something unintelligible and pointing into near space. The reply he eventually did make was equally unintelligible. It could have been Quechua or Aymara or even English. Sensing a lack of comprehension, he reverted to a complex hand signal which was even less meaningful than the several sentences which preceded it. I gave up and returned to hang around the car-hire office.

At 10 a.m. – with great panache – a young woman was dropped off by a passing car and hurried to unlock the car rental firm's office. Documentation followed, at the end of which I emerged with the keys of a four-wheel drive Suzuki Vitara – a jeep with a lid on it. She flatly refused to hire anything else.

Puzzling. Potosí was on National Route One and I couldn't see why any of their other vehicles were not up to tackling the six hundred mile round trip. Bowling along at 60 or 70 mph down the major communications artery of the country should not involve much more than four or five hours of the day and – after an overnight stop and a look around the mining town – an equally brisk return along the same route might be expected to take the same amount of time. With an hour or two to spare, it might even be possible to fit in a quick look at Lake Titicaca not far north of the airport. Who was hiring all their cars? Couldn't be the equivalent of the Cuban Communist Party. It might possibly be the clergy.

The Vitara proved to be a throaty little vehicle well-adapted to city streets and hard-surfaced roads. It soon had me back at the top of the ravine and beginning the journey south across the altiplano. The now familiar landscape stretched away southwards – opening up into a great intermontane basin showing a distinctive pale yellowish-green surface colour and seemingly sparsely inhabited.

National Route One was a good road which dipped and rose over this gently undulating landscape as it pressed on across the sixty miles of altiplano to the town of Oruro. The traffic was surprisingly light. At intervals, low hills came closer to the road, at other times the basin widened and they merged into that distinct yellowish-green skyline.

Brown patches on the flanks of these hills indicated cultivation. A somewhat desultory cultivation, however, since many of the patches looked bare of crops. Perhaps potatoes lay hidden from view. Perhaps they were being left fallow for a year of two. Somehow, the more overwhelming impression took hold that they had simply been abandoned. In some, re-colonising grasses and weeds were moving on to once tilled soil but were seemingly taking a few years to do so. Growing was obviously a tough job on the altiplano.

Perhaps they were not all abandoned. Perhaps a strict rotation system was essential to maintain the integrity of the soil; the hillsides were at thirteen thousand feet, after all. Raising spuds on the roof of the world must be a very different ball game to raising them in an allotment at sea level.

The occasional village came and went. Mostly single-story; mostly breeze-blocks or bricks; mostly lived in but with tiny suburban fringes of crumbling dark-grey adobe dwellings which looked as abandoned as most of the fields. Instead of grass and weeds, the tell-tale signs here were windows and doors blocked off with slabs of dried mud of a slightly different colour to the adjacent mud walls. It was impossible to guess whether this was a Bolivian way of securing the premises, of keeping the draught out or of moving on to pastures new.

However, being blocked off with adobe did not seem the fate of all properties. Some of the communities close to National Route One seemed reasonably prosperous and the hundred or so houses which were clustered on either side of the highway usually had the focal point of a small Spanish-colonial style church, a two-roomed school and a steamy windowed roadside café. In these places, life looked as if it carried on much the same as anywhere in the provincial parts of Latin America apart from the substitution of mud for breeze-block and thirteen thousand feet for several hundred feet.

★

A landscape of muted colours: pale yellow-greens, darker browns and now the dark-grey adobe mud which could be observed in its natural state whenever a stream passed close to the highway. But with every mile, it was a landscape which grew slightly more arid and gradually more harsh. The brown patches grew less – whether recent or old. Cultivation was dying out for some reason. Swathes of dry, stony land appeared more and more frequently – eventually coalescing and becoming the norm. Imperceptibly, the pale yellow-green had become pale grey. Dust and stones took over – a sombre background that was only lightened when the occasional dash of bright red, green or pink at the roadside came into view and revealed itself to be one or more Indian women waiting to be picked up by the village truck.

They waited a lot – those brightly coloured Indian women. And the men, too. Bundles tied on their backs, bowler hats or ear-flapped caps on their heads; shawls or ponchos over their shoulders. And the battered vehicles which lurched to the side of the road to let them clamber over the travel-stained tail-flap were already jam-packed with others homeward-bound from market. But even on the truck, they all seemed to be patiently waiting.

Waiting for what? For an hour or so of journey – until they reached their homes and fields somewhere in the cold hills? Or was it a longer wait? Years? Centuries? Half a millennium?

Were they patiently waiting for the Latins to go, even? They were the people of this mountain plateau, after all. It was an illusion to think that the altiplano world had been colonised by Europeans and assimilated into Latin America. This was a place apart – a continent within a continent. Country boundaries had no meaning any more. It was altitude which ruled. There was absolutely nothing in common between Amazonian Peru and Andean Peru but a great deal of shared experience between Andean Peru and Andean Colombia, Ecuador or even Chile and Argentina.

If this Andean culture could be said to have a 'soul', however, it was the altiplano where that soul was centred. Europeans, Spanish-Americans and even those of coastal Indian stock who found themselves in the high Andes in the centuries after the Spanish conquest remained as a sort of visitor to these places. Even in La Paz, sheltering several thousand feet below the surface of the altiplano. Those sea-level dwellers who came up to the high Andes did not come to grow potatoes and maize; mostly they came to exploit and extract its mineral wealth or to exploit and extract its labour force. Now, in the late twentieth century, such mineral wealth was an attraction which was fading fast: mines had come close to exhaustion after five centuries, and many were abandoned; land-locked Bolivia was a long way from the world's industries; other more amenable sites had been located where the gold, silver, copper, tin and the other minerals could be extracted. The labour force, like the village communities along the highway, seemed somewhat abandoned. The Indians all looked as if they were waiting for the 'visitors' eventually to slip away. There were easier places in which to live. One day, perhaps, they would get the altiplano back for themselves.

The high Andes was an ecological niche. Over more than five thousand years, those of human stock who first moved up above ten thousand feet had physically adjusted to the different environment. Lungs were larger, bodies were shorter, blood composition had permanently altered. A kind of *soroche* in reverse took place when most of them ventured off the altiplano and down into denser air-pressures and warmer temperatures thousands of feet lower. Diseases took hold much more readily. A difficult adjustment had to be made psychologically as well as physiologically.

★

I suddenly began to have psychological and physiological difficulties in adjusting to what had become of National

Route One! The town of Oruro was still twenty miles away to the south but the hard-surfaced strip of highway which had been so efficiently heading in its direction abruptly came to an end in the middle of one of the stony swathes. A barrier of oil-drums and old sacking marked its passing. Beyond were diggings, piles of stones and then nothing but completely unmolested altiplano. Everything bore the unmistakable signs of a government road programme suddenly faltering and then running out of some crucial ingredient. It could have been tarmac but it looked much more like money.

Abandoned travellers had to make the best of it. A gravel-coated detour led off to the east but soon revealed itself to be a 'National Route One' in what was probably its original pre-tarmac form. The detour never returned to a proper road – it just carried on southwards into drier and drier country and into thick, choking dust clouds which became particularly dense whenever another vehicle passed in the opposite direction. The 60 or 70 mph average speed became a dream. Progress southwards dropped to under 20 mph – even less when the fact that the detour began resolutely heading eastwards was taken into account.

I was forced to ignore the bigger picture and concentrate on more immediate problems. Attempts to move faster worked encouragingly for a few minutes and then a skewed ridge of looser gravel sent the Suzuki spinning and sliding towards a deep and empty ditch which had begun to follow the highway. A cold altiplano night ditched in the dusty grey stonefields of Bolivia seemed unattractive. Then there were the culverts producing an additional hazard. Their appearance at regular intervals to carry non-existent water under the roadway always seemed inexplicably to coincide with the approach and passing of a fast-moving truck or long distance bus.

These speeding vehicles were surrounded by clouds of billowing white dust. Heavy tyres forged through the looser patches of gravel like the bows of ships crashing through a heavy sea. Instead of spray, great waves of stones spread out from either side of their progress across the land. As they passed, forward vision for any other travellers swooped down to zero. Choking white powder engulfed the immediate vicinity and a fierce side-swiping draught of dust accompanied the moment of their actual passing. Total disorientation became a problem in the middle of the encounter with little room for error. Somewhere to one side of the dust-storm was several tons of hurtling truck or bus; somewhere to the other side of the dust-storm was very loose gravel, the edge of the culvert and an uncomfortable plunge into that wretched ditch. Fear of the ditch neatly balanced threat of collision. The way forward and the danger of the passing only receded when the coarser particles had begun to settle.

It was unwise to slow down at these encounters. All too often, another truck or bus could be speeding up from behind!

The thin white powder which soon filled the interior of the Suzuki became a permanent feature: an acrid powder that smelt dusty; a dry powder which tasted dusty and a gritty powder that felt dusty – especially when it worked its way into the eyes and reduced vision even more. And the tension remained high. Whenever control had been restored and everything was quietly settling down, a slight rise and fall of the road ahead would announce another culvert – more often than not accompanied by the distant dust cloud of yet another approaching vehicle!

The twenty miles to Oruro took two hours. Bus after bus spewed its dust over the jeep; truck after truck shot past in its cloud of powder. Mid-afternoon came and went before this detour snaked its final miles across what seemed a particularly unattractive smoking wasteland of stones and hastily abandoned rubbish and the scruffy environs of the tin and wolfram-mining town began to line the road.

*

I filled up the tank, brushed myself clear of some of the dust and resumed the southward journey. Time began to be a worrying factor. No less than two hundred and fifty miles remained between Oruro and Potosí. Night driving on this kind of cold desert-like altiplano did not appeal. Thankfully, National Route One became hard-surfaced as it left town.

It began to point, however, into an ever more desolate landscape.

As Oruro fell behind and vanished, an empty landscape spread away from the road that – to the south – was characterised by a curious flatness. Distant hills still flanked the broad valley to its east and west, but this level southern horizon seemed to imply that a vast body of water lay just out of view beyond the curvature of the earth. A lightness in the sky added to the sensation that only a little distance further down the highway would provide a panoramic glimpse of a high-altitude lake.

It was indeed a lake that was being approached – Lake Uru Uru – but its waters remained tantalisingly mirage-like and unseen from the highway. The road continued towards an apparent shoreline but one which always appeared to hold itself mysteriously just below the line of the horizon.

The lightness in the sky grew stronger but started to interfere with the distant skyline. Before long, hills approaching closest to the now shimmering southwards view grew progressively more insubstantial. Eventually, they started to break into mirage-like fragments. Like all deserts, the distinction between clear-cut reality and illusion became ever more unclear as the miles passed and this landscape surrounded the lonely jeep. There was no other traffic on the road to provide a point of human reference.

Maybe water did lie out in that level expanse which disappeared over the horizon. Perhaps it came and went from year to year or from century to century. The smaller expanse of Uru Uru led southwards into a much larger Lake Popoo which was also supposed to hold water. All I could ever see was the elusive southern flatness broken occasionally by a floating hill.

*

In fact, opening to south, south-west and west was a huge area of level and virtually uninhabited country which marked the central basin of the altiplano – forty thousand square miles of it. Uncultivatable country – a landscape which not only included 'Lakes' Uru Uru and Popoo in its arid embrace but also the great *Salar de Uyuni* to the south and the *Salar de Colpasa* to the west. In its far north, even the real Lake Titicaca occupied part of the floor of this basin although, in that region, the softening effect of the yellow-green grass and the indifferent farming made it easier on the eye and less difficult to live in.

Walling this central basin in to the east were the peaks of the Eastern Cordillera; rimming it to the west were the heights of the Western Cordillera. Northwards, these cordillera coalesced into one Andean mountain chain and squeezed the true altiplano into a narrow central valley – the valley of Quito.

This basin was fascinating for a geologist – not least, because its vast forty thousand square miles in Bolivia looked like the site not of scattered lakes and salt flats but the largely dried out bed of one lake. Could a huge body of water have been raised high with the Andes and then drained away to leave only remnants like Titicaca and near evaporated patches of saline water like the invisible Uru Uru, Popoo and the *Salars*? Some people thought so. But where had the waters of that huge lake vanished to? And when? Could their going have been within the folk-memory of the Quechua and Aymara?

⋆

National Route One snaked on towards the mirage-like lakes but suddenly and without warning changed itself back from tarmac to that dreadful gravel. Surely it couldn't be gravel all the way to Potosí? My speed dropped to 15 mph.

The temperature had also dropped. Before the dust had required tightly sealed windows, the breeze coming into the jeep had been cooling fast. Now it was quite obvious that what little heat the afternoon sun of the altiplano held was quickly beginning to seep away.

Bare stony soil and clumps of rough grass again. There was little sign of other traffic. A mixed blessing, perhaps: fewer signs of humanity but also fewer dust clouds. No doubt, however, that moving further into a deserted landscape as the temperature dropped and night grew ever closer was bringing on a growing sense of loneliness. Perhaps the *soroche* was creeping back.

I began to wonder whether traversing the central altiplano alone was a good idea. Isolated in a vast dried out reservoir bed – it really wasn't the most inviting of places in which to spend the best part of a weekend. Bolivia was remote – despite the road, its high altitude near desert was probably one of the world's few remaining empty places. Human life seemed to shun it. Not only did the arid land appear to hold few opportunities for even primitive cultivation; it seemed doubtful whether animal life in general could have much of a time on its inhospitable surface.

It was also doubtful whether there would be much chance of a helping hand if an unexpected gravel bank sent the Suzuki spinning into one or other of the ubiquitous ditches. I now realised what had happened in La Paz. It wasn't the clergy at all. The cars were all being held back from the rigours of National Route One. That woman knew what Bolivia's main highways were like!

*

Despondent thoughts – but the prospect of returning was as dismal as the prospect of going on. The road continued along the eastern margins of Popoo but its surface seemed now to have built itself up into hundreds of close-spaced corrugations – each crossing the highway at right angles. Even at 15 mph and with time on your hands for pondering about such things, the phenomenon was difficult to understand. Usually, corrugations of this sort would be regularly scraped off, but in highland Bolivia such levelling of gravel highways did not seem to be an urgent task.

If the ridges had built up over time, what had made them cross the road at right angles? Could a combination of weeks of passing vehicles and a regular year-round freezing during the intensely cold altiplano night have done it? But frost needed moisture; and moisture in the vicinity of the invisible Lake Popoo seemed the one thing that was in particularly short supply. It was about as scarce as any sign of human life.

The intensely cold altiplano night! Twenty-four hours earlier I had been watching the late afternoon sun pick out patterns of white and blue on the tropical waters of the Caribbean thirty thousand feet below where they marked out the reefs of the Grand Bahamas Bank. Twenty-four hours later I suddenly woke up to the fact that I was back up at nearly fifteen thousand feet watching that same late afternoon sun sink remorselessly in the direction of a Lake Popoo. One view was from the seat of an aircraft traversing the balmy tropics; the other view was from a car seat shuddering along a dust road on the edge of frozen night.

It seemed irrelevant that this altiplano landscape was closer to the equator than the islands of the Bahamas had been.

⋆

Popoo was a lake – although still strangely elusive. Westwards, beige-coloured mud seemed to reach to the horizon and beyond. Highly saline mud. A kind of Dead Sea of South America. Water depths somewhere around its centre were reputed to be about eight to ten feet. Its shores did not seem much of a place to linger.

Popoo proved to be a place as well as a lake. Although, as its name suggested, not much of a place. About thirty or forty miles south of Oruro, a few adobe houses appeared – scattered amongst clumps of rough grass. Nearly all had windows and doors sealed off with crude chunks of dried mud. Community life here had totally evaporated: a quick chat with the neighbours or an airing of the bedrooms was a job for a builder not a housewife.

No neighbours and no housewives – Popoo was a ghost hamlet. Having passed it, the sense of loneliness and desolation increased. The shuddering strip of dust that was called a road continued to snake its way ever southwards. It was clearly leading ever further from the rest of humanity. I calculated that – at a very best speed of 25 mph – it would still be stretching ahead of the windscreen in eight hours time. At a more likely speed of 10 mph, it would be stretching ahead all night and the best part of the following morning. Stretching ahead, in fact, until arrival in Potosí for an early lunch – a Sunday lunch!

The ghost hamlet fell behind although grass, soil and the occasional rock at the roadside continued to maintain a somewhat spectral air – as had been the case for much of the unmetalled section of one of Bolivia's main arterial highways. Repeated raising and settling of the finer particles in the gravel – even with only occasional traffic thundering past – had sent them billowing outwards to settle on anything in their path. For ten or fifteen feet on either side of the road, a pale white cloak covered every stone and every blade of grass.

Westwards, however, this dusting had been defeated by the sheer scale of things. Over the shimmering flatness that was the mud or water of Lake Popoo, the air was very clear. Clear, but devoid of creatures. Nothing appeared to walk, fly, crawl or swim in its vicinity. Popoo was a ghost lake as well!

*

And then I suddenly noticed the railway line! Two reassuring strips of steel were following the road and must have been more or less in its vicinity since leaving Oruro. Perhaps the world had not quite abandoned the southern altiplano of Bolivia. But they were rather sorry looking strips of steel. On closer inspection, the rusty track had as much a near abandoned appearance as the small ghost-village communities it passed.

Trains did run – but not very frequently. The Popoo railway (I was later to discover) was part of a system which joined up no less a distance than the city of La Paz to the Pacific coastal town of Antofagusta in Chile. It was one of the world's great feats of railway engineering. Across a distance of nearly one thousand miles from the roof of the world, down the western mountain wall of the Andes and across the utterly dry Atacama desert to the ocean. Popoo was no Addlestrop but at least the tracks hadn't yet been ripped up.

Amazingly, just as the thought of steam hissing and throat clearing entered the dust-impregnated world that was the interior of the Suzuki, something happened. Not the appearance of a weekly train but the gravel changing to tarmac.

Smoothness at last – except that it wasn't! The vehicle continued its shuddering progress, showed a great reluctance to gather any speed and began lurching from side to side as I pressed harder and harder on the accelerator pedal in the suddenly renewed hope of reaching Potosí before midnight. With a slight increase in speed came an odour of burning rubber. Oddly and quietly insinuating itself amongst the acrid smell of the dust still lingering in the vehicle, it grew rapidly stronger. Smell took visible form. The smoke of burning rubber filled the Suzuki.

Rear tyre. The nearside rear tyre of the jeep. I stopped – finally realising what was happening. The nearside rear tyre was reduced to a few smoking shreds. Its axle-hub and wheel rim looked hot and bothered. It wasn't alone. More alarmingly, the companion offside rear tyre (although still intact) looked in a very sorry state. Not just loose gravel but sharp knives seemed to have been attacking it. Motionless and forlorn – how long was it before it too succumbed to 'torture of a thousand cuts'.

There was, of course, a spare. One spare – not two. If more torturers with knives lay up ahead to reclaim the Suzuki, then the situation was serious. And, if Popoo was typical of the facilities which lay in the Oruro direction of National Route One, then it was hardly likely that the Bolivian Motorists Association would hove on the scene, offer a hook-up to the nearest garage and then a lift home before nightfall.

That was the trouble – I didn't know what lay up ahead, except that it was getting progressively chillier and it was about fifty hours' walk to Potosí. Waiting by the side of the railway track to flag down a passing train looked as if it could take up to a week. It was difficult to imagine a train on those rails. What was the schedule? Freight creeping past in the night? Overloaded passenger carriages with people hanging off the doors? Was it only a ghost railway, in fact, with Lloyd Aereo Boliviano now doing all the serious transportation? I could be standing at Popoo for months! Suddenly, a Bolivian Railways timetable seemed a more useful aid for travellers than a map.

A rapid wheel change – there might just be some sort of railway station up ahead which could offer shelter and advice. With the shreds of rubber replaced by a proper wheel and tyre I climbed back and set off southwards again. Forward progress down the road began extremely cautiously but it soon became apparent that a speed less than 10 mph would put me in Potosí sometime in the middle of the following week. I increased to the reckless pace of nearly 40 mph. Five minutes later and the shuddering resumed. Was this the end of the offside rear tyre?

With some relief, it proved not to be. It was only the state of the road which had rapidly deteriorated. Dust-covered tarmac had faded into corrugated gravel. The tyre was still holding out – albeit looking no happier than a short while previously. Progress returned to some 15 mph.

Time passed and the corrugated road and the rusty railway continued further along the empty eastern edge of Lake Popoo. In the far distance, however, something was moving towards me!

A cloud many miles in the distance – billowing out like the smoke from a steam engine. The train from Antofagusta to La Paz? The cloud gradually came closer until it became apparent that it wasn't steam but dust and not a train but one of the long-distance buses. The white plume gradually made its way across the vast landscape until the vehicle causing it suddenly came into closer view. Roaring into the near distance it was clear there was to be no slackening of speed as another traveller was glimpsed occupying the same strip of highway. Despite the space all around, National Route One insisted on being fairly narrow and with a steep slope and ditch on either side. The bus covered the last section with a thundering roar, acrid white powder blanked out the world for a few minutes and the jeep was alone again in a deserted Bolivian landscape.

It was clear those buses were not of the stopping kind. With the dust-caked windscreen, it was quite possible to imagine that there was no one at the wheel, even. With high sides and made taller by roped-on suitcases, they gave every appearance of being on autopilot. Perhaps after hours on these straight altiplano roads, the driver took a break. Perhaps he walked down between the seats like the captain of a 747 – a joke or two here and there with the odd passenger and maybe even a quiet game of cards at the back of the bus. Meantime, the vehicle roared on across the roof of the world. Hoping that there would be anyone on the bridge who would stop suddenly began to seem as likely to succeed as flagging down the driver of the Royal Scot as it passed north through Watford station in the hope of a lift to Edinburgh.

More miles – the offside rear refusing to give up but the thousand torturers pressing on with the pain. Patch after patch of fierce corrugations; swathe after swathe of loose gravel; on and on down the edge of Lake Popoo for another thirty miles at the grand speed of 12 mph. The monotony of the scenery encouraged introspection; made me look inwards; made me look, in fact, to another problem.

The needle of the fuel tank had suddenly seemed to slip from three-quarters full to half-full in the blink of an eye. It hadn't, of course. It had been imperceptibly creeping around every second since that full tank at Oruro. Now the halfway point had been reached. A quick calculation suggested I'd need to refuel somewhere between Popoo and Potosí. The buses ran on diesel and no doubt had large tanks. The altiplano appeared devoid of petrol pumps!

Or was that a petrol pump coming into distant view ahead? It was time for a break. Some hovering dust and a few signs of human mark made on the landscape indicated what I guessed from the map was the railway station and small settlement of Challapata where the tracks veered off towards the Western Cordillera and the descent to Chile.

Closer to and Challapata began to look disappointingly small. A cluster of single-story brick and adobe houses positioned at the foot of dry brown hills. A cluster which had the curious characteristic of continuing to shrink the nearer I approached. Theoretically, Challapata was an obvious place to top up with petrol and possibly enquire about a spare tyre for a Japanese jeep.

Practically, it was clearly not on! As I reached the outlying buildings, a realisation quickly dawned: I was travelling in time as well as distance. Backwards! On this road from Oruro, I'd driven out of the late twentieth century, passed 'WW2' about the abandoned site of Popoo and was now somewhere near the dawn of the motor car. Challapata might have had a weekly train touching its isolation, and its rutted 'main street' coated once or twice a day with the fall-out of a long-distance bus but it was certainly not a global village.

Several fierce dogs bounded into the road and snapped around the Suzuki as I slowly passed amongst its few habitations – dogs which I sincerely hoped would not come anywhere near the offside rear wheel. It was a sentiment which had nothing to do with prevention of cruelty to animals.

Challapata was where highways diverged as well as the railway. Fortunately, the dogs angrily defended that part of National Route One which forked off to the south accompanying the rusty iron road to Chile. Perhaps they did the passing traveller a great service. No one in his right mind would go that way on a half-empty tank and a dodgy set of tyres. Dust and gravel all the way, the route led south for another thirty miles and then veered off west to tackle the dried-up desolation of the central altiplano. It crossed north of the dreaded *Salar de Uyuni* before climbing up over the Western Cordillera and slithering eighteen thousand feet down to the deserts of northern Chile and the Pacific coast. It was a road for expeditions. It was a road for the completely deranged.

I had already come to the conclusion several hours previously that the alternative was for the only slightly less deranged!

*

The other fork turned east at Challapata and began to climb up into the Eastern Cordillera. No sign suggested that Potosí lay at its end – the town was still more than one hundred miles away according to the map. It was a question of pressing on regardless. Tyre and petrol tank would need a guardian angel each to keep them in good heart. Asking for a third guardian angel to keep the driver in good heart seemed excessive.

At the beginning of the fork to Potosí was a long winding road which reached up to the sky. The journey to the silver mountain now had to pass over a landscape which was rearing up to sixteen thousand feet above sea level.

Whilst visible in the fading light of evening, these uplands of the Eastern Cordillera were certainly easier on the eye than the dreary central altiplano basin. As it climbed, the route curved tightly around a small dam and then ascended past its refreshing pond of dark water.

Obviously the region was not so arid as it appeared from below. Yellow-brown reed beds fringed the shores. Not far above and an Indian village appeared huddled in a fold of the hill – its single-story adobe buildings catching the very last of the setting sun. Blue smoke drifted in the air above reed-thatched roofs. Cooking was taking place in the walled enclosures outside each door, with the pungency of burning llama dung being tinted with the faint smell of food. Llama dung seemed not unlike the smoke of dried peat.

Higher still and several groups of the animals which had contributed the dung were clustered at the roadside – nibbling at whatever they could find. The route twisted and turned and revealed more small herds, these being quickly shepherded out of harm's way – usually by a tiny old woman who seemed to scurry into view from nowhere and just as quickly return to it with the llamas leaping downhill ahead of her.

Little seemed to have changed since that task was first taken up several millennia ago.

*

Black night on the *Cordillera do los Frailes.* A continuous twisting and turning. An endless following of a strip of dust – dust brightly illuminated by headlamps before being once more engulfed in the primeval darkness. Primeval because it was pierced by no lights. After the first hour of occasionally picking out the startled profile of an isolated llama or two, the world was now totally deserted. At higher levels, there were no more of the long-necked, slender-legged creatures looking up sharply from their ripping of the scanty roadside grasses and seemingly gravely affronted by the intrusion of artificial light. The occasional glimpse of a low wall of adobe or the corner of a thatched roof was no more. The *Cordillera de los Frailes* was clearly too desolate for even the hardy animals and people of the highlands. A full moon shone coldly on its pale grey-black surface; a dissected plateau of empty summits and dark valleys. At such a height, only stars glimmered above the distant hills. There was no trace of humanity for miles around; nothing whatsoever to indicate that any more small communities nestled in the shadows or sent their tiny old women to sit huddled in a poncho watching out over the flocks by night. If they did exist, those communities must have already retreated from the darkness of the high altiplano. Perhaps they had slipped out of the modern world and were now back in some earlier time. A long way back. Perhaps even as far back as Early Neolithic.

The tyre was still holding up, although the constant bends and turns in the road could not be doing anything other than worsening its condition. With a continuing increase in altitude came a worsening of the gravel surface. Severe corrugations in one place; banks of loose gravel in another. The imagined smell of hot rubber at one time; the cold blast of night air at another. Frequent quick checks had to be made as to whether the end had come. And no long-distance buses appeared to break the isolation of this upland road – they had also retreated for the night. Clearly, anyone with any sense avoided crossing the Eastern Cordillera by moonlight.

The needle of the fuel gauge dropped towards quarter-full.

⋆

Was this the right road to Potosí? The desolation all around and the absence of a sign at Challapata began to be worrying. Had I taken some unmarked route off the main highway and I was now twisting and turning ever higher and ever deeper into the middle of nowhere? Those desolate 'nowheres' were all too real in Bolivia. Like the *Salar de Uyuni,* some parts of the Eastern Cordillera could stretch for hundreds of miles: *sans* water; *sans* fuel; *sans* food; *sans* everything!

A rising sense of unease (panic) was slightly alleviated by evidence that the road – although still endlessly twisting and turning – was no longer climbing ever higher. Then a gradual descent into a wide empty valley opening up in the moonlight; a valley of dust and scattered clumps of coarse grass. A valley, moreover, which – at its farthest extremity – contained the very faintest glimmer of a light.

Humanity. The edge of Potosí? Well – sort of. Humanity, that is. It wasn't much of a place and it certainly wasn't Potosí. A kind of Challapata-by-moonlight. Single-story adobe houses, a few kerosene lamps, a truck or two parked at a drunken angle. A building which could have been a bar. No evidence of any fuel or of any reason why people might choose to live in such a god-forsaken spot. Apart from the trucks, this was frontier USA circa 1870. The time travel was still going backwards. No evidence of any people – although there were surely some inhabitants, somewhere.

A largely optimistic guess identified the place as Culta. If correct, the road was still then heading in the right direction although, just as I had reached that conclusion, it lurched off alarmingly to the south. The tiny community fell behind and a climb once more began into those empty moonlit hills.

★

I felt better after passing through Culta. The panic had gone. Perhaps the fall and rise in spirits was a function of the rise and fall in altitude across this landscape. Culta was one thousand feet or more lower than the worst of the *Cordillera de los Frailes.* It was just a pity that rising spirits could do little to reverse the remorseless movement of the fuel gauge needle.

Half an hour later and another tiny flickering light appeared in the midst of another empty valley of dust and coarse grass. It shone with the persistence of a star – a strange sight in a strange place. Then it turned reddish-orange. It was a fire!

A fire in the middle of a desolate landscape? A fire towards which the road led. A fire which could have been started by a human or... or what? Nobody lived in this dust; no other vehicles seemed to travel this road; no animals leapt away in the shadows. A fire which could be friendly and welcoming or a fire which could spell danger.

Closer to, and the ruddy glow of flames could be seen. And then sparks reaching into the cold night air. Then – only visible a few hundreds of yards from the scene – the faintly illuminated bulk of two large trucks. Then the black silhouettes of two drivers sitting huddled in their ponchos before the flames and staring motionless into the warmth.

They showed no interest in an approaching vehicle and outside their flickering circle of light, the dust, stones and coarse grass melted away into a cold darkness all around them.

★

The world seemed a slightly more welcoming place after the fire, although its distant appearance on this scene evoked feelings rarely experienced in modern times. The animalistic and primitive fear of the unknown in a world where there suddenly seemed to be too few people rather than too many. Devils or gods could have been dancing around that fire. It was not a rational universe up here on the night-time altiplano. It was a world of strange sights and inexplicable situations. The same world of the dwarves and the elves and the giants with cudgels. An empty world with no rescue from irrational fears. There were no clear-cut comforts and power-driven certainties in these Bolivian Andes; mystery and magic had taken over. It must have been like that in the Early Neolithic. Perhaps it was still the world of the people who lived in those mud houses on the climb up from Lake Popoo.

Another bright flash from a far off hillside – coming and going. Not a fire – something moving. A distant light sweeping like a torch beam – briefly picking out a faintly discernible patch of hillside and then vanishing. Several lights – moving fast towards me. The faint glow of illuminated dust clouds. Darkness and silence. And then a sudden great blast of light and noise as the white-streaked front of a bus roared around the hillside and passed in a hurricane of stones and wind. Not one but two – and then another and another and another and another.

Six long-distance buses passing in convoy – but no longer an unwelcoming, choking experience. More of them could thunder past if they liked. They pushed away those Early Neolithic fears. They meant that Potosí lay somewhere ahead. The time was 9 p.m. If the buses had left at 8 p.m.; there was only another hour to go.

There might even be just enough petrol left to get there – if the tyre held out.

Suddenly, the cordillera was becoming less and less desolate. Soon the road began descending. Then scattered pinpricks of light appeared on a long plunge down through a dark valley – not kerosene lights but electric lights. The power of civilisation was reaching up from slightly lower altitudes, from the world of the twentieth century, and pushing back the past. Further down the valley, a river showed that the central basin of the altiplano had been left behind, too. This tributary of the Pilcomayo was across the Andean watershed. Under a bridge, unseen waters were tumbling in the darkness and making their way to the Atlantic rather than to some dry *Salar* in the central basin.

'*POTOSI 48*' said a battered sign – the first since La Paz. The needle of the fuel gauge was well into the red. The offside rear tyre still hung on grimly.

The electricity faded out. The road began climbing. The landscape grew bleak and empty once more. The gravel corrugations came back and grew worse. The cheering spirit evaporated.

Then, just as the jeep slithered through what seemed to be the thousandth patch of loose gravel and shuddered out of what seemed the thousandth bend on the road to Potosí, its wheels gripped a hard surface.

*

The last seventeen miles into Potosí were a feather-bed, a magic carpet, a sleigh-ride through soft powder, a gentle surfing down a long winding canyon which eventually brought me out to a sea of lights spreading far up a hillside. I had arrived at the silver mountain. I had arrived at the highest city in the Americas and – during its seventeenth-century heyday – the largest. I had finally arrived at Potosí – the biggest boom town in the Spanish-colonial empire.

Potosí. Dusty modern shacks first. Then single-story breeze-block structures. Then some civic buildings as the hillside grew steeper. Then a seventeenth-century Potosí still largely intact with solid stone walls, narrow high-kerbed streets and ornate Spanish-colonial façades.

It was now 10.30 p.m. The old place was quiet and largely a-bed. Thick doors were firmly shut to the street. Winding and turning over the cordillera had put three hundred and seventy-five miles on the clock from La Paz to Potosí. The last thing that I needed after three hundred miles on soft gravel was to have a hard time finding somewhere to sleep.

★

A pale light breaking through shuttered windows. A new dawn in an old room. A room as high as it was long – unusually high and with the space and solidity of the eighteenth century. A clean room – the Quechua-speaking family who ran the inn were transparently decent. It was a room in a place which must have seen dust-caked travellers from the altiplano knocking wearily at its heavy door for two centuries or more – staggering gritty-eyed into its chilly night-time interior and being led by candle-light into one of the simple chambers leading off its covered courtyard. Or up to a second tier which was reached by a balconied access. Civilisation at last. Cloaks, riding boots and horsewhip dropped into a dusty pile on the stone floor, the worst of the white powder splashed off with icy water and an exhausted collapse into a low bed.

Nothing much had changed over the years. The temperature of the water in the shower was unbearably cold. It was still necessary to sleep fully dressed.

Fully dressed but still a cold night in that strange, damp eighteenth-century bed. The highest city in the Americas was no place for a light duvet or one or two soft blankets and a window left ajar. It was a two-mattress bed: one to go in the normal place below the occupant; the other to go on top. The kapok-filled top mattress pressed down with all the intimacy of a foot or two of heavy clay.

But I didn't mind. Heavy clay warmed up a little in the end. Everything was relative. The experience was infinitely better than spending each hour of the past ten counting the seconds as the moon looked balefully down on a freezing cold altiplano night and time edged shiveringly towards a frosty dawn on the *Cordillera de los Frailes.*

The early morning sun reached down the inn wall to the shutters and the day began more earnestly. The sound of passing traffic increased on the road outside.

On that same road, the dust-caked jeep stood where I had parked it for the night. The narrow but empty cobbled passage of late evening had become a busy thoroughfare on a working morning. Oddly, the Suzuki seemed to lean into the traffic. Closer inspection revealed that the torturers of a thousand cuts had completed their interrogation in the small hours of the morning. The offside rear tyre was totally flat.

Ever more traffic squeezed past the problem. The surface was cobbled and uneven. A complex problem of a flat with no spare. I released the handbrake and rolled painfully downhill towards a more peaceful place – the tyre flapping and slewing as the wheel-hub chewed its way into already exhausted rubber. The slope levelled into a semi-horizontal space and the jeep stopped.

How many tyre dealers did Potosí have, I wondered?

★

The sudden discovery that the silver mountain overlooked that horizontal space came as a great surprise. Towering above was the mass of Andean rock that was the foundation of the city's fame – rising two thousand seven hundred feet over the surrounding rooftops and revealing a pinkish-yellowish tint to its bare surfaces. The famous Potosí mine – the passages of which reached up to almost sixteen thousand feet above sea level. A raw-looking mountain, honey-combed with workings which were the relic of centuries of effort – the massive expenditure of labour which had gone into extracting the treasure of one of the New World's richest ore bodies. Centuries of lives and deaths had been sacrificed to that mountain. One half of all the Americas' silver had been hacked out of the rock that stood illuminated by the morning sun when it had reached peak production in the last quarter of the sixteenth century.

In fact, from the Potosí mountain wound a long river of silver which connected this high and remote spot in the New World to all the cities of the Old World. As fast as silver was poured into the coffers of Spain it poured out again. Wealth from Potosí paid for Philip's Spanish Armada (he even used the ships of the flotilla to carry troops for the invasion of England). It paid, also, for Spanish adventure into the Low Countries. By mule train over the altiplano; by sea up the Pacific coast to Panama; by mule train again from Pacific to Caribbean; by semi-annual flotilla from Cartagena to Seville. From the Spanish Crown to the merchants and banking houses of Amsterdam and into the burgeoning commercial systems of Post-Renaissance Europe. Gold was not really the great prize of the conquest of the Americas. The supply of gold was finite – the treasure of the Incas and the Aztecs could not last for ever. After the first few years of discovery, what was mostly being carried back in those galleons was silver. For a time, the supply of silver was almost infinite – Potosí's pinkish-yellowish mountain contained staggering quantities of it.

Not all such silver reached home, of course. There were the human predators in the Caribbean increasingly ready to divert the flow. Potosí silver leaked away east as well. As time passed, an unofficial stream began to dribble down the Andes and laboriously cross the continent by mule-train and river to the developing colonial centres of Buenos Aires and Rio de Janeiro. From these Atlantic ports it found its way into the Portuguese New World. Much Potosí silver underwrote that country's ramshackle sixteenth-century expansions into India, Indonesia and China.

The value of Potosí silver was high when counted as a fuel of European expansion. Its cost may have been even higher when counted in terms of human life. Altiplano Indians died by the thousands to keep the flow going. The *mita* of Potosí was the largest, most highly organised and the most infamous of the forced labour systems of the Spanish colonists – a system of near-slavery grafted on to the totalitarian Inca state. For almost two hundred and fifty years, Potosí sucked in virtually all the able-bodied male Indians living in the central Andean area. Few between the ages of eighteen and fifty escaped the obligation of one year of labour in the tunnels and shafts of Potosí. This European thirst for silver warped and almost destroyed the careful balance which the Inca state had preserved between labour and the need for food production.

Many died because the intense high-altitude work was too heavy for them. Respiratory diseases became common, as those carrying loads of up to 300 lbs hoisted their way slowly through the long stages of near vertical ladders; each time exchanging the heat of the mine for the cold of the Cordillarian day or night. Some simply slipped and fell under the weight of their burden – six hundred feet down the shaft they were laboriously climbing.

As much as the *mita* wrecked patterns of existence and the agriculture of the altiplano, the deterioration in the general health and well-being of the altiplano peoples allowed smallpox and other newly introduced diseases of the Old World to find ready victims. The Quechua and the Aymara peoples staggered under the blow but the galleons continued to ply the Atlantic remorselessly until the end of the eighteenth century.

★

How many tyre dealers did Potosí have? Not many – and most of them seemed to be asleep or out of town.

I asked the inn to call a taxi. It arrived within minutes. The driver – an efficient man wearing the usual cap-with-earflaps – took a quick glance at the hapless vehicle. He promptly jacked and blocked-up the offside wheel with a large slab of colonial masonry he happily prised out from a nearby wall; loaded wheel and wheel-hub (of the 'spare') into the back of his car; asked his accompanying woman friend to squeeze alongside them; started his ramshackle old cab and bumped over the cobbles and into the traffic of the hilltop town.

We began to descend through the centuries. Clearly, the dusty twentieth-century shacks at the bottom of the hill were the only hope of providing replacement tyres for a Japanese jeep.

But first we let his friend out somewhere between the seventeenth and the eighteenth in a dense area of narrow streets where the colonial heart of Potosí still stood virtually intact. Government house, city hall, treasury, cathedral and mint slipped past or could be glimpsed in the near distance before less historic nineteenth and early twentieth-century schools, shops, markets and municipal buildings marked our further progress downhill and into modern times.

Well – modern times of a sort. First port of call in the late twentieth century scruffiness which huddled around the bottom of the hill was a two-story house in a backstreet. It had drawn curtains and gave off a strong air of somnambulance. The taxi driver thumped on a brightly painted door and threw stones at a second floor window. We waited. It seemed a funny place to find a tyre agent.

'*No esta!*' shouted a voice from across the road. '*Mercoles... semana proxima!*'

Crikey. The middle of next week! We went on. More backstreets and more second-story houses. Doorways proclaimed specialisation: three or four car seats in one place; exhaust systems in another; hub-caps in another; steering wheels at a house on a corner. Everyone appeared to be asleep, however. No sign of human occupancy presented itself until a thin lad emerged from the hub-cap house and hopped painfully down the street like a wounded bird.

At last, at the very bottom of the twentieth century, there stood a house festooned with tyres and inner tubes. It was clearly a long way from the *Casa Real de Moneda*. The mountain of silver now lay hidden from view by buildings. The jeep's wheels were rolled inside and tried for size against a random selection of tyres.

One was an approximate fit. The new tyre was both narrower and smaller than the shredded nearside rear, but National Route One would not notice the difference and Bolivia did not seem to be the place where a Suzuki Vitara with a slight tilt to starboard would be singled out as an object of amazement and mockery. The taxi driver negotiated a price and I agreed. He clearly had the matter in hand. We still needed an inner tube for the punctured offside rear, however, and we moved onwards and outwards to the very edge of town.

Potosí levelled out and sprawled into more widely spaced industrial buildings. The dust, rocks and rubbish of open country were close at hand. A workshop caked in soot and rubber-parings came into view as our last hope. A bus-breakers yard – it stood hidden behind the travel-stained hulks of several of the long-distance monsters. This was obviously where they came to die after they had been driven to the point of utter exhaustion.

The appearance of a man caked in soot and rubber-parings started a rummage amongst the axles, engine-hoods, tyres and deflated tubes of normal-to-gigantic size for something which might vaguely suit a Japanese jeep. After several anxious minutes he could be seen standing upright and waving a tube which looked whole but decidedly off-the-peg. With an impassive expression and a deft manipulation of tyre levers, a bucket of water and a hissing air hose, it fitted and restored the wheel to its inflated normality. With a look of triumph, the taxi driver bounced it back to his waiting cab.

The problem was solved – after a fashion. The sorry-looking outer tyre of the offside rear remained sorry-looking, but at least the jeep could function. Not long afterwards and we were once more in the seventeenth century under the silver mountain. The colonial stone had been replaced and the taxi driver was turning the last of the bolts securing the spare wheel to its rightful position. The task was done.

That myth about taxi drivers. That the job is a career move from the Waffen SS. It's not true. There are one or two misanthropes about, of course, but the general run of drivers are helpful souls who know their patch far better than any outsider and who sincerely try to do their best. My Potosí driver did his best and I was extremely grateful. We shook hands and I asked his name, but he replied in Quechua and it was difficult to catch. 'Christopher' seemed good enough.

*

Tyres and tubes had taken up the best part of a morning. But now that I had five operational wheels, another problem began to loom large. The return journey to La Paz! There was no question of re-entering all that dust, of course. Quite another route was planned where I neatly envisaged setting out from Potosí on the road to Sucre and thence connecting with a main cross-Andean La Paz to Santa Cruz highway somewhere east of Cochabamba. According to the map it was all quite simple.

A few miles longer, perhaps, but – with good hard-surfaced roads – my speed was going to be much faster. I'd be in La Paz by late afternoon.

It all sounded just a little too neat for Bolivia. In La Paz by late afternoon... With a newly prejudiced eye the plan slowly dissolved under closer scrutiny of the map and the reality of actually starting out for Sucre. Why should the route from Potosí to that town be any different from the dusty nightmare from Potosí to Oruro? And if it was so much better – why didn't the long-distance buses go that way? And – worse – why did the thin red line that twisted and turned between Sucre and Cochabamba have a symbol which suggested it to be a less well-maintained 'minor road' version of the National Route One I had been travelling along the previous day?

All in all – better the devil... It had to be National Route One again.

⋆

Dust by daylight. The climb up to the *Cordillera de los Frailes* under bright cold sunlight. The river Pilcomayo's dark valley now appeared much more precipitous than when shrouded by the night: unprotected roadsides slithering away into its steep-sided ravine; bridges with no walls on either side; unexpectedly sharp turns; downward swerves past fallen rocks. I hadn't noticed all that the evening before. Only the welcome pinpricks of electric light after the desolation above.

And, as the climb continued, more colour and personality in the landscape than the moon was prepared to reveal – fortunately! The red sandstone bluffs of the lower part of the route were simply scenic; the curious outcrops higher up less so. A combination of weathering and shadow turned grey sandstone into semblances of huge skulls: skulls which leered grimly out towards the highest part of the cordillera – towards the desolation which I had once more to cross.

Once up there, it was no longer a place to be feared. By day and by sunlight, the cool, arid wilderness had taken on a stark beauty. High altitude turned the clear sky an intense blue; outcropping strata gave the ground the rich colours of a palette. The road wound through bedded sedimentary rocks: against that high-altitude sky was a landscape composed of huge steeply dipping bands of pale green, of green and purple and of green, purple and orange. The colours reared out of the dusty roadside verges and soared away to meet the distant skyline. The view had improved – the road was regrettably unchanged. New layers of dust crowded in to coat every surface in the interior of the Suzuki thickly with yet more of the fine, acrid powder.

★

Six hours later and Oruro had almost been reached when that ubiquitous dust finally worked its way into the jeep's carburettor. Night had fallen, the fuel level indicator was again well into the red and the engine was probably running on combustible silt rather than petrol. Oruro had become the faintest of distant orange glows on a skyline that was otherwise black with desolation. With a succession of jerks and coughs, the Suzuki limped to a halt. Fuel, food and relaxation were so near and yet still so far.

Somehow, the jeep was made to jerk and cough those last few miles. I reached Oruro and a replenished petrol tank seemed to push the silt into the background. I couldn't risk a night-time stoppage on the next stretch of dust-road, however. A gloomy, deserted but fairly modern hotel came into welcome view overlooking the main square and it was with great relief that I escaped the possibility of an altiplano sojourn by taking a room.

The place was so quiet and the way had been so long that I only just managed to avoid tipping fast asleep into the last dregs of a voraciously emptied bowl of soup.

★

Morning and the bright colour of *polleras* – the red or green puffed-up skirts worn by Aymara women. Colour everywhere. An occasional dash of that lurid pink satin. Bowler hats: a flattish style here; a more domed style there. Brown and grey as well as black. Sometimes a stove-pipe hat and sometimes a steaming cauldron. Light refreshments, freshly boiled maize-cobs or magic potions? Community tea-ladies or copper-skinned witches?

Woven shawls worn around tiny shoulders – vaguely reflecting a Spanish woman's clothes of the eighteenth or early nineteenth century; archaic and miniaturised. Piles of potatoes and peppers laid out on the ground. Hardware and ceramics. Carts and barrows. Ponchos and caps-with-earflaps. Market-time again – this one spreading amongst the low outskirts of the town as its single-story buildings quickly petered out in the litter-strewn dust. Then there was just the dust.

★

At a garage on the lip of La Paz it took three men, pressurised air, a constant jet of water and an hour's brushing and scrubbing to get the worst of National Route One from the outside, the underside and the inside of the hired Suzuki.

I had made sure that the road north to Lake Titicaca was hard-surfaced.

★

Golden reed beds – the same stuff that Thor Heyerdahl had made his raft from. Bundles being gathered and taken up to the road. Some modern boats – patrol boats of the Bolivian Navy (the lake was shared with Peru), sloops and pontoons leading out from the Huatajata Yacht Club, a hydrofoil. Rippling blue water turning emerald green as it shallowed and met the shore – an utterly different world and yet less than two hundred miles from the desperation of Lake Popoo. The world of Lake Titicaca.

A high altitude Garden of Eden rimmed by snow-capped peaks. That intensely blue sky again. The sun reflecting back off distant waters where Titicaca passed north-westwards and into Peruvian territory. An Island of the Sun hidden somewhere in that band of glitter – the island that was the centre of the Inca creation legend.

★

Had it all been like Titicaca once – the dreariness which was now the great central altiplano basin? Blue waters and golden reeds stretching down past Challapata and covering the desolation of the *Salar de Uyuni*? Had it all gone from being Paradise to being Hell? Did a folk memory of a lost world linger amongst the peoples up here? Had the waters slowly evaporated as the ice of the Weischselian glaciers gradually melted at the poles and the global climate became progressively warmer during the last ten thousand years?

Did that world of the Neolithic remember when the whole of the altiplano was like Titicaca and not like Popoo?

Or had it all happened quite suddenly? An earthquake. Another upward thrust of this part of the Andean mountain chain. A fault movement allowing one of the headwater streams of the Amazonian river system to creep high into the Eastern Cordillera and breach the eastern wall?

If such a catastrophic event had taken place – witnessed or unwitnessed by the early Amerindian farmers of the highlands – then there was only one place where that enormous perched body of water could have poured away to the ocean; only one place where it would have left signs of its going.

*

It was a fine night for flying. Through the cabin window, the stars of the southern hemisphere glittered in a velvet-black night sky as the Lloyd Aereo Boliviano Airbus took off for Santa Cruz, Manaus and Caracas. A roundabout route but one which avoided the long detour to Miami.

Below, as the runway ended and the aircraft began to climb above the edge of the La Paz chasm, the lights of the city started to appear. First a trickle, and then a flood and then a torrent – thousands and thousands of lights spilling off its edge, pouring down its slopes, swelling and merging with other lights as the city centre was passed. The surge continued downwards and eastwards to where it followed the valley through the gap in the cordillera and along a path which led unerringly into the great Amazon river system and the Atlantic Ocean.

Chapter Eight

Weekend in Brazil

Two streams of early morning commuters hurrying along a broad tarmac surface before converging and then turning to climb a long ramp leading them into town. A scene which, for the most part, could have been anywhere – a flow of passengers disgorging from the 7.20 from Bexleyheath and Barnhurst and bracing up for a short walk from Cannon Street to the City. Or office workers heading for another day in Wall Street under grey Manhattan skies with the prospect of a crowded lunch bar and the journey in reverse some eight or nine hours later. Some of these commuters held briefcases, others light bags. The few who carried sacks did – admittedly – add a slight touch of the exotic to a scene which might have been repeated in any large city but they were vastly outnumbered. It was the mood that made for the general impression; the mood of early morning London, New York, Paris or Tokyo. That lack of conversation or light-heartedness; that bending of the will towards daylight hours being spent amongst filing cabinets; that trade-off of freedom for money.

And such a pity. The sun shone brilliantly down on the Amazon jungle.

*

The coffee stand was placed at an angle near one end of the tarmac. Whether it had originally been sited in that slightly skewed position or whether some event had caused the flimsy structure to be moved sideways was unknown. Few commuters seemed to have time or inclination for a pause at the counter and a quick cup of coffee. Only occasionally out of the morning's stream did the odd customer briefly shake off the remorseless grip of Time and tersely order a small polystyrene cup of the black liquid, dash it down like a slug of whisky, slap a coin or two on to the plastic counter and then hurry off to rejoin those who had not stopped. Coffee drinkers merged back into a flow of people that continued to sweep up the ramp before fanning out from its end towards whatever responsibilities might await them. A misshapen beggar – supported by a wheeled box instead of legs – pleaded for coins as they passed. It was a normal working day in Manaus.

The red-haired lad who served the coffee was still half asleep – lazily wiping the counter clear before leaning out to gaze at a flat-bed truck which was edging in reverse towards him. Choking diesel fumes and a near-miss briefly shook out a livelier interest and opened up the prospect of business. Several men scrambled out of the cab of the truck and the lad was soon fully occupied with levers, hissing steam and the chromium jugs of an Italian espresso machine as he serviced their demands. Coffee was again collectively swallowed like hot spirits – the smoothness of the process being slightly unsettled by a driver who suddenly appeared and demanded action. Waving fiercely at the load carried by the truck, he shouted urgent orders. It was clear that the job of untying and releasing the much-knotted ropes of a grubby tarpaulin should begin immediately. Beneath it, lumpy produce lay hidden from view.

The untying began with alacrity. Rope-ends were soon being hurled vigorously over the truck to invisible recipients on the far side who – when they had loosened or unknotted their end of the bindings – warned of the return of the rope with shouted words.

It was noticeable how each of these terse communications had a curious '*ssh*' to them – as if an East European language was being spoken. Romanian, perhaps. Or Bulgarian.

The language was Portuguese. The town of Manaus stood an ocean and half a continent away from grey Romania or quiet Bulgaria. The truck, the skewed coffee stand and the earnest early morning commuters were all afloat. Under the tarmac, in front of the town, opening up beyond and dwarfing this little knot of human activity contriving to carry out its daily business, was a great presence; a huge flow of warmish grey water; a continent's outpouring. All this early morning activity was taking place on the River Amazon – the largest river in the world.

Fresh water – draining out of an area much larger than Eastern Europe. An area bigger than the whole of Europe for that matter. Water which silently moved day and night at a rate of some 170 billion gallons an hour towards an Atlantic Ocean that was still one thousand miles downstream. Ten times the Mississippi. And when it reached the sea, the Amazon continued pouring out its fresh water to lower salinities for more than one hundred miles offshore.

The tarmac surface on which the commuters hurried and on which the truck was being unloaded was merely the crowded deck of a large steel pontoon – a human device firmly tethered but fighting a constant war against the endless surging of a four knot current. A river that was almost superhuman in its scale. Mid-stream at Manaus, the Amazon was nearly three hundred feet deep.

⋆

The superhuman scale of the Amazon had first made itself apparent a few miles downstream at the place where the Careira ferry crossed it and formed a communication link between the vast rainforest area stretching north to the Venezuelan border and the uplands of the Gran Sabana (the 'Lost World') with the even vaster expanse of trees rolling south to the Mato Grosso.

At Careira, however, it was not a river which presented itself, but a sea. In this first glimpse of the Amazonian waters, they appeared to spread away southwards into a grey infinity. There was no sign of a distant bank – the Amazon reached to the misty horizon and merged with it. It was a sea which was mysteriously absent from any maps of central Brazil.

⋆

The Caracas-Rio flight touched down at Manaus and was immediately engulfed in a hot, tropical darkness cut by the familiar ordered patterns of runway lights and modern terminal facilities. The Amazon jungle had been pushed well back from the world of international airline travel. Few passengers seemed eager to disembark at this brief stopover on the Caracas-Rio flight.

The modern airport of Manaus was as bustling as if the hour had been 4 p.m. rather than 4 a.m. Perhaps it was easier to do business in the slightly cooler hours of darkness than during the higher temperatures of the day. Even this night air of tropical Brazil, however, was singularly hot and humid. The equator lay only about two hundred miles north of the city, there were no Andean mountain ranges in the vicinity and – at an elevation that lay only a few hundred feet above sea-level – it was intent on making its presence felt.

A short taxi ride and I found a hotel and slept until mid-morning. Oblivious to the outside world in a poky back-room, deep in the side streets of a tiny island of civilisation, I missed the sun rising over half a continent of trees. A low cloud cover muted its insufferable tropical brilliance. The day was jungle-hot but dim and damp.

The low cloud cover thickened and deepened as morning became noon. As I drove out of Manaus in a hired car with an intention of travelling (as far as was possible in a few hours) down the Brazilian Pan-American Highway and well into the southern rainforest, the sky over that part of Amazonas began to rumble and flash.

⋆

To journey south along the Brazilian Pan-American Highway, it was first necessary to cross the Amazon. After this ferry crossing at nearby Careira, the route (according to local maps), headed boldly into the infinity of trees and then – some hundreds of miles further on – grew faint and uncertain as it reached one of those blank green spaces in which the map-makers of tropical South America could find nothing worthwhile to indicate. Was this virgin rainforest? No towns lay along even the clearly marked part of the route. Even small named dots indicating roadside settlements seemed suspiciously small. In fact, from the way it was cartographically represented, that vagueness and uncertainty which took over the highway the further south it went began to assume a slightly sinister air. Although most of the population of Brazil lay in that direction, a certain lack of determination clearly emanated from the map. It was as if all the incentive to get to Brasilia, Rio or Sao Paulo had begun to falter somewhere south of Manaus and had been defeated by the sheer enormity of the sea of trees.

Fortunately, I wasn't going that far. A few hours would not achieve much progress into the largest equatorial rainforest in the world. With the fastest of speeds, penetration by road could only be a few tens of miles. It might only be a few miles – possibly little more than the distance which the daily river-commuters covered on their morning boat-rides into Manaus. Travelling by river was much easier – as long as the river went where you wanted to go.

The ferry had first to be found before that territory stretching away from the south bank of the Amazon could be reached. And Careira proved unexpectedly difficult to locate amongst back roads which wound about on the red lateritic soil of suburban Manaus. That was the first surprise – the fact that the swampy Amazon basin was not all flat. Its surface was surprisingly undulating and the recent parts of the town seemed to have extended unexpectedly far into the low rainforested hills – houses and gardens fighting hard nonetheless to hold their ground against a virulent and luxuriant tropical vegetation which looked as if it was always eager to return and re-occupy the man-made spaces cut out of its midst. A mile or two beyond was another surprise – on the far edge of Manaus lay a sleepy industrial estate.

★

The residential suburbs and outlying tentacles of civilisation which formed the extreme edge of Manaus were part of the industry of the late twentieth century. Concrete, steel and pre-fabricated sheds. Its centre was defiantly nineteenth century. Extending up from the river piers and docks built by a Scotsman to service the rubber boom were busy streets of neo-colonial buildings – some grand, others not – which led inevitably to the town's famous opera house and the symbol of its heyday – when Caruso was brought by sea to sing at the grand opening; when the clothes of those who listened to him were laundered in Lisbon; when the Amazonian Indians struggled to tap impossible numbers of trees in the hinterland to feed the demands of the times. Boom and then bust. Other parts of the world began to provide rubber. It could be made synthetically.

Perhaps Manaus was rising in another boom. Air transport made the territory feel more part of the rest of Brazil. Those light industries on its edge were acting as the modern supply centre to the vast frontier state of Amazonas. Rubber had gone but gold and diamonds still passed out to the world, and cast cement pipes seemed to be needed in great quantities.

The industrial estate gave way to a confusion of stacked timber and truck-scarred roads. At the end of a bumpy trail making its way through ever more distant yards and shacks, the foreshore at Careira suddenly came into view.

*

I first caught a clearer – and curiously alarming – view of the Amazon over the top of a pile of cement castings. Alarming because this was the view of a river which appeared to have grown so great that it stretched to the horizon. It was impossibly big. Sweeping away from a massive ferry barge that could be seen pressing up against the Careira loading jetty was an expanse of yellow-grey water with no boundaries. It was water which simply continued southwards as a grey and menacing inland sea until it dissolved into a misty haze that merged with the sky. Surely, the river could not reach as far as the horizon?

A huge lake was the last thing to be expected so far inland. The absence of a far shore-line certainly gripped the attention and was disorientating. It made you want to rush back into the town centre and check whether some disastrous seasonal flooding had taken place. Was half of Manaus under water, too? Had a kind of catastrophic, Noah-like deluge occurred where the river spread out across the rainforest and drowned it to the far horizon?

Subliminally, the ferry boat added to this fleeting impression. It could have stood in for Noah's Ark and was hardly adapted for casual users. Positioned at the end of a short jetty roughly constructed of concrete and earth and providing only a very crude-looking access, stood an immense flat-topped craft. A barge – positioned bows-on and with its engines running as if pushing the river-banks ever further apart. A few mud-spattered trucks stood on the deck giving the impression they had suddenly been abandoned in disarray – each dwarfed to near toy-like proportions by the sheer scale of the vessel. Brazil was a big country. The river and the those who plied its waters were clearly big, too. The car I had hired to venture into the southern rainforest was one of the smallest on the road.

Like a beetle attempting to mount a flight of steps, I revved up the Fiat Uno I had rented and accelerated on to the ramp with the hope of joining the trucks. Everything went well for a few seconds until the encounter with the junction between bank and boat took place. At that crucial point (a fairly steeply-angled crest), the base of the tiny Fiat clanged noisily into the steel plate which reached landward from the barge and rolled back from the experience as if mortally wounded. Something had happened down below. Something rather serious. The car seemed unable to repeat the effort and rocked weakly landwards with loss of power. It was as if it had been kicked in the stomach.

The engine room had taken a direct hit. I discovered later that the Fiat had received a severe blow to the sump which had then fractured the engine casing. There was no time for a look under the bonnet, however, – mechanical concerns were quickly blotted out by more pressing external forces. A brief glimpse southward showed that the misty horizon – the one seemingly so far away – appeared to be rushing closer by the second. Before the implications of this phenomenon could be fully assimilated, the car began to be rocked further back along the jetty by sudden and very fierce blasts of wind; erratic movements of warm air which, as they grew stronger, quickly whipped the waters beyond the aircraft carrier into a frenzied white-flecked turmoil. Yellow-brown surf started to swirl feverishly up the sandy bank and reach between the hulls of the much smaller craft beached there. Higher above the waterline, dry sand was lifted into dusty clouds – the windscreen of the Fiat quickly receiving the full impact of this rapidly moving grit. A few moments later and Noah's

Ark was in trouble – its outline half-dissolved into an approaching mist with the horizon not far behind. As the craft was reduced to a dim outline it suddenly vanished altogether in wreaths of diesel smoke quickly tugged inshore by the howling wind. Above the roar of the latter came the faint shriek of a rapidly-increased throttle. The skipper was running full astern into the blast as he tried to keep the unwieldy vessel afloat and under some sort of control. Trucks swayed on its deck. Wakes of white water could faintly be seen adding to the turmoil of the suddenly furious Amazon.

Then the full impact of the 'mist' arrived at the Fiat. A tropical storm was sweeping over the huge rainforest and pouring even more moisture into the mighty river. As the first curtains of thundering spray cascaded over the small vehicle – vigorously encouraged by more sharp and powerful gusts of water-charged wind – an uncomfortable tossing began. Still stranded just below the highest point on the jetty, the car was exposed to the full blast of the wind. For a few minutes, an entire atmosphere seemed to have been replaced by a solid cascade of rain which poured down in such torrents that the little Fiat's beating windscreen wipers did no more than flail about in its submerged midst like a gnat lost in a waterfall. Rain caused the loud drumming which now came from the surface of bonnet and roof. Rain, aided by the continuing wind, swept upwards as well as poured downwards. Rain came in turbulent squalls which tossed it in all directions. Near-invisible objects passed by inside the howling mass of wind, water and sand: tatters of plastic sheeting; rope strands; half-rotted leaves; and miscellaneous rubbish from the foreshore – all rattling and flapping around the Fiat on their rapid passage into the forest. At the river's edge, unseen surf was energetically pounding the beach with an ocean-like thump and roar.

Visibility improved between gusts. Not far beyond the struggling Ark lay another barge of similar size – beached but beginning to slew about in the surf as if all the noise and water were on the point of making it panic like a great steel horse. A slight increase in wind strength and it looked ready to rear off and canter away down the one thousand miles of rainforest to the sea. Also dimly visible in these brief lulls was a third barge. This suddenly appeared offshore in the thick of the storm and was now stern to the land with its propellers churning the Amazon waters at top speed. The crew were clearly performing a balancing act between the force of the wind and the current of the river. It looked as if it was the ferry from the south bank.

The cataclysmic storm added yet another dimension to the enormous scale of Brazil: clearly there was no such thing as 'scattered light showers' to be found in the rainforest. But – as is the way with tropical downpours – a few minutes later it was all over. The rain and wind continued on their way across the state of Amazonas. The sky brightened. The air felt warm and freshly washed and wet surfaces began to steam away their acquired moisture. Southwards, the low and indistinct outline of the opposite bank of the Amazon came into view. In mid-stream but already dwarfed by the scale of the river, that incoming ferry suddenly abandoned all idea of landing on the Manaus side and churned away towards the far shore.

First impressions of the Amazon began to fade. The yellow-brown sea covering a vast area of the rainforest south of Careira had now shrunk to a recognisable river. The storm had created the optical illusion of an endless stretch of water but its passing had brought the rainforest of the south bank back into its proper position. Nonetheless, this river was prodigious; passing Careira was one-fifth of all the flowing water in the world – an endless movement across the continent from the Andes in the west to the Atlantic in the east.

★

There was something awesome about being so close to that flow of water. There was also something seriously wrong with the Fiat. Since the crunch of the sump against the steel plate, its power was negligible – enough to limp back into Manaus but certainly not enough to speed into the unknown territory which lay across the water to the south. And the ferry still showed no sign of moving. The journey was off.

As I handed the sickly vehicle back to the car-hire firm at Manaus airport, a vague explanation (in limited Portuguese) about bumpy roads did not sound very convincing. It clearly wasn't enough to stop an additional $100 repair charge being added to the bill when they found out that the engine manifold had been cracked by collision with a heavy metal object. Crossing the Amazon was a job for the big boys.

But heavy-duty trucks had little to do with the real communication routes in Amazonas. The ferry at Careira was an unimportant sideshow. Water was the means of transportation and the commercial hub for the east/west and north/south routes of the great equatorial basin was the port which lay a short distance upstream.

Manaus was a fluviatile crossroads: a place where ocean-crossing cargo ships met tiny canoes; where bulk cement was being unloaded in close proximity to river vessels taking on furniture or bananas. The size and depth of the river meant that ships could reach deep inside the land mass of the South American continent and almost travel across it to the foothills of the Andes. For Manaus was nowhere near the end of its navigable possibilities. Virtually everything travelled by water in tropical Amazonas and the Amazon was not one river but an amalgam of many. Three huge flows of water met at (or just downstream of) the town: the River Negro coming in from the north-west (with headwaters intermingling with those of the Orinoco in Venezuela); the Solimos arriving from the west and the Andean foothills of Colombia, Ecuador and Peru (where one of its tributaries was the Urubamba curling in the canyon below Machu Picchu); the Madeira coming from the south-west and high Bolivia. Major rivers in their own right, they all formed 'the Amazon'.

River boats could reach far up these substantial inland water-highways. The Madeira stretched southwards for nearly two thousand miles from Manaus and the point where it joined the Negro/Solimos. Further east, the Amazon connected with its tributaries of the Tapajos, the Xingu and the Tocantins – all pouring the waters of the interior plateau of Brazil and the Mato Grosso into the one great river and each with long navigable stretches. These tributaries, substantial rivers themselves, slid through a huge expanse of barely inhabited forest – the latter two each being longer than one thousand miles from source to confluence. Big country stuff again.

It was such river highways which had created the nineteenth-century ease of travelling *in the same ship* from London or Amsterdam (or any of the other ports of Europe) to small towns some two thousand three hundred miles inland from the Atlantic coast of Brazil without the need to disembark once. It was possible to travel from Tilbury in eastern England to Iquitos in eastern Peru.

Air transportation had seen to that sort of long-haul sea and river-faring. Not many ships and passengers did it these days. No longer did shiploads of soiled clothes take such a long journey from the better off of Manaus to the laundries of Lisbon and back again. Those Southern American east-west maritime routes to Europe had made way for a new direction. The late twentieth century was the time of north-south air transportation. The middle and upper-classes of the continent had abandoned Portugal and Paris: now they bought their clothes and their microwave ovens in the shops of New York.

It remained true that this vast interior of the South American continent – or, at least, a very narrow strip of it along the rainforested margins of the Amazonas river system – was still easier to reach from afar than were many parts of the interior of Europe.

★

The trouble was in thinking up a good reason to go. Moving up the Amazon in the second half of the twentieth century (like moving up the Congo) was still not a fully air-conditioned experience. It remained a future dream that specially equipped tourist vessels would ply long distances at a fast speed whilst their passengers gazed comfortably out through cool glass as a thousand or so miles of rainforest slipped by. Accessible it was, but the forests of the Amazon had still not been tamed in the same way as other difficult parts of the world had been put in their place. The elderly train travellers of Australia now crossed the once-feared Nullarbor Plain playing bridge. No one was allowed to cross the big country of Brazil with quite such insouciance. It was still only working river boats that plied backwards and forwards across the water transportation routes of Amazonas.

There were a considerable number of these vessels docked at Manaus. Capacious but not yet wholly of the late twentieth century, their powerful engines were probably modern enough but their white-painted and rather stately superstructures were open-sided and had more in common with Mississippi paddle-steamers then Parisian fly-boats. Decks were loaded with goods and baggage and the passenger cabins looked small, hot and uncomfortable.

It was a fair bet that the riverside communities they put into once they had left Manaus were likely to be small, hot and uncomfortable, too.

★

Perhaps the ever-present daytime tropical heat and humidity was why thirty or forty river boats crowded nose-to along the edge of the pontoon at Manaus as the commuters made their early morning way into the town. They all seemed to be setting off under the cover of darkness for their river journeys. And they all looked much the same at first glance. Reaching abruptly up in an amidships position on a sixty or seventy foot hull length was a high bridge which bristled with aerials and overlooked an often miscellaneous cargo. Sleeping people (in hammocks) were lodged amongst clusters of bananas, sacks of vegetables, armchairs wrapped in polythene sheeting and piles of battered suitcases.

Distinction came with the chalked destination-boards propped-up close to their bows. Such boats were going all over the place – they were the 'long-haul' buses of this part of Brazil; the Greyhounds of Amazonas. Journey times were quoted in days rather than hours and huge distances were involved: Manaus to Santarem, to Benjamin Constant, to Porto Velho. Getting to some of these places involved travelling along more than a thousand miles of river. A thousand miles from this central Amazonas pontoon and a week of swinging at insects from an open deck as the boat chugged its way manfully upstream against the current or slid more easily downstream through the watery highways of the jungle.

One boat – the *Navi Aypura* – stood bows-on near the coffee stand. The work of removing tarpaulin from the truck was complete and the consignment of bananas which had lain hidden from view was now covering much of the planking of the lower of the two open-sided decks. *Navi Aypura's* destination was east to Santarem – over 500 miles downstream and sometimes a two-day journey and sometimes a five-day trip. Much depended on high or low water in the Amazon system and on the time of seasonal flooding. This was one of the long trips which began at nightfall. En route to Santarem (the namesake of the much larger town near Lisbon in Portugal) a stop was to be made at Juruti – mapped as a tiny riverside dot with nothing in the way of roads or tracks leading off into some 40,000 square miles of rainforest. It was completely detached from the rest of the world. Only the river was able to supply those who lived there with an armchair or a sack of non-tropical vegetables. There was no sign of any laundry-bags on the *Navi Aypura*.

Nearby, other boats stood a-loading. Bows-on to the pontoon were the *N/M Almte Monteiro* and the *Avelino Real* – vessels, readying themselves for the long haul upstream to the west. Some early passengers had evidently secured a berth – or maybe Manaus was simply a leisurely stop-over. The heads and feet of sleeping figures protruded from deck hammocks as supplies were humped and pushed noisily around their motionless, canvas-enveloped bodies. They almost seemed dead to the world – perhaps they had already undergone a four to seven-day journey; perhaps they were mentally readying themselves for another week of throbbing diesel engines and biting insects; perhaps they really were dead. You could see why people preferred air travel.

And perhaps that was why passengers for the really long journey up the Solimos were leaving embarkation until the very last minute. It was clearly no picnic going from Manaus to the Peruvian border. Although there were short breaks at Jutai, Tonantins, Amatura, Tabatinga, Fonte Boa and Benjamin Constant, the amenities were hardly likely to match those of an international airport. Take Fonte Boa, for instance. There couldn't be much relief for the traveller in Fonte Boa – it appeared to be a place more lost in rainforest and even less accessible by roads or tracks than Juruti. In fact, it made Juruti look like a suburb of Santarem. No less than one hundred and forty thousand square miles of trackless trees surrounded the place. Crammed with species, perhaps, but little in the way of cinemas or traffic lights. The 375 mile circle of emptiness (as perceived by *homo sapiens*) was big enough to accommodate not only the British Isles but Eire and a large chunk of the north-west European continental shelf. Things looked a little more promising in Benjamin Constant – but to reach the first sizeable community encountered by Peru-bound vessels meant a trip of one thousand miles inland from the pontoon at Manaus. That was as far upstream as the Atlantic lay downstream.

There was more sleeping going on with the *N/M Ana Maria VIII*. Quite a few huddled deck-hammocked forms were strung amongst its cargo of furniture although this boat was not to cast off from the pontoon and head south-west for another two days. Perhaps it was already filling-up with those wrapped in that endless dream of the South American continent – the dream of riches; of gold; the dream of the conquistadores. The *Ana Maria VIII* would eventually cast off and head along the six hundred mile passage of the Madeira for the gold-rush community of Porto Velho. A frontier town not far from the Bolivian border where the Madeira was fed by a river called Madre de Dios and where life was cheap, the rule of law of little account and those deemed a nuisance soon vanished in the huge area where the rainforest of Brazil merged with the rainforest of Bolivia.

Water joined it all up from this hub at Manaus. Land routes had been tried, of course, but to little avail. Amazonas was an unforgiving terrain once the surface cover of dense vegetation had been stripped back in the interests of the motor vehicle. Grandiose Brazilian government plans for Amazon roads which seemed such a good idea in distant Brasilia, Rio or Sao Paulo – the Trans-Amazonian Highway or the Northern Perimeter Highway – had all turned into expensive white elephants as post-construction washouts removed section after section in the torrential rainstorms of the type which had briefly hit Careira. That unfortunate mix of military security and private speculation had prompted a lot of it. Big wall maps and pointers must have been heavily employed to show how Brazil was surrounded by no less than seven neighbouring Latin American countries; that Brazil covered a territory almost as large as the United States; that borders needed defending; that once a road had been built into an area it was ripe for land speculation. Penetration of the rainforest was needed more for private cattle-raising than for rushing troops to meet marauding armies emerging from Guyane; Suriname; Guyana; Venezuela; Colombia; Peru; or Bolivia and setting out to crush Manaus before moving on to the more populous areas. There were armies creeping across these borders, nonetheless, but they were not soldiers; they were shadowy figures more concerned with slipping back again with quantities of unnoticed Amazonas diamonds, gold and other mineral wealth or timber which the Brazilian authorities would have dearly loved to have secured for themselves (or, perhaps, for the State). Some gesture of patrolling the Amazonian garden fence was necessary, but the place itself had easily thrown out such a puny man-made concept. Expensive road systems were too ephemeral for economic or military control, the trees hid from the air most of what was going on below their canopy and that left only the rivers. Water transportation still ruled in Amazonas.

⋆

A spontaneous urge. Sign on for a hammock berth on the *Navi Apura.* Or on the *Avelina Real* to Benjamin Constant. Admittedly it was a commitment difficult to disengage from. There was no catching the next boat going in the opposite direction if twelve hours of passing trees and muddy banks proved less than enthralling.

Perhaps it was fortunate that no boats were casting off from the pontoon at that point – a round trip could take the best part of two weeks. Out of those reputed eight thousand species flourishing amongst the riverside trees of Amazonas there it was no doubt that the insects would take over the show. Mosquitoes, bees, hornets and wasps abounded in the jungle – not to mention the local variety of small biting flies called *piums*. And these were only the vanguard of a huge reserve of insect hostility. *An Amazonian Fortnight* or *Beached at Benjamin Constant* would have to be someone else's baby.

But a few hours later – when the opportunity to take a shorter boat trip presented itself and the threat of insects had to be met head-on – it proved to be an empty one. The mosquitoes, bees, *piums* and even the larger forms of flying, crawling and swimming wildlife all seemed to have completely vacated the tiny part of the Amazonian river system through which I and a few others sped downstream along the river Urubu from the small village of Presidente Figueiredo. Perhaps the noise of the 12 horse-power outboard which struggled to push us all through shallow water had frightened everything away. Or perhaps animals and insects preferred the big-time river rather than its smaller tributaries.

Both the river Urubu and the village of Presidente Figueiredo were undoubtedly small-time stuff. Much smaller and considerably less grand than their names suggested. In fact, the Urubu was hardly even a river and could be much more aptly classified as a sluggish and clogged tropical stream rather than anything remotely associated with its mighty colleague somewhere in the trees to the south of us. And the collection of shacks named after a previous Brazilian president! Well, it was fortunate that he was dead and had never troubled to head some sixty miles along the Venezuela-bound road north of Manaus to visit the collection of nondescript dwellings poised on the river-bank around the bridge over the Urubu.

A minibus had brought us to the bridge where we had been led down past the refuse tip of Presidente Figueiredo to the muddy waterside and settled into an open boat. A boatman dealt with the engine whose prop-shaft he frequently had to lift clear of logs and hidden obstructions as the hull scraped or banged its way through what were evidently very shallow waters. The Urubu dawdled south-eastwards from the village to the mighty Amazon with all the alacrity of an English country lane heading towards a motorway – a dribble heading towards a torrent. Any faster movement of the water would have promptly run us on to some shoal hidden under its surface. We began to move slowly into the landscape of trees and water as a back view of the rackety huts with the big name receded and vanished around a bend. The Urubu quickly grew deeper and wider.

Soon the small boat had stopped slithering over sandbanks and scraping amongst fallen branches and began to make its way more grandly through the Brazilian rainforest. In some places, patches of tall trees closed in and the river waters crept under darkly-shadowed foliage with no sign of a bank; in other places there were calm stretches where the light penetrated as far as the surface of the warm coffee-coloured waters and the trees fell back and seemed lower. And as we went on, the fact that Urubu was only a tiny sibling of enormous parents – the Negro, Solimos and Madeira – began to have some positive aspects. We were a little overloaded, after all. Much better to tip into five feet of opaque water than to tip into three hundred feet of it – especially after what had been hooked out of the big rivers. Especially after what I had seen not long before on the hot marble slabs of Manaus fish market.

There were varieties of *piranhas*, of course, and electric eels on these slabs. Everyone knew about such Amazonian fish, as they did, too, about the twenty-foot water snakes of the region – the anacondas which lurked in the rivers of the rainforest. Perhaps we had bumped or scraped past an anaconda already as we started out along the tributary; perhaps it was just a series of submerged branches. There was some reassurance in the possibility that – to some extent – a person had to go out and find an anaconda; crash about in untrodden places or try for a dip in quiet forest pools. It was the opposite with many of the other creatures – they found you. And being found by a *pirarucu* (perhaps surrounded by the tipped-out fruit, vegetables and meat of the weeks shopping) was not a pleasurable contemplation.

The boat had nine passengers – two of whom were very large local ladies who had balanced themselves in the bows of the narrow boat and seemed to present a distinct boat-handling hazard. Despite being wedged in by what seemed like the groceries for an entire community, one tight turn and a log submerged in the wrong place could clearly have them out and – in the process of leaving – tip and submerge the rest of us at the same time.

The *pirarucu* was a huge pike. Big rolls of its yellowing flesh had been presented to customers of the fish market – the creature being a source of protein and a staple of the local diet. The outer flesh of the fish was accompanied by even bigger piles of its still-glistening intestines on which a morning's heat had already begun to work a process of decay. Maybe *pirarucu* flesh was all the better for a day or two of bacterial action. Nobody seemed to mind the smell and nobody seemed to mind the fact that the creature rose up from the depths of the river to eat anything and everything. Those stories of *piranhas* stripping a cow or a human to the bone in less than an hour; it was probably the *pirarucu* who did the stripping in the Amazon and left only morsels and a clean-up job for the smaller fry. It seemed the subject was not one that a polite enquiry could receive a satisfactory answer – too delicate a topic for after-dinner conversion.

Other creatures of the marble slabs were smaller but more bizarre. Catfish abounded – great piles of them everywhere in the open-ended shed with its glistening, scaly floor. The catfish came in all sizes and one of the smallest of them had a particularly unpleasant habit. A tiny fish known as *Vandellia cirrhosa* (or *Cardiru*) evoked the biggest wince – a fish too small to form part of the food cycle of the Amazon but a creature which wriggled into the urogenital systems of any humans unfortunate enough to suddenly find themselves in Amazonas waters and a fish that was then very reluctant to re-emerge. The opaque Urubu sweeping downstream of rubbish-strewn back entrances to Presidente Figueiredo looked a very likely habitat for *Vandellias* to flourish in their thousands. Once one of them was installed in a new home, it was the devil's own job to dig it out again.

Dominating the market, however, was what seemed to be an excessive amount of human-like intestines tumbling from the slit undersides of most of these freshwater fish. That and their strange bathyal shapes: in one place a creature with prehistoric leaf-like patterns to its armoured plates; in another a flat and silvery fish with the shape of a wood chopper or meat carver; in another, one looking as if it had survived unchanged from the Devonian Period.

Curiously, the few tourists in our boat-trip down the Urubu were outnumbered two-to-one by locals (like the shopping ladies) who seemed to be using the transportation of the poorly-subscribed and rather amateurish Amazonian tour to complete their weekly chores. These people had travelled with us from Manaus and, although it was likely they were all being carried along free by the overheads, we (the tourists) soon realised that none of us had any idea of where the trip was leading. Why were these ladies taking shopping into the trees? What lay at the end of the Urubu – another Presidente Figueiredo? It was all very puzzling.

⋆

Taking tourists into the rainforest was a highly competitive growth industry in Amazonas these days, however. Whereas the rubber planters had desired nothing more than to leave their poor Indians labouring amongst the endless trees and crowd into Manaus to enjoy the opera from Europe; it now seemed that the eco-conscious of Europe (and North America) all wanted to get back into the jungle as quickly as they could. Visitors were many but competition to draw them into the trees was intense – in fact, Manaus was a city bursting with eagerness to earn dollars by taking newcomers wherever they wanted to go in the region. Tours were organised by hotels, tours were organised by travel agents, 'tough tours', 'soft tours', tours organised by almost anyone who had access to a small boat with an outboard motor. The tours were also widely variable in length – few hours up a creek (like the Urubu) contrasted with several days to a month penetrating deep into the remote back-country which extended all around the town. On the scale of the Amazon basin, such journey's were, of course, barely leaving its outskirts. The fact that, whether short or long, each trip usually had a guide who spoke several languages reflected the growing attraction of this last great wilderness to those pulled towards the life of the jungle: German, French, Italian, Spanish or English-speaking tours could be arranged. In the centre of Manaus, placards and signs advertised 'Amazon Cristovo Tours' with 'TWENTY YEARS EXPERIENCE IN THE FLOREST'. 'OVER NIGTHS IN THE JUNGLE' could be arranged.

Brazil, like Venezuela, was not a place where this competition for custom stopped during the hours of darkness. Procurement agents worked through the hot tropical night at their job. Particularly those in the terminal building at the airport. The young woman who had persuaded me to join the trip up the River Urubu the previous day had begun the process (unsuccessfully) at 4 a.m. when I was part of the few Manaus-bound passengers spilling off the Caracas-Rio flight. She had more success at 1 p.m. when I returned to face the music over the sickly Fiat and the failed crossing at Careira.

How profitable could it possibly be with only four tourists garnered in a similar determined manner? I had wondered this as we started off down the tree-choked headwaters of the River Urubu and the outboard was being throttled up to weave and duck through a particularly bad patch of half-submerged branches, rotting stumps, shallows and floating logs which looked like alligators. The question raised itself again after an hour had passed and we were still cruising down the river having already used up one tank of fuel as the motor pushed the heavy extra load of locals to their unknown destination. Presumably due to the competition, the cost had not been great (although payment was preferred in US dollars) – but the minibus had to be paid for, some lunch was promised and a boat and boatman occupied for what was apparently to be almost a whole day in the forest.

As a second hour on the river began to pass, I realised that preconceptions about the tropical rainforest were being shattered. It did not seem particularly hot – or humid – for one thing. And that beleaguering by pests was not taking place. The speed of the boat over water shaded by trees created a freshness in which – providing we did not sink or overturn – Amazonas could be viewed with a reasonable degree of comfort. The three Germans – two nurses and a student chemical engineer – who made up the additional non-indigenous population of the boat had all been placed amidships with the intention of clearly acting as a kind of counter-balancing force to the weight of the Indian ladies and their groceries in the bows. Other locals and the boatman contributed to a balancing of the stern where they carried out a spirited conversation in Portuguese around the outboard tiller.

⋆

The need for close attention to the weaving and twisting of the river started to ease as the Urubu grew ever more wide, deep and less choked. But where the banks parted – so did the shade of the overhanging trees recede into the distance on either side. It became much more evident that the tropical noon was nearing and the heat of the day intensifying.

But still the insects kept away. Sometimes the bank to one side or the other was clearly defined with patches of bright yellow sand beyond which a few yards of heavily forested dry land could be seen before leaves and lower branches obscured any view. More commonly, however, dark brown waters continued to disappear from view into a maze of muddy roots and the near-darkness of thick vegetation. Wildlife was absent – the roar of the outboard presumably frightening away what creatures there were although a heron or similar bird could be occasionally glimpsed in the distance as it took to the air in fright.

Those sandy banks were another preconception shattered, however. The rainforest was not all swamp and rotting vegetation. In fact, most of the Amazon basin was permanent *terra firma* and lay well above water. Locally on the Urubu, this was confirmed by low sandy bluffs becoming visible above the sand banks as the river passed through an area where the ground to one side rose fifty or sixty feet to a plateau that appeared to have been cleared of large trees. These drier places were lived on and even seemed to be under some form of crude cultivation. Sometimes, a thatched hut was visible overlooking the river with a muddy track leading down to boat or canoe at the waters edge. Sometimes distant brown figures waved from above or retreated from our bow wave as they briefly stopped pummelling washing at the riverside.

Such scenes suddenly made the media image of the wild rainforest difficult to hold in view. What was going on all around was global domesticity rather than the cut and thrust of nature in the raw. With the bags of groceries in the bows and the week's washing occurring on the banks, it felt as if mighty Amazonas had been tamed into commuter-land. Where were the anacondas, the alligators, the biting sandflies, the terrible piums, the dreadful mosquitoes? Were we getting value for money?

Unperturbed, the River Urubu grew ever wider and became more and more placid – lazily making its way south-eastwards with banks of mud and tangled root systems that were now quite distant from the speeding boat. Our V-shaped ripple spread farther out behind us until it reached the indistinct boundary between land and water and was lost in vegetation. The forest beyond was a ragged thatch of foliage through which – here and there – only occasional trees stood out with majestic trunk and sweeping branches. Sadly, they seemed leafless and dead.

Hidden from view, more cultivation was afoot in this part of the river. At one spot where the bluffs returned to line its course, the boat closed with the bank and briefly nosed alongside a dug-out canoe. No human presence was part of the scene but an arrangement had obviously been made; someone had placed a sack of freshly-cut pineapples in the tiny vessel – pineapples we were meant to collect. A brief silence as these were quickly hauled aboard and then a roar back into mid-stream and a continuation down the wide and placid river in the direction of the Amazon.

Over two hours had gone by. The river was clearly making its way towards a confluence with its big brother. The prospect of our crowded boat suddenly being projected from this quiet and gentle tributary into that one hundred and seventy billion gallon an hour flow was not inviting and I began to look anxiously around each bend hoping it was still the Urubu which came into view and not the swirling torrent of the world's largest river.

Thankfully, the Amazon was never sighted. The trip and the 12 horse-power engine were not intended to spin into that flow. Before we reached it, other moored and deserted canoes came into view and a narrow path led steeply up the bluff which overlooked them. We came smartly alongside these and were encouraged to step stiffly across to dry land.

⋆

Several large and open-sided circular huts stood out of view at the top of the bluff in an area hacked from forest growth that was beginning to force its way back into the clearing. Two of the huts had wood-shingled conical roofs below which sheltered a clutter of hammocks, drying clothes, boots and knapsacks – evidence of twenty or thirty people that the forest seemed to have swallowed up. The roof of a third hut covered tables and chairs arranged around a serving counter. No one explained this mirage of organisation amongst the dug-out canoes and river washing of the Urubu, but we had clearly arrived at some kind of Brazilian government-funded camp for visitors to the rainforest.

The two large Indian ladies were the last to struggle up the path with the boatman behind them – all heavily weighed down with the shopping bags and pineapples. This group and the other non-German passengers of the boat disappeared into a more complex fourth hut from which came yells of greeting and the emergence of a man of East Indian appearance who – surprisingly – began to speak in English and not in Portuguese.

'I am your guide to the rainforest and will you please come this way to the waterfall,' he said, beckoning the three Germans and me towards the surrounding wall of foliage. It seemed the rest of the way – to a waterfall in the rainforest – was to be on foot. Lunch would have been more attractive but was to come later. Why were all Third World tours the same: only the organisers knowing what was going on; everyone smiling and pleasant but giving answers to questions which appeared to make no sense whatsoever?

Take the waterfall, for instance. It made absolutely no sense telling us that we were going to visit a waterfall. How could a waterfall possibly exist in this vast Amazonian basin full of trees, swamps and rivers. We were not in the mountains. It was an area which – apart from the sandy bluffs – was an enormous lowland plain. Indeed, were it not so huge and fed by rivers which alternated in supplying floodwaters to it, the whole place might be submerged for most of the year. It was only the fact that the Amazon straddled the northern and southern hemispheres – with floods from the rainy season in the Ecuadorian Andes pouring into the river system at a different time to more southerly floodwaters coming in from the rainy season of the Peruvian Andes – that not all the incoming deluge arrived at the same time. Waterfall, indeed.

We began to brush our way through the foliage – at first gingerly and then with greater confidence as it became obvious that none of the higher branches held large snakes. Two other guides – young Brazilian men – suddenly appeared and made up the rear of the party. It became clear that the East Indian who was leading the way (a Guyanese) spoke well and was eager to improve our knowledge of the various trees whose trunks we moved amongst. Before long – in the cool, damp greenness which was the world under the canopy of leaves – it became clear that the two young Brazilians were obviously eager to improve their knowledge of German nurses.

*

For the three Germans this short journey was an acclimatisation trip at the beginning of a four-day hike much deeper into the forest: blond-plaited Gudrun and close-cropped Anna escaping from some sort of rigorous hospital training course and a more ordered life in Cologne; Mattias, a student chemical engineer from Dusseldorf with a pigtail and earring who appeared to be permanently dazed by the experience of two months' production-line work in a Sao Paulo canning factory.

There were many trees in that forest: the path wound deeper and deeper into the gloom and the sunlight and the blue sky could only be momentarily glimpsed where a recent fall had occurred. More that a touch of Hans Christian Anderson came over the scene as we made our way in silence and single file around the base of huge trunks – Gudrun close behind the Guyanese like some sort of tropical Gretel, and Mattias bringing up the rear and occasionally reacting to a new tree as if it were built of gingerbread. They were certainly very useful – those trees. Every time the leader held up his battered machete and called for a halt something more interesting was disclosed. Around the flanged trunk of a great teak we all struck one of the soaring ribs with the back of the implement and heard how the Indians used it as a drum to communicate across the rainforest; we grouped again at a rubber tree as he made a slash with the blade and persuaded the white sap to flow. We passed around and under mahogany and Amazonian cedar trees; we lit resin oozing from bark and fingered oil which (he claimed) could run an internal combustion engine. We reached a tree whose bark was used by the locals as an aphrodisiac; we reached another whose sap was like milk; another whose secretions could be used in perfumes, another which had medicinal value. There was quinine, cocaine and caffeine all around in the gloom, as well as the possibility of a cure for cancer.

And then – amazingly – we came across the waterfall; a liana-covered rocky ledge about fifteen feet high over which a stream of clear water gushed into a pool. The guides said we could swim in it and began taking off their clothes.

*

Later that day, as the Varig plane started its climb to cruising height for the eleven hundred mile journey to Rio and the coast, it wheeled north-eastwards above the Urubu. From high above, the tiny river could just be picked out as it wound through the dense carpet of green – a thin parting in the foliage compared with the huge glittering band of the Amazon when that too came into view under the wing. We had not been far away from the main river when we began the trek into the forest. The circular huts of the government camp were too small to spot through the triple plastic of the aircraft window but somewhere down there – swallowed up in trees which stretched over to the far horizon – were Gudrun, Anna, Mattias and their Brazilian guides. It seemed a pity to leave the Amazon so quickly. I wondered whether the members of the trekking party were enjoying themselves as they moved deeper and deeper into the forest. They certainly had under the waterfall.

*

The rainforest proved surprisingly difficult to shake off – even in the intense cosmopolitan atmosphere and world-class urbanity of Rio de Janeiro. Not only had Jane Fonda, John Denver, Placido Domingo, Shirley MacLaine, the Beach Boys and the Dalai Lama hit town, but more than a hundred presidents, prime ministers, sultans and kings were also in the city. It was very different from Presidente Figueiredo – despite the global villagers each arriving to speak up for the forest. The only ones who had ever seen it were likely to be the members of several groups of Amazonian Indians who stood about in a special uniform made up of patterned boxer shorts, a spear and a feathered headdress.

Perhaps timing could have been better for the flight from Manaus to Rio. No sooner had the aircraft doors slowly swung open and the crumpled occupants of the cabins begun to straggle out into the terminal building than they were surrounded by eager faces and a cluster of clipboards.

'Any botanists? Are you a botanist, sir? All botanists this way please.' The clipboards waved about – dividing Japanese ecologists from Indian environmentalists; Philippine journalists from Laplanders worried about holes in the ozone layer. I should have known that all this was going on. Suddenly, almost every passenger on the plane had sprouted a stick-on label or a badge; groups were already coalescing under banners. Abbreviations were rife. UNCED '92 began to move off – a largish group; ECO 92 got itself together on the way to the baggage hall; BCSD seemed to be well met by clipboard; GLOBAL FORUM fell behind when they realised that they had lost an important part of their corporate body – misdirected into the transit lounge and waiting to be met there.

We had landed on the Earth Summit.

A discreet security-guard of honour lined much of the raised road which led from the airport and into the downtown hills of Rio. With so many global leaders congregating in the same spot and President Bush arriving to ratify a global warming treaty, no chances were being taken. Groups of rifle-clutching Brazilian soldiers in full combat gear guarded every overhead bridge; each fly-over was the site of a military communications post (where much winding of the handles of khaki field telephones took place); every tunnel held troops.

It was later reported that the Earth Summit security net was being drawn this tight so as not only to deter potential terrorists but temporarily to brush away from the media's eyes the homeless of Rio as well. The thieves had all been encouraged into some sort of unknown oblivion with assaults and petty theft down by eighty per cent. The ragged street kids were having to compete for attention with the one thousand youth activists dressed in waste paper from the Global Forum who were marching backwards to a Word War II monument. Jacques Cousteau was warning that the world's population was increasing from its present 5.5 billion and heading towards a figure of 16 billion by the year 2070. There was UNCED's failure to deal with militarism's destruction of the environment. There was the question of social and ecological breakdown.

There was the problem of finding a simple bed for the night amongst such towering issues.

*

How beautiful Rio appeared in the early morning light. I had a room overlooking Copacabana beach and as the rising dawn entered the bathroom and a mirror reflected the glory of the tropical sun creeping over the South Atlantic horizon and colouring the tall granite hump of the Sugar Loaf, I knew why they had all come here rather than Blackpool.

Copacabana was fringed by the long sweep of high-rise hotels and luxury apartment blocks familiar from any tourist brochure. But its reality matched the photo-image. This glorious sea-front – first tinted a pale rose colour, then milky orange, then quickly passing through a brighter cream to reach the dazzling whites of full daylight. My room stood high above the shiny dark crowns of the palms along the red-paved promenade. Beyond them ran that broad arc of sand where the thump and hiss of the ocean had been audible throughout the night. Seaward of the beach had begun to develop a misty haze as the heat of the day started to bear down on the surface of the sea. Copacabana – for the most part – slumbered on.

The air was warm but fresher than the rainforest. The small form of an occasional jogger passed between the palms. From the city behind the beach, the hum of traffic began to rise into a muffled roar. Rio wasn't all picture postcards, palms and visiting environmentalists, though. A big city curled around the foot of the Sugar Loaf and the other tall hills in the bay. Copacabana was only one of its suburbs. Eleven million people lived here; the shanty towns which were called *favelas* crowded up the steep tropical hillsides not far behind the beach-front luxury. Not all was perfect in this lovely place.

*

From the airport, the heavily guarded route into the main part of the city had twisted and weaved amongst steep slopes or plunged deep into the heart of the curious hills (amongst city office blocks or brightly-lit shops) to emerge shortly afterwards along palm-fringed boulevards offering views of flower-beds and expensive yachts. Occasionally, a postcard-familiar scene would briefly frame in a surge of recognition before being blocked off once more by the embrace of another short tunnel or the demands of traffic streams which unexpectedly merged at speed. It was clever

– this kaleidoscopic picture of Rio from a car; the highway channelled and tunnelling through the best parts of the city and out to Copacabana before the newly-arrived had time to realise there was more than bright lights and affluence all around. In fact, the highway had done such a good job under cover of darkness that I had no idea in the morning light how one part of the place linked with others; where the centre of Rio lay; or how the famous statue of Christ on Mount Corcovado could be reached.

It was easy when you knew how, of course. The first principle in the process of gaining a feel for the layout of a strange city was to join the increasing flow of boulevard traffic as it made its way north-eastwards and back in the general direction of the airport. The morning rush hour from suburb to city centre had begun. Cars poured out of Copacabana along the coastal road, met other cars in the vicinity of Flamingo Park (where I briefly glimpsed what must have been the war memorial destination of the backwards marchers clothed in waste paper), slowed as traffic signals and other complexities diffused any sense of progress and then came to a halt as a great mêlée of buses, taxis, cars and pedestrians coalesced around the church of La Candelaria at the seawards end of Avenida Vargas. I had clearly reached the downtown area and this was clearly the real Rio. The sense of easy elegance and the grand perspectives of the tourist brochures had gone. Even the morning sun seemed to have been left behind. Trapped by trucks and amongst rushing people weaving their way past the now-stationary vehicles where they fumed in streets of the dusty masonry, it began to rain. There was nowhere to escape and park along the narrow side streets lined by towering commercial buildings. This was not the Earth Summit; this was straightforward city life.

I found a place in the end – but not before creeping slowly through the side streets around the monastery of San Benito, edging further along the shoreline and into a complexity of grubby dockland streets before noticing a gap in cars parked near the Federal Police Headquarters.

It was a gritty, grey sort of spot. Over-reaching the car roof was the concrete underside of an elevated Avenida Rodrigues on which more traffic moved at speed. And, not far ahead was the other side of the railway tracks from affluent Copacabana. A legless man in a battered wheelchair had made a home around the base of one of the concrete pillars which held up the road above. Outside the dark recess of a cardboard and tarpaulin shelter, he slowly wiped a few pots and pans with a filthy cloth before pushing himself inside. Avenida Rodrigues kept the rain off but it was a noisy, dusty place to spend a life in. Disability and a semi-hidden position under the roadway must have saved him from the security round-up.

Once beyond the cover of the elevated roadway, the rain could be felt in earnest. As I scurried past the entrance to the Federal Police Headquarters, I realised that matters were starting to reach a point of serious wetness. A raincoat was clearly the thing in this coastal city – even if the downpour was warmish to the touch and soon evaporated away by the heat of the tropical sun. The several men with professional cameras who lingered at the entrance to the headquarters had all thought to bring some rainwear and were obviously familiar with the ways of the city. As I passed, I could see that they each had the world-weary air of press men – people whose job it was to make the best of waiting about in the hope that an anticipated event would actually take place; someone of interest would emerge through the grandiose entrance whom they could snap for the Rio evening paper before clearing off to some Brazilian 'El Vinos'.

No, surely not. Could they be waiting for the final chapter in the Great Train Robbery to be written? Could they be waiting for that photograph of Ronald Biggs handcuffed to the Metropolitan Police of London? Was he being finally extracted from beautiful Rio and returned to the somewhat less picturesque streets of South London?

I couldn't stay to find out. The rain was coming down with such intensity that it would now take a good hour in the sun to dry out – assuming the sun was going to re-emerge at some time in the day. Even a search for sanctuary in the nearby Monastery of San Benito was thwarted by a funeral. It was an event where almost everyone seemed to have arrived by taxi and the fleet of hired vehicles was still waiting for them to emerge. But there wasn't a great deal of space outside the church and an incredible number had somehow been manoeuvred into a very small hilltop forecourt. They were parked like peas in a pod – so much so that where a few serious and soberly dressed latecomers rushed on to the scene they had great difficulty in forcing a route through both cars and tightly knit groups of umbrellaed chatting drivers. And that wasn't the end it – having reached the church it was clear to all concerned that the place was packed to capacity. There really was no space for another group of dark suits and black veiled hats inside.

As the rain built up to a crescendo, I edged closer into the tall overhanging façade. It was most unfortunate that it happened to be a funeral but whilst the dead were bone dry – some of the living were getting soaked to the skin outside. Lovely place for a send-off, though. Hardly a square foot of boring plaster or dusty stone could be seen – gold and gilt glistened everywhere; richly-ornate ecclesiastical decoration covered almost the entire inner surface of the church. Whoever it was, was clearly going out with a first class ticket.

Funnily enough, the richness of the church interior was in direct contrast with the austere-looking black-robed monks of the monastery who seemed to have nothing to do with the event. At intervals, one of these would emerge from a kind of guard-house at the side of the façade, ease his way through the taxis and drivers and stride off towards the wet city streets as if the seventeenth century had not long been over. If they could face up to the rain, then so could I – it was obviously an unfortunate time to visit San Benito.

*

Following a monk, however, was not necessarily the key to Rio de Janeiro although the rain did seem a little easier in his spiritual slipstream. Traffic was still in a state of near-gridlock around La Candelaria but, on the off-chance that a change of church might offer a better prospect of shelter, I decided to disengage and slip inside. Shelter was clearly not uppermost in the mind of the monk of San Benito, however, who continued striding straight past as if the Benedictine order had somehow contrive to make itself waterproof. Half expecting to find another packed interior I cautiously opened one the huge doors and prepared to meet the same incongruous mixture of sobriety and gold which lay up the hill.

Nothing of the sort. The church was a rather bare expanse of dusty stone and dark wood. Only two people were at what seemed to be their devotions. They huddled in a far pew and I had to walk softly past them in order to exit the church on the Avenida Rio Branco side of Candelaria. As I drew closer, I realised they were not Brazilians but from Japan. And as I drew closer still I realised they were not communicating with God but with their more earthly relatives. Both were discretely writing postcards.

Outside, the never-ending rain was proving to be a real nuisance. On the crowded Avenida Rio Branco, the many pedestrians were being forced to keep as close as possible to the façades of the buildings to avoid not only the deluge coming from above but the constant splashing from the road as a combination of passing traffic and large puddles sent near-horizontal bow waves sweeping along the outer edge of the pavement.

It was of no help to movement that the narrow strip of relative dryness which everyone was trying to pass along at the same time was also inhabited by a long string of street traders – constantly trimming the improvised control lines which held up their sheets of polythene or cardboard and kept the rain off their wares. Wallets, guide-books, handbags, cassette tapes and collapsible umbrellas all occupied the same limited space as pedestrians and it seemed that, in this enormous country of Brazil – all 3,286,488 square miles of it occupying nearly half the continent of South America – too much pressure was suddenly being placed on a foot or two of pavement running down the eastern side of the Rio Branco. Something was going to have to give. People were forcing themselves along as if on a narrow ledge above a huge drop.

It gave. A man on the inside brushed against one of the stalls and dislodged a cheap camera which fell to the floor. An argument began: the passer-by claiming that nothing amiss had occurred; the stall-holder shouting about damage and the need for payment. It was an age-old scene and could have taken place in the Roman Empire as much as in Rio de Janeiro. Hands waved, voices were raised, fingers jabbed in the air, more people began to get wet as they edged around the altercation.

I didn't stay to see the end of it. A better shelter came into view in the form of a savings bank where – behind steamy rain-splashed plate glass windows – long queues of damp people led up to a welter of clerks, forms, passbooks, rubber stamps, adding machines and printed announcements of the prevailing interest rate.

Although no one came out with a new rate there and then, those announcements were rarely allowed to fade and grow yellow with age and city grime. The Brazilian economy saw to that. It was in a mess like its neighbour to the south, although perhaps not quite so deeply mired in debt repayments. Nonetheless, a similar process of Brazilian monetary incarnation and re-incarnation echoed that of the Argentinian Republic. Old cruzeiros spawned new cruzados until new cruzados were replaced by even newer cruzados before prematurely ageing to become... new (old) cruzeiros again. Over a period of four years from March 1986 to March 1990, one of the newest of the cruzeiros had come to equal one million of the old ones.

I was in a savings bank where all this manoeuvring hit the pockets of the ordinary people and it was surprising how orderly they were. Nonetheless, it did not seem wise to save up for a rainy day in Brazil; there was time enough in the passage of a single shower to lose a lot of money or even go bankrupt.

And all that was without the 'special arrangements' imposed by the administration of Fernando Collar in mid-1990 whereby a withdrawal limit of the equivalent of

US$1,000 was imposed on bank and cash deposits for eighteen months. I left the packed interior of the Rio savings bank in the search for another haven: a calmer place to shelter in; a place where you came out with much the same financial status as you entered; a place where you were not amongst the bloodied foot-soldiers in the battle of the World Bank versus Latin America.

Southwards, the huge Petrobras building stood nearby and behind it was a curiously rural spot where a grassy knoll rose up and was topped by a kind of covered platform towards which shiny tracks seemed loop in a wide bend from the west before leaving in the direction from whence they had come. Curiously, as they curved out of view, the lie of the land gave the distinct impression that they were either taking off into mid-air and oblivion or were making a very steep plunge into a nearby valley – this defile separating the low central hill over which Avenida Rio Branco continued to head southwards. Steeply rising suburbs could just be made out in the rain to the west – forming the far side of the valley. Before much further thought could be given to the spatial relationships of this iron road to nowhere, the conundrum was partially resolved by the appearance of an ancient tram creaking and screeching slowly into view and towards a halt at the extremity of the loop. It stopped at what now fell into place as a sort of scaled-down central station. I could feel the River Urubu and the Amazonas waterfall problem creeping-up afresh – nothing seemed to quite make sense.

The tram was ancient – an antique – and so densely packed inside with people that they were bulging out of the windows along each side. Magnifying this bulging effect – although the tram itself was top-heavy – were latecomers who had standing-room only. They clung to brass handles with feet tucked sideways along a narrow wooden running board extending along the entire outside length of the single carriage. An open back compartment contained a uniformed ticket collector; an open front compartment contained a uniformed driver. With much noise and the clanging of a bell, the latter signified that the incoming commuters could begin to disembark – which most did before the tram reached a complete halt by making a running jump on to the cindered track and continuing with much the same momentum as they each made a careering run through the downpour and off into the city.

The tram had hardly become motionless in front of the platform when a homeward-bound crowd quickly materialised from nooks and crannies in the shelter of the station and began to climb aboard. I climbed aboard with them – if only to establish quite what took place when the elderly vehicle once more completed its turn and once more encountered the empty space beyond the knoll.

Something quite unexpected happened when it did. Rather than rocketing downhill, we took off into space like some air-borne coffee grinder. A clear view of the ground from a centrally placed seat in the interior was difficult as not only did canvas flaps partially obscure the view (and keep out the worst of the rain) but some latecomers had joined us on the running board just as the tram reached the point of departure from *terra firma*. What could be seen of a downward view did little to disprove flight, however. There appeared to be absolutely nothing below us except roof tops and a very busy road – although whatever we were supported by did seem to be able to project some very rusty wire netting that was clearly intended to collect any passengers from a straight fall of a hundred feet or so but which clearly would not. Through the broken strands of this netting I caught a brief glimpse of a file of Amazonian Indians making their way towards an Alternative Earth Summit meeting – each with the regulation boxer shorts, feathered headdress and sharp-pointed spear. Surreally, they disappeared underneath us like a line of colourful mackerel-hooks.

The grinding continued monotonously towards the suburbs of the far hillside although taking on a gradually more laboured tone as rooftops grew closer. Alarmingly, people started dropping off their outside perches just as the laboured tone turned to a high shriek. The tram had encountered solid land. It began climbing a steep flank – tackling the incline like an angry bee which had just escaped from the indignity of a rolled-up newspaper. More outsiders fell off and whatever had borne us aloft was required no more. We started a zigzagging route which painfully made its way up a hillside occupied by quaint paved streets and old colonial houses – a little dilapidated and half-buried in dripping tropical foliage. The rain was easing, however, and – as the climb progressed – the view improved to such an extent that the San Benito Monastery, the Rio Branco, the Sugar Loaf and even the broad sweep of the Atlantic could now be fitted into a mental framework of the city. Everything, in fact, began to fall into place except what had supported us on the mysterious passage through the air as we left the station on the knoll.

The seats inside the tram were really benches made of wooden slats. The appearance of a third uniformed crew member swinging along the outside and collecting fares caused a closer look at what the role of the individual in the back compartment was supposed to be. He was riding shotgun! A soldier with a rifle was guarding the takings... or was he part of the Earth Summit security net? Once again the River Urubu syndrome surged in. As the conductor collected his fares it was clear that the price of a tram ticket did not seem to match up with the damage that a close-range bullet hole could do. At 550 cruzeiros it worked out to 15 cents US and those on the outside travelled free. And yet here we were, trundling along like some Wells Fargo stage making its way to the bank at Dodge City?

Completely ignoring our security guard, many of the interior passengers began to depart as we slowly climbed or briefly clanged to a stop through a suburb of Rio called Santa Teresa. No one seemed to wait for the tram to stop, so a mêlée usually resulted as early departures tangled with early arrivals. There was not much space between the rows of benches and no way of moving from front to rear or vice versa without recourse to the running board or a stiff climb as we continued to mount the hillside.

Passengers leaving and boarding had that complete mixture of skin colours that was typical of the coastal cities of this old Portuguese colony. White, brown and black and a great many shades in between – but mostly dark brown or black. Luxuriant Brazil was very different from monotonous Argentina; it was mostly white or grey there. Indeed, some of the land mass of the huge country came fairly close to Africa – still a week or two's sailing time but across a much shorter oceanic gap than elsewhere. The north-eastern ports of Recife and Natal were closer to the West African ports of Freetown and Monrovia than any other part of the Americas was. Indeed, it was a lesser distance from the Old World to the New World of Brazil across the mid-Atlantic than it was from Rio to the major cities of Latin America.

★

The unfortunate business of slavery, of course, had served to bridge the gap and to first bring Africans to Brazil. The thirst for unskilled labour to work the sugar plantations. The slaves came quite quickly as the Portuguese had already penetrated well down the African coastline before the Spanish and other Europeans had started their exploratory journeys. And then, after Columbus had returned from his voyages and the potential wealth of the New World began to quicken the pulse of Catholicism and the Iberian peninsular, by a quirk of geography Portugal was able to add the great mass of Brazil to the lands 370 leagues east of the Cape Verde Islands which the Treaty of Tordesillas had agreed was part of their worldly domain.

As they sorted out the commercial implications which this 'territorial deal' of the early sixteenth century had given them, the connecting of what they knew of Africa with what they were beginning to discover in America started the sad flood of humanity from one side of the Atlantic to the other. And, as the rule of monarchy seemed to linger longer in Brazil than anywhere else in the New World, so, unfortunately, did the practice of slavery. Seventeenth-century attitudes lingered on to the nineteenth in that vast country. Attitudes like '*...without Angola, no slaves; without slaves, no sugar; without sugar, no Brazil...*' Perhaps they linger on now. Officially, slavery was ended in the 1880s; unofficially, its practice is reported to persist in out-of-the-way places still – throughout 1980s and into the 1990s.

The African mix had certainly livened things up. For they also said in Rio: '*Without the Africans, no Carnival; without the Carnival, no Samba*' (and – for that matter – none of the beautiful mulatto women who walked the streets of the city).

Perhaps, too, the twentieth-century Brazilian writer Jorge Amado had most sensitively pinned down the difference between the two huge states which dominated the non-Andean part of the Latin American continent – Brazil and Argentina. Perhaps he had caught their underlying mood best when he wrote that, '*The black man saved Brazil from melancholy and sadness.*' Melancholy and sadness: you had to see more of the country than this tropical Rio suburb to understand what he was talking about. But it was true. He – and she – had.

★

There was more exchanging of passengers as we climbed higher and higher and rose through a kaleidoscope of back gardens and front porches; of basement walls giving way to the tops of palm trees; of huge damp flower-pots holding orchids; of tiny tiled gardens; of purple bougainvillaea; of pale-green shutters peeling to dirty white; of the dark russet colours of thick roof tiles; of more basement walls. And, as the elderly vehicle mounted through Santa Teresa, it took on the extra role of a provider of local services: in one place, several plastic cans of water too heavy to carry were balanced on the running board as we creaked past the frontal basement part of a building site, and lifted off again as we groaned on up past the back of an incomplete second floor. In another place, an orange-overalled road sweeper hooked on with broom and bucket for a lift from one street level to another. Near the end of the route, a bevy of noisy schoolgirls crowded on to the benches and feverishly scribbled notes in exercise books as they swapped lunch-break for what was presumably to be an afternoon of tests.

Their convent school lay at the very end of the run where the tram screeched around a short section of rail, reversed, settled down for a few minutes of rest and then – like a tired skier – gradually gathered momentum for a brake-squealing descent. It went down towards the now distant centre of downtown Rio like a knife-sharpener working overtime. The old brakes just about held it back from a rocketing, careering, shrieking, record-breaking plummet towards that mysterious valley crossing and another noisy arrival at the grassy knoll.

I solved the enigma when we reached the bottom of the hill. It was easier to see now that the rain had stopped. That airy gap was bridged by a white-painted mock-Roman arched viaduct which looked slightly narrower than the width of the tram and was almost impossible to glimpse from inside unless you leaned out past the canvas flap and peered sharply downwards. We rolled along the top of it. There was no retaining wall. The tram and its passengers (we had acquired the same complement of free-fare hangers-on at the foot of Santa Teresa as had been dropped off on the outward journey) trundled high above a busy valley floor. That rusty wire netting was the only barrier between us and impalement on a factory chimney or the spears of any passing Amazonian Indians. Perhaps that was why the running board was free.

We rocked slowly from side to side as we crossed over. With bated breath, I wondered when the last ride to heaven was scheduled for. The time, sooner or later, when some part of the iron and wood contraption could hold out no longer and a full complement of free and fare-paying passengers plus the driver, plus the conductor and plus the soldier with rifle who rode shotgun, would pour through some unsuspecting rooftop or crash in a welter of brass and bell-clanging across a fast-moving traffic stream. It was almost better not to know how it was done.

The rain had stopped by the time we did the final turn at the station near the Petrobras building. The thankfully solid and firm pavements of Avenida Rio Branco were once more in full use; the funeral was over at the San Benito Monastery and the Press had gone from the Federal Police Headquarters. The poor man in the wheelchair was deep inside his canvas shelter and the car I had hired was already covered in a kind of wet dust which seemed perpetually to spray off the Avenida Rodrigues as its traffic passed overhead.

On the descent I had caught a brief glimpse of The Hunchback.

The Hunchback – the steep hill called Corcovado which was topped by a huge *Estatua du Cristo Redentor* – rose out of the foliage and rooftops of Rio somewhere south of where I had retrieved the car. It was foliage and rooftops which proved difficult to pinpoint once in the hurly-burly of the shore-side tunnels and traffic streams but I eventually reached the narrow road which disentangled itself from the latter and began to zigzag up through the former.

Charles Darwin had noticed how noisy the thick foliage of Rio could be as it dripped dry from the heavy wetting of a tropical rainstorm. As each zig turned into a zag and I followed the narrow road from the rump of the Hunchback and on to its densely vegetated shoulder, the weather did not seem greatly different from 1832 when '*...one morning, in the course of six hours, 1.6 inches of rain fell. As this storm passed over the forests which surround the Corcovado, the sound produced by the drops pattering on the countless multitude of leaves was very remarkable; it could be heard at distance of a quarter of a mile, and was like the rushing of a great body of water...*'.

When it could be glimpsed through all this dripping and pattering, the view from Corcovado was magnificent. Below, the city draped itself around the foot of the tall green hills and reached up their flanks until the slope became impossible and only trees and shrubs could cling on to the near-vertical granite. This whole rugged landscape then appeared to slowly sink into the Bay of Guanabara. Those same tall hills became islands and those islands became progressively lower in the water until none reached above its surface. The Bay of Guanabara gave way to the distant sheen of the Atlantic Ocean.

All this was even better at the top where everything came into view: the Sugar Loaf; Copacabana; the lake of Ipanema and then – far to the west – the green blur of the Great Escarpment. Beyond it, the vast expanse of continental Brazil began in earnest.

But, under the mightily outstretched arms of Christ, other matters had clearly begun in earnest. The Earth Summit was coming to the summit of Corcovado. A security net suddenly appeared in the form of a reel of field telephone cable which was unceremoniously flung across the parapet below the statue. The heavy thud as this hit the ground was followed by the sound of steel on stone and the scuffled boot-noise of four or five Brazilian soldiers weighed down with the same sort of khaki communications equipment that had been positioned along the road in from the airport. More soldiers were out of view and occupying a very precarious vantage point somewhere below us. It seemed they were already on the phone. Buzzing, much winding of handles and some shouted commands took the edge off what otherwise might have been a place of peace and serenity at the foot of *Cristo Redentor.* A twentieth-century racket clearly had the edge on non-technological nineteenth-century ones. I didn't wait to see whether it was the Dalai Lama or John Denver who was due to arrive for the view – the place seemed to be filling up with troops.

★

That green blur of the Great Escarpment was intriguing. What lay behind it? More tropical forests clinging to the high ground called the Brazilian Highlands? The state of Minas Gerais – an inland territory given the curious name of 'general mines'? A place of gold, diamonds, aquamarine? It was certainly the place where the attractive crystalline chunks of amethyst, tourmaline and topaz that were being offered for sale to tourists near the top of the Hunchback came from. And somewhere beyond was Brasilia – the capital of this varied country. It was difficult to leave Brazil without getting to its capital city but, by road, Rio to Brasilia was a 600 mile drive. A long way but – as I descended past an Earth Summit cavalcade grinding up to the top of Corvocado – it didn't seem a bad idea after all.

★

It was not, however, a very good idea in a huge country like Brazil, although the initial stage of the journey was no problem. The road from Rio wound north-westwards and began its climb up the face of the Great Escarpment and through stunningly beautiful country. Steep ascents, sharp bends, winding valley sides – all the time through a rugged landscape sparkling under the soft warm sunlight of late afternoon. Sparkling because the colours were intensely vivid: verdant tropical greens everywhere but now splashed with orange and yellow where trees were in blossom. Great masses of purple bougainvillaea came into view from time to time; the fronds of a palm would take on an unexpected polish as sunlight bounced off them at a lowered angle. And where the route climbed further into the Brazilian Highlands, it made its way along narrow valleys when one entire side would be formed by a steep shoulder of smooth granite – a grey rock-face which dwarfed patches of bared red soil where tiny plantations of sugar-cane and coffee shared level space with the road. Above all this, the sky was a deep blue.

An entrancing place – but for all the trees in bloom, the bougainvillaea and the blue skies, it must have been quite a struggle hacking a route up through this kind of country in the early colonial days. The various 'booms' of Brazil pushed people on, of course. Like the present, the economic past of the country was all ups and downs. First the coastal sugar-cane boom of the seventeenth century with the slaves pouring in from West Africa – a boom which went bust in the eighteenth. Then, to some extent coming to the rescue, the gold of Minas Gerais booming in the early eighteenth century and collapsing towards its end. Travelling for several hours in a north-westerly direction over the country of the Great Escarpment and the Brazilian Highlands was to pass from one boom to another – from sugar to gold. Then came the expansion of coffee growing in the mid nineteenth century – a boom which had sagged towards its end although (like the gold) still making its mark on the twentieth century. Then the infamous rubber boom built on the backs of the Amazonian Indians at the end of the nineteenth century and which had left Manaus and its opera house stranded in the rainforest by 1913.

Hacking a way up and over the Brazilian Highlands must have been a tough experience – even driving north-westwards into Minas Gerais was tough. As the sun began to set and a road-sign announced that the capital was still 500 miles away, I realised I had bitten-off more than I could chew. The interior of Brazil seemed to go on forever. Some of the melancholia of Jorge Amado began to creep into my soul. Darkness fell and I also realised it was too much of a journey to wind back down the narrow valleys of the Great Escarpment to the lights of Rio. The sheer size of the place was demoralising. Too far to return and certainly too much of a journey to carry on through the night and reach the distant city of Brasilia.

Surprisingly, not long after, the glow of an enormous megalopolis became visible as the uplands began to level out into what seemed to be a vast plateau. Over it, a glittering carpet of lights spread westwards until they dimmed and became faint. Was this a dream? What was going on? It couldn't possibly be Brasilia – and there was supposed to be nothing else but five hundred miles of darkness and road.

Closer to, the route plunged down into the edge of the grid-iron of wide boulevards which had marked themselves out by patterns of street lamps. Office blocks were brightly lit, buses ran, traffic lights winked, the city went on and on. As the road descended from higher ground and the way onward to the capital became confused amongst some of the thoroughfares, I also became totally baffled. The place was as large as Manchester, lit the sky with a neon glow and yet I had travelled north-west on the assumption that there was nowhere of any significance on the route until Brasilia. Where on earth was I?

Could this be Belo Horizonte – somewhere assumed as a main street accompanied by a scatter of houses and gardens?

Everything in Brazil was huge. It was that main street and scatter of houses and gardens but also happened to be the third largest city in the country. However, here was a temporary solution to the melancholia – the not wanting to go back and not wanting to go on. I could spend the night in Belo Horizonte and think of something new in the morning.

*

As it was the third largest city in Brazil and home to over two million people, that newly-absorbed fact did nothing to offset another bout of melancholia which came on when looking for a hotel room amongst the streets of Belo Horizonte. I quickly grew tired of the over-familiar experience of searching the boulevards and back-roads of an unknown city for somewhere to sleep. No hotels advertised themselves in this metropolis of Minas Gerais and the place was hardly on any tourist route. In fact, a proper hotel never materialised. I spent the hours of darkness in a modern building offering apartments to rent – apartments which would have suited a family of four who needed a fully functioning kitchen, a dinner service for twelve, wine glasses and place mats to match and six carving knives. Flower-pots and a huge packet of washing soap were also available.

But why, though? For what reason would a family of four be spending time in a Belo Horizonte whose main functions were car manufacture, steel-making and processing the various mining products of the Brazilian Highlands. It was the River Urubu all over again. Nothing made sense – particularly this huge city that only Brazilians knew about.

It did have a beautiful airport, however – far out beyond the edge of the city and uncomfortably wreathed in the white mist of early morning. Oscar Niemayer had designed its long curve of sculptured concrete and the floors of the glass-enclosed passenger lounges were lovingly cared for by staff who seemed to have been at the job since dawn. Everything was functioning – despite the early hour: architecturally perfect coffee kiosks; plentiful seats and a choice of airlines; a car-hire office more than willing to take my Rio vehicle. Even the ubiquitous pod-mounted television screens were busy, although it was a little early for John Denver and *Country Roads*. This place was a stopover between the city of the Earth Summit and the city in the middle of nowhere – Brasilia. I let the plane take the strain.

⋆

Brasilia was intended to herald the twenty-first century, although such a concept was a tad early when the twentieth still had half its course to run. Building began in the late 1950s in the empty undulating landscape of the state of Goias; the low trees, bushes and rough grassland that was interior Brazil when it wasn't covered by tropical rainforest. A brave place to site a green-field capital city and to hope that the world would beat a track to its doors. Rio was the former capital: imagine closing down the European Community building in Brussels and re-locating to a new building six hundred miles away with the amenities of Volgograd or Kharkov. It was Sunday morning and the place was suspiciously devoid of politicians, ambassadors and senior government officials.

But, of course – they all had to be back in Rio. It was the Earth Summit.

And another thing about Brasilia – it was all so familiar. As the aircraft from Belo Horizonte banked slowly above the city and began its final descent, the grand design was laid out for all to see: the winged bird; the soaring plane; the giant bow pointing at the heart of the South American continent. Lucio Costa had turned thought into form with his grand 'strings' of the main highways of the Eixo Rodoviarios Norte and Sud drawing back the straight arrows of the Eixo Monumental to the west and the Eixo Ministerios to the east. Oscar Niemayer had created more of his sculptured concrete with the 'feathers' that were at the end of those arrows – the Supreme Court, the Congress building and the President's Office. Even the government departments of Brazil were thought turned into form as observed from the air – toy office blocks each standing at ease and at arms length as they lined the Eixo Ministerios: Education; Air Force; Navy; Transport & Communications along one side; Social Security; Agriculture; Sport & Culture along the other. Brasilia was what the 1950s thought the future would look like. It was what Fidel Castro had in mind; it was the world of John Kennedy, of Yuri Gagarin, of Sputnik 1. There was more than a touch of the Festival of Britain. Brasilia fitted with Bratsk; it was far better than the suburbs of Leningrad or Moscow but still identifiable with them. A centrally planned city with living space carefully worked out on a drawing board; a tree here; a fountain there; a bus station carefully disguised; a symbolic tower; places for people to stroll. Brasilia had preserved all this; it was like Mussolini's enormous model of Ancient Rome. But could people be expected to actually live in a model?

There were not many of them on the ground, certainly. It seemed central planning in reality had created some familiar problems: no one wanted to stroll in the strolling places; no one bustled down the soulless pavements; no one seemed to want to do anything at all. In the middle of Brazil were streets redolent with a forgotten atmosphere; that atmosphere of boredom and ennui; that overwhelming familiarity of a Fifties Sunday afternoon.

Brasilia wasn't entirely shut down, however. A kind of fair struggled to create jollity around the base of the TV tower where some craft stalls and a few fast-food stands were clustered together at the edge of one of the extensive car parks. Nearby was a kind of memorial museum to President Juscelino Kubitschek.

'*Fifty years progress in five years*' was his slogan, and Brasilia was his baby. Massive loans underpinned the growth of his vision – the five years being from 1956 to 1961. It was a brave idea but the economic ebullience at the beginning of the 1960s quickly faded; not least because it cost an awful lot of money to air-lift cement, steel, glass, food, fuel and one hundred thousand workers into a barely inhabited expanse of rough grassland and wait for a city to emerge.

⋆

It is to the credit of the Brazilians that it did emerge and that it has become a national symbol. Its completion and continuation perhaps speaks more about the prospects for a twenty-first century Brazil than the cynical '*Fifty years inflation in five years*' which was a consequence of the massive debt that it helped to bring about. Brasilia in a less big country would now be a ghost town of rust-stained concrete and pot-holed roads leading nowhere.

Kubitschek died in a car crash in 1976. His memorial museum lay half-sunken so as not unduly to interrupt the Eixo Monumental as it swept westwards to the bus station and the Supreme Court. Beyond it, there were no more of those enormous Belo Horizontes at the end of a day's drive – nothing much in the way of civilisation until Benjamin Constant was reached on the other side of the Mato Grosso. And that was seventeen hundred miles away!

Chapter Nine

Weekend in Argentina

'STICK IT UP YOUR JUNTA', 'ENEMY BANGERS HAVEN'T A CHANCE'. Was it a good idea to visit Buenos Aires on exactly the tenth anniversary of the Falklands conflict? All those headlines as Maggie was turning down the fifth or sixth Haig Peace Proposal knowing full well that two aircraft carriers, five guided-missile destroyers, seven frigates and a host of other surface or subsurface ironmongery was heading like a maritime 7th Cavalry as fast as it could for the Argentinian islands of *Las Malvinas.*

The queue reached towards the desk of an immigration officer who looked placid enough. But was he one of the Argentinians who must have read some of the British Press in March, April and May of 1982? Those headlines: 'COLLISION COURSE FOR WAR' in the *Daily Mirror*; 'WE'LL SINK 'EM' in the *Sun* and the somewhat ambiguous '*...any ships found in our 320 kilometre war zone will be treated as hostile and liable to attack*' of Minister of Defence John Nott – the latter hurriedly adding that it applied particularly to vessels belonging to Argentina.

Was the presentation of a British passport on the very day of the anniversary of the sinking of the *Belgrano* going to be taken as an act of hostility? Was it all going to flash back into his mind like one of those electronic information boards? '... ALERT!... A BRITISH PASSPORT... LAS MALVINAS... STATE OF HOSTILITIES... COUNTRY STILL OFFICIALLY AT WAR WITH UK?'

Did he still feel furious about the 'GOTCHA' that the *Sun* waved in triumph when the news came in about the sinking of the *General Belgrano*? Admittedly things were toned down a bit when it was discovered that the aged cruiser had been outside the Maritime Exclusion Zone, was moving away and that 368 Argentinian lives had been lost. Then it began to seem less of an escapade and more like a real war. *HMS Sheffield* was sunk by Exocet missiles; he probably knew about that, too.

But then some of the rumbustiousness returned. 'WALLOP: ISLAND BLITZED; SPY SHIP HELD; ARGIES JET FLEET; OUR BOYS SAFE'. 'WE'RE GOING IN' said the *Mirror* 'SMASH AND GRAB INVASION'. Then, on 21st May, came the *Sun*'s 'MAGGIE SENDS IN THE TROOPS' as the Task Force landings began in San Carlos Bay.

The queue gradually shortened and the man at the desk grew closer. How much had he and the inhabitants of the seventh largest country in the world and the third largest city in Latin America known of what was going on as the forces of one small island on the edge of the North Atlantic began to battle the ten thousand men who had occupied one small island on the edge of the South Atlantic? What about 'HIGH NOON: BRITAIN SET TO SHOOT ARGIES'? Was there not that hastily withdrawn evening headline which had briefly suggested that it might be a good idea to 'NUKE BUENOS AIRES'?

The electronic information board again – coming through with an update: '...STOP PRESS... HOSTILITIES FORMALLY ENDED OCTOBER 1989... NOW MAY 1992... NO PROBLEM... ALL FORGOTTEN'. But the *Daily Mirror* could still be there in the background stirring up trouble: 'WE'RE WINNING', 'GALTIERI TO GET THE BOOT'. And – as the *Mail* wistfully watched its sales slump back to pre-war days – 'GOODBYE GALTIERI'.

Flick, bang, scribble. With a frown, the man inserted the rectangular blue stamp of the Republica Argentina and handed back the passport. No mention was made of Gotcha, Sticking it up yer Junta, Bangers, Wallop and Nuking Buenos Aires. Just as well really – twelve million angry people could still be out there, otherwise.

★

There was no shortage of people in the terminal building – even if they had put the business of scrap recovery and the rights of the Falkland Islanders to *vivir en libertad* behind them.

People living in a recognisable world: an Atlantic world; more grey than tropical green. Not a very exuberant world – not Caribbean or Pacific. No shorts and palm trees. Not much colour – clothes were heavier and more sober and faces sadder, too. Little sign of Africans, or Amerindians, or even Hispanics. The faces were urban. European. But not even West European. Greyer faces. Faces from eastern Europe: Poles; Hungarians; Russians; Slavs; Serbs. The sky outside was grey, as well. Lightly overcast – like an urban Atlantic sky should be. The sky of Liverpool, of Glasgow, of Boston, of Manhattan.

Admittedly these were first impressions. The seventh largest country in the world measured up on the basis of a few hundred of its people in an airport terminal and a brief glance out of the terminal building window. But that familiarity was hardly surprising. The *gaucho* culture of the swashbuckling, guitar-playing riders of the pampas had long since been swamped by an enormous influx of late nineteenth- and early twentieth-century immigration from Europe. As the flow of 'huddled masses' across the North Atlantic from there to the United States began to lessen, so it grew stronger across the South Atlantic from there to Argentina.

But those many hopefuls passing over the North Atlantic often pressed on from the eastern seaboard and were encouraged to populate the prairies and farmlands of the interior. In Argentina, most newcomers seemed to have preferred the attractions of the city of their arrival: Buenos Aires.

Indeed, nearly all the twelve million people living in this sprawling metropolis which now extended over a considerable portion of the flat coastlands around the *Rio de la Plata* were direct descendants of this huge wave of European immigration: second or third generation Italians; Spaniards; French; Poles; Germans or Russians. Nearly forty per cent of the population of Argentina lived in the capital. And, even in the second half of the twentieth century, Europeans were still coming: the swampy but fertile area between the Parana and Uruguay rivers that was called Mesopotamia had filled up with Germans and others during the 1950s.

⋆

The country was a very different place before this great wave of immigration. In the first half of the nineteenth century, Argentina only had one million people – a thinly spread scattering of mostly farmers and ranchers who had moved in previous centuries from other parts of the old

Spanish empire. In that empire, the vast land mass of the pampas had formed only a part of the Viceroyalty of Rio de la Plata. This was a colonial administrative area reaching right across the continent to Bolivian Potosí and La Paz; engulfing what is now Paraguay and Uruguay and extending south to include all the Patagonian 'cone' of South America below the island of Chiloe. Huge estates and personal fiefdoms – the culture of *estancieros* – had spread over the grasslands of the interior where the horsemen of mesticho and pure Indian stock roamed with their herds and their songs.

As the second half of the nineteenth century began, however, this 'Life on the Open Range' that was Argentina became progressively more a folk-myth than reality. Railways (British built) snaked in from the coast, fences began to cut back the free movement of cattle, grass gave way to other crops, small towns with grain elevators grew up around railway halts, the lean long-horns were replaced by beefy short-horns. Argentina set about exporting grain and meat across the Atlantic in a systematic fashion and soon became highly successful at it. As the Spanish empire faded away, so the pampas became the larder of the British empire.

*

Those were golden days for the Republic of Argentina – the days of the meat, wheat and hides pouring off the great interior grasslands and through the railways, ports and refrigerated steamships shuttling from South to North across the Atlantic. Stewing steak, 'luncheon meat' and the forerunner of the hamburger supported the human 'muscle' necessary to maintain the continuing industrial revolution of Britain and the United States. In the other direction, money and investment flowed back and continually improved transportation and processing. 'Fray Bentos' – a small river town some one hundred miles north of Buenos Aires – was probably less well-known in Buenos Aires than as the name on a label of a tin of corned beef in the grocery stores of Britain and the US. In the heady days of the early twentieth century, this flow of food out and wealth back gave Argentina some of the highest levels of prosperity in Latin America. Neighbouring Uruguay, too, grew rich on processed meats and other foodstuffs. The burgeoning populations of the eastern seaboard began to enjoy social benefits that were the envy of a Europe racked by the trials of World War I and casting nervous glances towards the gathering storm of World War II.

A secure, settled and prosperous future was beginning for those in the former Viceroyalty of the Rio de la Plata. Then it all somehow fell apart.

★

No – the Atlantic greyness of the people in the airport terminal building was not simply the fact that they had originated from eastern Europe or lived an urban life under faintly overcast skies. It had little do with 'TROOPS SMASH INTO ARGIES' or 'GOTCHA' or anything else of the brief adventure with *Las Islas Malvinas,* either. Mostly, it was caused by money.

In 1992, the Argentinian economy was in more of a mess than that of Brazil. The flow of wealth back from the North Atlantic had dried up. Refrigerated container vessels plying between Buenos Aires, New York or London were reduced to a trickle. Another South American boom had gone bust.

The 'bust' had begun before the military adventure of early 1980. The Argentinian economic mess had been around for twenty years or so – beginning, in fact, soon after the end of the Second World War. At this time of change, Peronist nationalisation and price fixing had annoyed Argentina's major importers. Rising levels of foreign borrowing then created difficulties over debt-servicing. The international oil crisis and the growth of the EEC had compounded the problem.

Although, by 1970, some attempts had been made to fix the slide in value of the currency with 'old' pesos taking away the growing burden of inflation by being made into 'new' pesos, the problems continued. For every hundred of the 'old' pesos – a 'new' peso replaced it. By 1983, however, these 'new' pesos had begun to weary of the task of supporting the economy and began to need to go about in vast numbers to have any chance of surviving. Not long after the Falklands War, things had deteriorated to the state where ten thousand 'new' pesos were corralled together and told they constituted an 'even newer' peso which was optimistically called an 'argentino'.

Then the 'argentinos' fell sick. By 1985, they too had to band together for support: one thousand of them were deemed to constitute a new 'even newer' peso which was called an 'austral'. A lovely name but doomed: as the 1990s loomed on the horizon, no less than ten thousand australs became... one peso!

*

Pesos came back in March 1991: one of the new ones now being worth ten trillion of the very ancient pesos of the early 1970s. Inflation steamed full ahead like refrigerated carriers of corned beef to Connecticut and Coventry had once moved up and down the Atlantic. It had reached a peak of 20,266%. The Argentinian economy was not exactly helping out with that secure, settled and prosperous future.

⋆

Surprisingly, the newest peso with the uncertain shelf-life was pegged on a one-for-one basis with the US dollar. But as I changed US$100 in the expectation of receiving one hundred pesos, nearly a million in freshly-minted australs were instead pushed across the bank counter. A fortune – or so it briefly seemed at the time. A thick wad of crisp high-denomination notes. But only fools think money-changing facilities at airports are giving anything away for free. Added to the australs were a few grubby low denomination pesos which almost seemed as if they should be cast in a nearby bin – leftovers from that time in 1970 when it all began to get out of hand.

By the time I was on the open road leading west from Buenos Aires, had enjoyed a brief cup of coffee and had paid several tolls on the short stretches of elevated motorway which moved downtown traffic to the distant edge of the city – the australs had almost all gone. Thousands of them were needed for the simplest of transactions. The grubby pesos held their ground a little better but, at a rate of 20,266%, they were being consumed almost as fast as the elderly 2.0 litre Peugeot I had hired was burning up fuel. Much more fuel and thousands more australs would be required if I was to get to Corrientes.

*

It seemed a good idea on the flight down from Caracas to go to Corrientes. A long way and a lot of driving, of course – about six hundred miles a day for three days – but the big republics on the eastern side of South America were roomy places and couldn't be tackled with a faint heart and an afternoon's spin in the motor.

The plan was to leave Buenos Aires as quickly as possible and get into Mesopotamia. Then to follow the big rivers: the Parana first to the town of Resistencia and the border with Paraguay. Perhaps a brief sortie into that country or then on to Graham Greene's novel. Then east and north to the border with the southernmost part of Brazil – a long way from the rainforest and a long way from Rio. A long way from anywhere, really – which was why the Jesuits of the seventeenth and eighteenth centuries wanted to set up their utopian communities in the empty country where Paraguay, Brazil and Argentina met. Then south into Uruguay – having a look at the fertile lowlands of the other side of Mesopotamia before crossing back into Argentina at the bridge over the River Uruguay at Fray Bentos.

From there it would only be a comparatively short run in to Buenos Aires. Tough, with long hours at the wheel, but this was the flat side of the South American continent: good roads; no potholes; no winding Andean ascents and descents; no misty rugged terrain; no dangers. But I'd forgotten about monotony and boredom. I'd forgotten the lesson of interior Brazil; forgotten what Jorge Amado had written; forgotten the journey to Belo Horizonte. I'd forgotten about melancholy and sadness.

*

Buenos Aires was creeping west over the pampas and had already colonised a considerable area, but eventually the sheer scale of the flat lands defeated even the march of buildings. The vast interior of Argentina began to open up. The next significant population centre on the straight road leading north-west along the line of the River Parana was the city of Rosario – nearly two hundred miles across the pampas. It was before I had covered half of this journey, however, that I started to realise that the landscape of Argentina was going to defeat the grand circuit through four countries and around the margins of Mesopotamia. Perfectly flat farmland stretched away beyond the horizon for three hundred miles to the west, three hundred miles to the south and nearly one thousand miles to the north. A landscape of maize and flax which swallowed the Peugeot like a tiny boat trying to cross a Pacific Ocean. Nothing broke the uniformity of this landscape and nothing would. Endless crops – growing in fields which met other fields until they rolled over the horizon to meet even more fields. Overhead was a huge prairie sky of pale Atlantic blue. Here and there were cumulus clouds which sailed slowly and ponderously across the billiard-board flatness – their shadows brushing leisurely over the squares and rectangles of crops and then fleetingly touching the scattered stands of tall eucalyptus trees before moving on to more fields and crops. Near and far, clusters of these trees dotted the prairie and provided shade and protection from sun and wind. Close up, their foliage caused deep shadows to gather at the foot of papery trunks; far away their outlines hung suspended just above the distant edge of the world like the vague outline of the altiplano hills shimmering beyond the unseen Lake Uru Uru.

In highland Bolivia, it had seemed difficult to cope with anything other than the dust and the corrugated surface of the road; on the hard-surfaced empty highway to Rosario the mind was much freer. Any danger could be seen miles ahead. It was easy mentally to rise out of the car and see it speeding far below as a tiny toy moving across this vast checkerboard of cultivation.

But maybe it was better to be bouncing along at thirteen thousand feet with every new mile bringing another new circumstance. The Andean highlands or the Venezuelan interior kept a driver fully occupied. These 'wet' pampas were a tamed landscape – fertile and well-watered but never rising high enough to offer even a glimpse of the huge rivers which drained them. The Parana – emptying an area over half the size of the Amazon basin – could not be seen even though the road ran close to its western bank. Somewhere just across the horizon its waters made their way through a deserted corridor of marshlands. A few hundreds of miles to the east, these hidden waters flowed out into the Atlantic through the even larger corridor of drowned pampas called the *Rio de la Plata.*

★

The straight road to Rosario pressed on. Stands of eucalyptus rolled up over the horizon to the north-west and sank away from view on the horizon to the south-east. Rectangular fields of maize and flax appeared ahead as regularly as they receded away to the rear. The car could well have been stationary and the Earth moving under its wheels for all the sense of progress that this landscape imparted. Like some vast conveyor belt: eucalyptus stands and rectangles of maize and flax tipping off the edge of the world left behind, turning upside down, moving slowly below in some vast hidden cavern and then tipping upright again ahead. The same trees and the same fields – endlessly repeated. An eternal journey.

Was it worth stopping and marking a eucalyptus trunk just to check?

Beethoven had to come to the rescue in such circumstance. He always did where there was a straight road, a huge and open sky, the possibilities of infinite speed over endlessly repeating landscapes. Funny that – only Beethoven. None of the rest would do – except, perhaps, Kachachurian but he was stationary, cold and savage. Kachachurian was not this landscape; his music was like looking out from a hill or cliff or high tower but not moving. Mozart, Brahms, Vivaldi and Bach lived indoors, in rooms offering movement but on too delicate a scale. Their harmonies were for city streets or for helping to take the edge off heavy traffic.

There was a curious excitement about what Beethoven had to offer – at speed. His orchestral music pushed aside the weariness of journeys to nowhere and was the opposite of soulless. The Third – the third and fourth movements of the *Eroica* – had a bright cheerful dynamism set against a backdrop of grandeur. He never visited South America, a man caught in the ebb and flow of the Old World, but it was the colour and scale of the landscape of the New World that the music of his Third Symphony best captured.

The sheer monotony of the pampas was a challenge even for Beethoven. I remained on the conveyor belt of eucalyptus, maize and flax at the end of the *Eroica* and had only covered one hundred and eighty miles of the planned eighteen hundred! Only a tenth! As late afternoon began to edge into early evening, the thought of revisiting the endless eucalyptus, maize and flax on any return to Buenos Aires seemed grim.

★

Plumes of smoke on the north-western horizon! Something was changing. A fast-moving prairie fire engulfing all in its path? The last smoldering remnants of civilisation destroyed by a global nuclear war which had somehow taken place whilst I was on the conveyor belt? Whatever lay ahead was a welcome diversion. Thank god Margaret Thatcher hadn't thought of moving inland after 'WHITE FLAGS OVER STANLEY' had been reported by the *Daily Mail*. After a week or two roaming around the pampas, the entire Task Force would have surrendered to clump of eucalyptus trees rather than press on to the Andes.

It was Rosario under the smoke – not devastated or heavily singed but looking reasonably prosperous and lining the edge of a River Parana which had finally decided to show itself.

★

Everything in Argentina seemed a bit over the top. First Buenos Aires had gone on forever before the route north-westwards through open country could be reached. Then the open country had gone on forever before Rosario could be reached. Then Rosario – the country's third largest city – turned out to be composed of extensive suburbs, wide tree-lined boulevards, spacious parks and a downtown area thick with rows of administrative and commercial buildings.

Then there was the River Parana – slipping past a spacious waterfront as a wide grey expanse of water which looked as if it had already decided to become the River Plate despite being a considerable distance inland from the Atlantic Ocean. And then there was the huge stone monument to General Belgrano.

'GOTCHA' and 'WALLOP'. The *Sun* again. That uncomfortable business of being outside and steaming away from the exclusion zone. The high Argentinian death toll. HMS *Sheffield* and the Exocets soon after.

It wasn't just the waterfront of Rosario that kept bringing it all up. He was everywhere. The Belgrano University. The Belgrano Private School. The *Base Belgranos I, II & III* in the Argentinian Antarctic, the Belgrano Laundry...

Belgrano seemed to have founded the Republic of Argentina single-handedly and then played a role in most of its infrastructural development until the late twentieth century. Even now, he could be inaugurating the Belgrano Software Programming Institute or opening a chain of Belgrano Betting Shops. Pity. The great man – and the use of his name – seemed to be a bit over the top, too.

Manuel Belgrano was a military leader in the Argentinian war of independence. In fact, the waterfront monument marked the site where he first raised a flag for it. But the real battle for liberation from Spain was commanded by José de San Martin who devised the plan which eventually resulted in the famous handshake in Guayaquil ten years later with that other man of the times – Simon Bolivar. Bolivar's victories had released the north from the grip of Spain; San Martin's victories had released the south. Belgrano's fighting career met largely with defeat.

In fact, it was as a result of this lack of success on the part of Belgrano, that San Martin was eventually called upon to supersede him in the struggle against the Spanish. He was the younger man but performed the task admirably. It helped, of course, that he knew his new foe inside out. San Martin had gained his military experience in the Napoleonic Wars – serving for no less than twenty years, but as an officer for Spain. This background no doubt developed in him a strategic ability which he quickly demonstrated by pursuing success not by all-or-nothing head-on confrontations, but by a series of glancing blows.

First step in the freeing of Argentina was the liberation of Chile. Second step was the liberation of the Viceroyalty of Peru. Third and final step was Argentina – achieved in 1821. However, that fateful meeting to discuss the future of the South American continent with Bolivar twelve months later led to the curiously hurried departure of San Martin for Europe. Within two months, he had embarked for Brussels, then Paris and then a long retirement in Boulogne-sur-Mer – a man who had somehow detached himself from the cut and thrust of the new world of South American politics. Perhaps it was the earlier twenty years in the Spanish army; perhaps San Martin was the wiser man. Bolivar – left with the possibility of the United States of South America in his grasp – watched it quickly slip away. By the time The Liberator died of tuberculosis near Cartagena eight years later, no less than nine fledgling republics had squabbled their way into existence around the central rump of colonial Portuguese Brazil.

San Martin did the deeds but ended his life in Boulogne; Belgrano handled the defeats but found himself immortalised all over Argentina: in universities, schools, Antarctic bases and coin-operated laundries.

*

Few people seemed to be about in Rosario. It was Saturday afternoon but the city centre and the waterfront were almost deserted. One or two strollers walked the paths and wide pavements near the monument, but a motionless fisherman and a motorcyclist undertaking some sort of temporary repair work to his machine were the only signs of static humanity. The fisherman had the stance of a garden gnome – intensely absorbed in watching his line disappear into the grey waters of the Parana.

They were not particularly inviting waters sweeping past the stonework of the embankment. Silt-laden, opaque and somewhat slower-moving than the Amazon. No boats plied for trade or waited to travel upstream or downstream. This Parana seemed as deserted as the city. Only bright green pieces of weed bobbed past on the last stretch of their long journey from the Mato Grosso to the sea.

Suddenly the angler jerked into life, whipped his rod back, leaned as far as he could over the embankment and struggled with a long pole and net. Something heavy and active required lifting on to the masonry. The motorcyclist looked up and then quickly stepped over to help. The writhing object was landed safely on the paving stones – a sizeable catfish flicking and jumping about as it fought the black nylon which held it. Unappealing side whiskers jabbed out through the mesh – the wriggling movement intensifying as the fish's life began to ebb away. The fisherman looked around for an object heavy enough to give it the *coup de grâce* but saw nothing capable of dealing with what was clearly an unexpectedly large catch. Stepping over to his machine, the motorcyclist came back holding a heavy adjustable spanner – offering it to the fisherman with the very faintest trace of an acolyte offering up a sacrificial knife. The fisherman took it and clubbed the solid body of the catfish into inertia.

The city seemed even more deserted after that. Limp flags hung about the Belgrano monument. The Parana swept on. The fisherman began to pack up. Something like the third or fourth movement of Beethoven's *Third Symphony* was needed to break the mood. There was nothing for the soul on the waterfront of Rosario. Only death.

⋆

Ground mist. Early morning on the pampas south of Rosario. The same early morning ground mist which had hidden the runways of Ezeiza airport from the overnight Caracas-Buenos Aires flight yesterday. Although only thirty or forty feet thick, its impenetrable whiteness had blanketted out the necessary positioning lights – causing the Viasa aircraft to suddenly abort its slow descent towards a hidden Argentina and wheel off to port to touch down in Montevideo. There was no mist in Uruguay: the smallest country in Latin America occupying what was essentially one big farm (about the size of England and Wales) on the flatlands to the north of the Plate. It wasn't allowed – with a three million population which was almost entirely made up of former immigrants from Europe, clear skies, a Swiss-like calm and an atmosphere of freshly-scrubbed cleanliness prevailed.

They were nice enough at Montevideo but they wouldn't let us out of the transit lounge. Two hours elapsed before the mist to the west and on the Argentinian side of the Plate had dissipated sufficiently to allow a plane to land. Two hours in such a place after twelve hours or so in the air is like two hours in a doctor's waiting room.

The mist lifted slightly faster at Rosario. Except where it was heavily impregnated with smoke. I had made an early start from the downtown hotel and planned a retreat back to the huge metropolis at the mouth of the Parana. Driving across the pampas took too long – they would have to be flown across.

Thoughts of another day on the eucalyptus conveyor belt could not be entertained. There was an alternative route which swung further to the south and then picked up the main highway reaching into Buenos Aires from Mendoza and the Chilean border – nearly six hundred miles to the west. The route from Rosario led first to the town of Pergamino. However, there was still this mist to contend with.

*

Smoke billowed over a dimly perceived industrial suburb of Rosario. A clutter of down-at-heel residential and commercial buildings, fenced off industrial plants surrounded by wasteland, shanty villages made of packing cases and sheets of scrap metal, piles of rubbish and evil-looking pools of water. The social programmes of a secure, settled and prosperous future had clearly faltered. Potentially rich Argentina – the bread basket of South America – was struggling as much as the Andean countries.

The smoke drifted away but the earth was still wreathed in white vapour. As I left the city, the ground mist of the pampas swirled back to restrict vision. The road was poorer than that of the previous day. Potholes frequently loomed dangerously out from the limits of visibility. Somewhere in the mist were the ubiquitous eucalyptus trees, the maize and the flax but nothing of them could be seen – only a foot or two of glistening grasses and the grey outlines of bushes. And, as the sun began to beat down on its surface, the mist grew worse. It became very light and hovered only ten feet or so above ground. I suspected the tips of trees were now showing through into clear air but sufficient vapours continued to hug the ground and envelop the moving car that it considerably slowed any progress.

Suddenly, not many miles from Pergamino, it was gone. Like a curtain being drawn and instantly flooding a night-time room, the full brightness of day came in an instant: the air was clear; the level pampas stretched as far as the eye could see and the country road ahead diminished to a fine point on the completely flat horizon. Overhead, a huge blue sky. All around, near and far, clumps of eucalyptus, fields of maize and fields of flax.

Or was it something else? A plant with small browning leaves which not only grew in lines of low bushes in the fields but which also appeared to be deliberately planted on any spare strip of rough land at the roadside or even in the gardens of the occasional prairie house.

Was this the Argentinian herb tea called *yerba mate*? The drink of the *gaucho*? The accompaniment to the self-reliant life on the open range and a diet almost entirely made up of fresh steak seasoned with salt. The *mate* washed down the steak. It was the southern cowboy's equivalent of salt pork, beans and coffee.

The southern cowboy: ironically, a roving life of cattle-herding on the prairie which was about as short-lived in Argentina as it proved to be Oklahoma, Kansas and Nebraska. And both had been killed by the same enemy. The romantic image of days in the saddle and nights of song around a flickering campfire were as much doomed by the slow march of European immigrant farmers eager to put the pampas under plough as they were by farmers and then railroad gangs who pushed lines of communication into the west and into areas that had previously seen only waving grass and the high arch of the blue sky.

*

But was it really romantic out on the grasslands of the nineteenth century? Hindsight always picks up the brightest colours and conveniently delegates all the duller aspects to a kind of forgotten background. When Charles Darwin rode along the banks of the Parana to Rosario in 1832, it seemed to him a very different place. Hardly the same country at all. A place of thistles '*...in some parts as high as a horse's back, but in others* [where] *they had not sprung up... the ground was bare and dusty as on a turnpike road.' 'When the thistles are full-grown,'* he wrote '*...the great beds are impenetrable*' and with tracks known only to '*...robbers... who inhabit them and sally forth at night to rob and cut throats with impunity.'*

Darwin found – as well as too many thistles – that the pampas were incredibly flat. Rather boringly flat, although he was too polite to note that down.

> *...For many leagues north and south of Rozario, the country is really level. Scarcely anything which travellers have written about its extreme flatness can be considered an exaggeration. At sea, a person's eye being six feet above the surface of the water, his horizon is two miles and four-fifths distant. In a like manner, the more level the plain, the more nearly does the horizon approach within these narrow limits; and this, in*

> *my opinion, entirely destroys that grandeur which one would have imagined that a vast level plain would have possessed.*

A bit more scientific, perhaps, than being caught up with the conveyor-belt theory and the repeated flicking-up of clumps of recycling eucalyptus trees, but then – in 1832 – the former was still in its early stages of development and the latter were still in Australia!

⋆

Pergamino hove into view: a few streets in a grid pattern leading off the main street; a grain elevator or two near the railroad tracks. Not much going on except the occasional scrunch of rubber tyre on gravel, sometimes a bird flying past and sometimes an ant narrowly escaping being squashed under the rockers of a veranda chair. Pergamino didn't have to be in Argentina, it could have been anywhere: Maple Creek, Saskatchewan; Plainville, Kansas; Strawn, Texas.

But Lujan was in Argentina. On the main Mendoza-Buenos Aires route. A place which also arrested Darwin's attention when he saw the Argentinian version of a wagon train heading west.

> *...I should never have thought it possible for a bullock waggon to have crawled along: as it was, they scarcely went at the rate of a mile an hour. We passed a train of waggons and a troop of beasts on their road to Mendoza. The distance is about 580 geographical miles, and the journey is generally performed in fifty days. These wagons are very long, narrow, and thatched with reeds; they have only two wheels, the diameter of which in some cases is as much as ten feet. Each*

is drawn by six bullocks, which are urged by a goad at least twenty feet long... the whole apparatus looked like some implement of war.

It was said to be a forerunner of one of these medieval contraptions – carrying an image of the Virgin Mary – which became stuck in mud at Lujan in 1630. Despite extra men and bullocks being drafted in, the clumsy vehicle proved impossible to shift. Eventually, it was (conveniently) decided that the Virgin had willed that her image should stay there.

★

A nice bit of lateral thinking as it turned out. The image is still there – and on the altar of a church whose neo-Gothic bulk could be seen rising out of the eastern horizon long before the rest of the town made an appearance. Also, instead of a lot of wasted energy arm-wrestling with the Almighty to get the Virgin Mary to move along, the faithful now came to Lujan.

A busy church and a busy town servicing its pilgrims – full of that rather odd mix of candle-ridden claustrophobia, affliction and candy-floss tackiness which tends to accompany such shrines. Day-trippers from the metropolis were putting a heavy strain on the facilities; it being Sunday, a great stream of coaches, cars and ambulances had arrived from Buenos Aires and the church was full of queues of people in pullovers or plastic rainwear waiting to kiss the wooden foot of a crucified Christ whilst others took a slightly more hygienic option and prayed.

Not only was the church of Lujan full, most of the tables in nearby cafés and restaurants were taken by visitors since the serving of lunch had reached its busiest period. All around those same urban, European faces filled Argentina. Everyone seemed quite elderly – even younger people. The spirit of the rollicking *gauchos* was gone; Lujan would probably have been too pious for their tastes even when they did roam the grasslands to the west. These city folk made Argentina seem as if it had passed from its dynamic youth to the beginning of an active and prosperous middle age and then jumped straight into retirement on a slender pension. Life could only be tough at an inflation rate of 20,266% unless you had access to international hard currency accounts. Everyone was waiting for the great political figure who would hove on the Argentinian scene, set the economy to rights and allow the country to leave the twentieth century in the same expansive way that it had entered it.

But time was running out. Menem had flair but did he have the rest? Galtieri had tried the 'smoke and mirrors' trick of *Las Malvinas* but that had ended in tears.

★

In the 1930s and 1940s, it looked as if Juan Peron might be the man for whom the Argentinians were waiting. And 'Evita', of course. Peron was the 'man of the people' who had developed his power base on a platform of wealth redistribution. A man who came at a time when the prosperity of the country was deemed to be gathered into too few hands. An Argentina whose industrialisation, transportation and export capability was under the control of too many foreign owners. Peron wanted to shift wealth towards wage-earners and away from stock holders and profit-stripping. He was in favour of nationalisation.

Having spent time in Italy as a military attaché, he was a man who was also very familiar with how Mussolini had made the trains run on time. Also an author of history books, a champion fencer, skier and boxer, stood six feet in height and was a proud of a mix of Mestizo, Italian and French ancestry. He might have been the man to take the economy on to new heights. But posterity suggests he was also the man who put the first knife into the goose that laid the golden egg.

★

As the rest of the world grappled with war, Peron staged a successful military coup in 1943 that led him to the role of Vice President and Minister of War in 1945 and President of Argentina in 1946. For a few years, the curious phenomenon of Peronism sat in the driving seat of the country's politics: an authoritarian but paternalistic mixture which was part communism, part Tamany Hall and part capitalism. The time of Evita and *los descamisados* – the shirtless ones.

But Evita (Peron's second wife) died of cancer in 1952 and Peronism started to look more and more threadbare. Accusations of corruption, demagoguery and oppression grew louder. Spells of military control interspersed with Peronist rule began as economic conditions started to slide during the 1960s and 1970s. There was the 'dirty war' in the late 1970s. Then – after South Georgia, San Carlos, Goose Green, Bluff Cove and all that – there was that remorseless rise to an inflation rate of 20,266%. Perhaps the song *Don't cry for me – Argentina* should really have begun with the words: '*I'll cry for you – Argentina*'.

★

Once more I found myself in Buenos Aires, where election signs asking its twelve million population to '*VOTE MENEM*' still covered many of the walls of the suburban residential areas. The suburbs which had covered the pampas. Instead of maize or *yerba mate,* there was now a wide vista of urban buildings reaching to the horizon. Instead of the open road, elevated motorways streaked through mile after mile of white buildings fenced in by rectangles of tree-lined streets. Instead of the vertical relief provided by the eucalyptus trees, the verticality of TV aerials, illuminated signs and the occasional church tower stood in their place.

This was the city which had made Graham Greene's Corrientes seem provincial. This was a city which, in its heyday, had sufficient wealth, boulevards and cosmopolitan elegance to rival Paris or Vienna. This was the city of café life where *Señora* Plarr (the mother of Eduardo the half-friend of the British Honorary Consul) had sacrificed her beauty to *alfajores* stuffed with *dulce de leche* in the tea rooms of the Calle Florida. This was where those well-sculptured cheek-bones and that slender neck had disappeared under three chins and the heavy pouches of constipation. The shirtless ones were still in Buenos Aires, too. Fringing the outer edge of suburbia had been more of the places the Argentinians called *villas miserias* – the cardboard and corrugated-iron towns of the new generation of *los descamisados.*

★

Despite inflation and a cut-back on conspicuous consumption, Buenos Aires was still cosmopolitan. And – like all great cities – it remained a place of strong visual contrasts. Particularly where a late afternoon sun broke through the foliage of boulevard trees in the more affluent part of the city and illuminated the glass and gilt entrances to exclusive apartment blocks. Expatriates? Or those who were somehow still managing to remain secure, settled and prosperous under the shadow of 20,266%? At dusk, in the vicinity of Belgrano University, waiters in pavement bistros preparing for their patrons by chalking up the dinner menu. In the semi-darkness of early evening in the Plaza de Mayo where the *Madres de la Plaza de Mayo* still gathered every week to mourn the loss of sons and daughters who vanished in the 'dirty war'. In the full-darkness of mid-evening a red-robed cardinal in the nearby cathedral intoning an Easter message to a packed congregation – perhaps including *las madres*. And in the late evening the wrought iron entrances to the underground Metro system rising amongst the plane trees and pavements as they did in the squares, avenues and arrondissements of Haussmann's Paris.

★

It might have been easier to find a bed for the night in Paris. All that time – from late afternoon to late evening – I had been searching for a modest hotel. Traffic swirled and stopped, turned and accelerated continuously through the long thoroughfares or the narrower residential streets of the huge city. Nothing materialised. Only the large illuminated name of the city-centre Hilton constantly enticing the weary traveller to throw in the towel, hand over his credit card and wait for the room rate to rise at the same speed as Argentinian inflation.

The Hilton it had to be – but even getting back to the foot of the illuminated sign was complicated. Sunday night in a Catholic country was a night when everybody was in town. The place was the complete opposite to a Saturday afternoon in Rosario. Late traffic slowly ground its way through throngs of people and a forest of flickering neon. Crowds were everywhere in those central streets. It was the Soho of South America, the Omonia Square of the New World: pedlars, sellers of almost every major newspaper, a shop stacked high with a global range of canned beer; pizza parlours; hamburger stands; cinemas with queues for the next performance, bars, strip clubs and so on.

Something turned up just before I reached the Hilton – a cheaper option.

★

I still had it in mind to get to Corrientes, but the only suitable way to reach into the interior and back again on the same day was a flight to the town of Posadas – also a river town on the Parana, also a frontier town with Paraguay but upstream of Corrientes and nearly two hundred miles to the east.

The town of Graham Greene or the towns of the Jesuit Priests – it was going to have to be a choice. One was a living place, but given colour and texture in a novel of the mid-twentieth century; the others were dead and ruined but a fascinating insight into the eighteenth century.

I chose the ruins. They lay on the edge of the northern pampas where the vegetation grew thicker and the endless grassland finally petered out. This was the part of Argentina called *Misiones* and it stretched for some one hundred and fifty miles east of Posadas.

★

No mist on early morning Mesopotamia but cloud cover hiding most of the pampas until Posadas was almost reached. Then, just over an hour after leaving the capital, the aircraft sank through a swirling blankness and out again into that now familiar sudden clarity. Like the vapours on the Rosario-Pergamino road hiding a sunlit sky above, this descent had somehow come through clouds to a sunlit surface several thousand feet below.

It was still flat – extremely flat. More like a billiard table than a billiard table. It even seemed to be covered in felt – albeit more grass-green than felt-green. There were no fields and only widely spaced plantations of dark trees to give the impression that a mighty hand had sewn on a few patches to the cloth and had made a bit of a dog's fist of it.

We dropped down a thousand feet or so and still the felt refused to transform itself into a landscape of ditches and rocky patches. The aircraft could land anywhere on this landscape. The entire surface of this part of the Earth had turned itself into a runway. Only the fact that there was no sign of Posadas anywhere in the vicinity was disconcerting.

The last few hundred feet and it wasn't a billiard table, of course. A slight undulation would have made any giant's game somewhat unpredictable; the occasional drainage ditch would have disagreed with any aircraft's landing gear. But flat grassland, nonetheless. Verticality was provided by heaps of bright red soil suggesting termite or ant colonies and the low brick terminal buildings of Posadas airport.

★

Another landing; another Argentina. The Atlantic world had gone. All those urban Europeans with pale faces under lightly overcast skies; they had gone, too. This was South America again. Hispanic South America.

The South America where it can cost $7 to hire a car, or $70, or even $700. I couldn't believe it. The man insisted that the newest pesos were worth one-for-one with the US dollar! This was up-country Argentina; whatever they did to the money in the big city was their business. It was a holiday weekend, the prices were all printed out on a chart, exchange rates were not his concern and did I want the single Ford Sierra he had for hire or not.

You can't spend an entire day in a tiny terminal on a billiard table in northern Argentina. Not after flying all the way down South America to see the country and then flying another five hundred miles north to get away from its monotony. The room for negotiation was somewhat cramped too. How can you walk away from a rotten deal in disgust, breeze through the doors of the buildings and then be confronted with grassland stretching to the horizon in every direction. I mentally came back inside, acknowledged acceptance and we left the terminal.

It wasn't even his car! And it wasn't parked somewhere nearby. A precious hour passed whilst we drove towards the town of Posadas, which seemed to be hiding where the ground sloped gently towards the River Parana, bumped down some back-streets of red gravel and stones on its residential fringe, unlocked a corrugated-iron door and then both scraped it heavily back on creaky hinges to reveal a dilapidated garage and a dust-covered car. Then a process of laborious paperwork began. It was some kind of subcontracting deal: a garage-owning friend brushed out the interior of the Sierra, established that its petrol tank was empty and not full and wiped away the dust on the windscreen. Another detour would be necessary to fill up with fuel in Posadas, another hour lost. Any change of plan to Corrientes was now out of the question – it would have to be the Jesuit Missions.

*

The Sierra was a poor swap for seven hundred dollars in plastic money. Someone had surgically stubbed out a cigarette on the section of perspex above the fuel gauge indicator in such a way that it was impossible to see through to the needle. The same heavy smoker had extinguished his fags in a number of other less crucial places where small circles of melted plastic or holes in vinyl remained to tell the tale. An odour of cigarettes lingered in the vehicle although it was otherwise clean. The brakes were clearly unreliable.

Posadas was a busy Monday-morning sort of place. Rather endearing and typically Latin American in that all the navigational signs seemed to have been removed during the Falklands War and never put back. It was not necessary to put them back – everyone knew the ways in and out of town.

Except me. One way out of town which a queue of trucks and buses seemed to be lining up for was the way into Paraguay: an Argentinian customs post, a short ferry-ride across the Parana and then another Paraguayan customs post. The same green country on either side.

In inadvertently joining the queue of traffic exiting Posadas by crossing the Parana, I suddenly realised that the view of Paraguay across the river must have been a very similar view to that wistfully taken by Dr Plarr. Across that same River Parana – wondering in that same way what was going on over there. No more than a few short decades earlier, wondering about the iron grip of Stroessner.

Wondering, in fact, how the country had managed to survive into the twentieth century at all – considering its disastrous history since independence. It wasn't just the thousands like Plarr Senior – left to rot in remote Paraguayan police stations during the 1960s and 1970s as the General's 'police', military and official assassins ransacked behind any unlocked door they came across. Worse had been experienced during the terrible War of the Triple Alliance when – during the late 1860s – the tiny population of the country fought off the torturers and murderers of their own leader (Marchal Francisco Lopez – the 'Napoleon of South America') as well as the combined armies of Brazil, Argentina and Uruguay. At the end of it – out of a population of 800,000 – fewer than 200,000 survived. Most of these were women, only 14,000 were male. Of this reduced number, those who were above the age of twenty years and still alive in the 1870s amounted to 2,100 persons!

★

It was all history now – the War of the Triple Alliance and Stroessner. Paraguay had recovered. The dictator had gone – replaced three years earlier (in 1989) by a *coup d'état* which changed one general for another; this time a General Rodriguez. Elections were promised in 1993. Paraguay had more to cry about than even Argentina.

The country across the Parana looked green like Argentina, was mostly flat like Argentina and had the potential like Argentina to become one of the prosperous members of the twenty-first century global community. It was much smaller, of course, and in the early 1990s still had a few medical problems as well as its propensity for megalomanic military governance. On the north bank of the river were said to linger traces of tuberculosis, typhoid, dysentery, hepatitis, dengue fever, hookworm, venereal disease, goitre and leprosy. The fact that most of these were up in the Chaco and in the Mato Grosso parts of the country gave some consolation but it still seemed a damned sight safer on the south bank.

Most visitors to Posadas finally found the road leading north-east out of the town and into the province of Misiones. The pampas were no more. Savanna began and then low hills started to rise to the east; the southernmost beginnings of that huge Brazilian plateau which stretched endlessly north until it enveloped the Brazilia which lay a thousand miles away. Soon, the countryside was neither grassy nor flat. Verdant sub-tropical forests had taken over.

This was beautiful country after the pale prairies of the south. It must have seemed like a paradise to the Jesuits as they left behind the melancholic uplands of the Brazilian plateau or the stark Andean highlands. The dark greens and bright greens of sub-tropical foliage, the red soils, sometimes an outcrop of a red or purplish-red sandstone, a wide blue sky overhead – this was the country of an Amerindian people called the Guarani.

*

It was amongst the pastoral setting of hills and vales, tre and rivers that the Jesuit fathers of the seventeenth and eighteenth century gained permission from the Pope and the secular authorities (no one was quite sure whether this part of the South American interior was under the Spanish crown or the Portuguese crown although the former claimed the territory), to build their 'New Jerusalem'.

This social experiment was an attempt to redress the balance; to live with the indigenous peoples of the Americas rather than force them into labour gangs, it was a little like communism, a little like Utopia, a little like Sunday School, a little like New Harmony Mills. It worked amazingly successfully – for one hundred and fifty years and until the Jesuits themselves were disbanded by a Pope Clement XIV fearing the power of large multi-national organisations. The green forests spreading across the broad upper valley of the Parana (where the three modern countries of Argentina, Paraguay and Brazil all come together), once held thirty or more large Jesuit-organised communities of Guarani artisans and craftsmen, farmers and stock breeders. In their heyday, communal houses and great sandstone churches rose amongst the foliage, the bells of Matins and Aves tolled through the trees, choral music and choir-song echoed across wide plazas and the entire population celebrated the consecration of the sacrament amongst gold, gilt and candlelight. For a time, the 'New Jerusalem' had been built in the New World.

⋆

St Ignacious Mini was one such place. Its end came not long after the withdrawal of the Jesuits. Late eighteenth-century *bandierantes* swooped in from the Brazilian coast and herded the singers, musicians, craftsfolk and stock-breeders away to slavery and despair. New Jerusalem vanished like a mirage.

Except that its ruins still remained in the forest. And the twentieth century had brought many from far and wide in coaches and cars to see what it might have been like.

A difficult viewing. No ghostly echoes of the Society of Jesus were visible until deep inside the ruins. The modern community of Guarani craftsmen had made sure of that and had turned out an amazing range of baskets and bags, pots and plastic wall-plaques, imitation mandolins and wooden leaves. They also did colour film, fried chips, cheeseburgers, Marlboros and six-packs of iced coke. Lads would park a car for a pittance and postcards of seventeenth century *reducione* life was available for a few dollars more. Had *bandierantes* pushed their way through the trees two hundred years later and found St Ignacious Mini they might well have sheered off and gone in search of some quieter spot.

Inside, however, some serenity had been preserved. Single-story buildings of red sandstone stood in rows like unroofed barracks; the grass-covered plaza remained wide and empty, the splendid façade of a large church still towered over its space; enough carved red sandstone masonry showed the skills achieved.

The church and the *reducione* had once served a community of four thousand souls. But the ruins offered little insight to what life had really been like under the priests. A kibbutz? A kind of paternalistic, theocratic internment camp? A refuge of tranquillity from a world of greed and slavery? A nineteenth-century British public school? Ampleforth? Round the clock muscular Christianity?

★

Those *bandierantes* might well have sheered away from the Iguacu Falls as well as St Ignacious had they come through in the late twentieth century rather than in the 1790s. Iguacu was the place where the upstream River Parana broke into countless streams amongst the trees before gracefully spilling down over a lip of rock several hundred feet in height.

It was undoubtedly one of the world's beautiful places. Rainbows linked the many cataracts and water seemed to be everywhere in the dense vegetation which surrounded the encounter of the great river with the rocks of the hard Brazilian plateau. A wide gorge curved back into the plateau: stretching away on one cliffed side was Brazil; stretching away on the other was Argentina. Tiny Brazilian tourists could be seen peering over the shimmering water haze at the Argentinian tourists who stood all around. Both were undoubtedly taking as much video footage of each other as of the cascading water. And buying six-packs of iced coke. And sets of those wooden leaves.

The brakes nearly did for me on the way back. There was twenty minutes to go before take-off. Darkness had fallen and the navigational aids pointing the traveller through Posadas had not improved since the morning. I wasn't quite sure where the airport was in the darkness of the surrounding grassland. Heavy traffic had begun a slow westwards journey in the direction of Corrientes. Time was slipping away. The plane for Buenos Aires was the last of the day and the only means of catching the early morning long-haul flight back from Argentina to Venezuela. I swung out behind a slow-moving truck and found the glare of approaching headlights dangerously close in the opposite lane. I braked sharply and the Ford Sierra lurched the wrong way. The headlights came very close, very fast. I swung the wheel hard to the right and slewed into blackness – the rear of the Ford probably missing whatever was approaching by inches. Nothing obstructed the skid through dust and red mud on the hard shoulder. Another swing brought the car back on tarmac and the sign for the airport entrance suddenly came into view.

The plane taxied down the runway and into the air. The man with a day's earnings of $700 drove his dodgy vehicle back to the garage. He probably couldn't see that the petrol tank was empty.

*

Argentina to Venezuela. Two thousand miles northwards across the interior of South America. Lifting off from the densely packed humanity of Buenos Aires and into the deserted centre of the continent. No morning mist over the pampas this time – the vast flatness of Mesopotamia spread out again far below under a cloudless sky. Then a fading of the green into the lighter landscapes of the dry Chaco country bordering the eastern side of the Andes: partly northern Argentina; partly western Paraguay. A fearsome loneliness down there. Desert land was only rarely crossed by narrow white ribbons of road snaking from one *estancia* to another. Then no roads – just short white strips close to the buildings which suggested that the late twentieth century now used a light aircraft as much as a pick-up truck.

Perhaps some of those inhabitants of the small clusters of buildings didn't want to be seen too much about town;

perhaps after World War II, some of them preferred the isolation.

Then, further north, came floods. Water everywhere – perhaps the tropical lowlands of Bolivia; perhaps the headwaters of the River Madeira flowing into the Amazon below Manaus; the network of rivers feeding into the Madre de Dios, perhaps the Mato Grosso.

Half of South America. I would have liked to see the other half – the northwards sweep across Amazonas and into the Orinoco basin but clouds began to coalesce over the equator. Soon there was nothing but a uniform greyness which persisted for the remainder of the journey and only parted to allow the runways of Simon Bolivar airport to appear in close view several hours later. The Atlantic had gone – the Caribbean flooded in.

Chapter Ten

Weekend in Chile

23°30'S: '*BUEN VIAJE AMIGO*' shouted a battered sign above the grave. The man – Alfredo Molina – who still gave passing travellers such a cheery salute on this desert road crossing the Tropic of Capricorn, had taken his last glimpse of it in 1962. On the 31st October, 1962 he had presumably crashed head-on with an oncoming vehicle or fallen asleep and jack-knifed into the dust at the side of the road. He was forty-eight.

Of course, apart from the sheer inconvenience of being dead, he was in as perfect a condition on a March day in 1992 as he was when he had suffered his misfortune thirty years earlier. Nothing lived in this place – absolutely nothing. No plants; no birds; no animals and no micro-organisms. The quiet work of decay was left high, dry and abandoned. Thirty years were as nothing to Alfred Molina – he would be in this spot for centuries. The mummified bodies of Indian women in an oasis village not far away had been there from long before the first Spanish conquistadores trudged down into the western edge of the New World. They were there still – in the tiny settlement of San Pedro de Atacama.

33°30'S and great wooden doors closing on a dim interior – muting the sound of traffic on the Avenida del

Libertador General O'Higgins. Stone pillars marching down the length of a nave – stout and ancient. A floor of grey flagstones leading off into side-chapels where the flicker of candles pointed to hopes pending, hopes satisfied, hopes dashed but stoically endured. A glass cabinet resting against the base of one of the pillars was covered with such hopes. Hopes expressed in the form of little notes tucked into its frame.

'*Gracia por los favores,*' said one in the spidery handwriting of a woman. '*Gracia por mi liberti,*' said another in the bolder hand of a man.

Inside the case was a torso. The waxy head and shoulders of Christ – *El Señor de la Cana*. Blood trickled down his upturned face from a vicious ring of thorns, and more blood oozed from deep open spear-cuts on his chest. A very particular Hispanic-Catholic interpretation of the pain and gore of the crucifixion scene. Latin Christianity had taken deep roots in this country of fertile lands, of vineyards and of tall Lombardy poplars.

39°30'S and rain blown inshore by the strong west wind. A wind which pushed the gulls far from the sea and away from Pacific harbours where yellow boats bobbed at their moorings and there was a strong smell of wrack and fish. A wind which swept them towards the lakes and the mountains. A wind which rustled through autumnal woods; sent yellow leaves scattering over the meadows; pushed across wheatfields and orchards; spun drifts of snow deep into mountain gullies.

49°30'S and glaciers creaking down to a cold ocean.

56°S and Cape Horn.

All this – at one end, a desert so dry that it was like the moistureless surface of Mars; at the other end, a landscape constantly soaked and pummelled by the full blast of the Roaring Forties. All this was Chile.

*

A country difficult to grasp mentally. A country two thousand seven hundred miles long and only one hundred and twenty-five miles wide. A country whose twelve million or so inhabitants had to squeeze into a narrow corridor between the mountains and the sea and yet had to contend with internal distances longer than the width of Europe. If Chile were placed like a stick with one end touching London, its other extremity would reach Niamey on the River Niger. If – like the hands on a huge clock – Chile were then swung eastwards from London, the tip of the seconds hand would sweep past Stalin's city of Magnitogorsk in the Urals and on across the Caspian Sea to Tehran. If Chile were a bridge with one end of its span secured to the Canary Islands, then the other end would reach Mexico – a bridge across the Mid-Atlantic.

More than 38° of latitude separated the frontier with Peru that lay north of the Tropic of Capricorn from the 'frontier' with Antarctica that lay south of Cape Horn. The worlds at either end of the Chilean Republic were vastly different from each other. And – in many respects – the Chilean Republic was quite different from the rest of Latin America.

*

The distance covered by the Lan-Chile flight from Caracas to Santiago might have taken the big new aircraft all the way to the ice-covered shores of Antarctica had it taken off from the Chilean-Peru border instead of Caracas. It was a long wearying haul through the night: three thousand four hundred miles across the equator with only one brief, hot stop at Lima.

Surprisingly, the time was still only 4.30 a.m. when the Boeing 767 bounced once or twice on a long dark runway and then rolled slowly to a standstill in front of the terminal buildings at Santiago airport. There it stood, surrounded by a seemingly flat and rather dry countryside with the blackness punctuated by only a few yellow lights. No city was evident but urban life was clearly not far away – the cool night air carried with it a faint odour of smoke and of exhaust fumes. A weary file of passengers made its way into the customs and baggage area.

Caracas to Santiago. From one city of four million people clustered in a valley high about the Caribbean to another city of four million people supposedly clustered below the majestic Andes and verging on the vastness of the Pacific Ocean. At this early hour, there was no sign of either mountain or sea.

Santiago was different from Caracas. A vegetation change had taken place – no longer was the ubiquitous profile of palm trees to be seen everywhere. Vague upright shadows in the distance suggested the Lombardy poplars of Tuscany. The broad fronds of banana plants were gone; dim ground patterns seen on the final descent of the plane had suggested the ordered cultivation of citrus fruits and of vines. People had changed, too – there was less noise; less chatter. We had entered the quiet sober self-containment of an authoritarian state and everyone seemed to be keeping their heads down; toeing the line.

It was just about the time when the human body was supposed to reach its lowest ebb. Perhaps a low ebb was not the best influence on first impressions of a new country. Perhaps the rapid overnight transition from CAP's exuberant but somewhat ramshackle democratic republic to Pinochet's stern dictatorship was too much of a contrast not to require some period of adjustment. Was Chile still ruled by police and army? Did the uniformed shadow of the General continue to stamp out the slightest flicker of liberal thought in this tucked away country? Did the clock still stand as it did in the months after September 1973?

The interior of Santiago's airport seemed only half-lit. Those of its staff who worked through the small hours of the morning could occasionally be seen – terse and apparently half asleep – going about their duties. It remained noticeable how nothing of the bright flamboyance of the tropics seemed to have survived the journey – even in the queue leading up to the passport control. Clothes appeared to have mysteriously taken on a heavier and more sombre tone from one end of the flight to the other – as they had done in high Bogotá.

But there was another thing – Spanish had become much more softly spoken. And, once through into the empty waiting lounge, any outsiders coming in to greet new arrivals somehow magnified the atmosphere of containment. There was little of the usual Latin expansiveness. Handshakes served for a greeting instead of hugs and kisses and slaps on the back; relatives quickly stood apart rather than becoming locked together in some heaving, fraternal mêlée.

But it was 4.30 in the morning. As time marched on towards dawn and the lounge emptied of the last of the Caracas arrivals, it began slowly to fill with the earliest of the outward-bound departures. These were people travelling internally – south to Valdivia or on to the Chilean part of Patagonia: people in plastic raincoats or sensible shoes; people with pale complexions who waited quietly at the baggage check-in for their 7 a.m. flight. With each new arrival came a little more of the smoky city air of the night beyond – a thin smoke building up progressively inside until it seemed that an urban pall was beginning to invade every nook and cranny of the spacious yet barely-furnished hall. That night beyond yielded up none of its secrets. Nothing other than darkness existed out there – darkness punctuated by a few yellow lights.

To extrapolate a cultural perspective across an entire country from less than an hour of two inside a terminal building at Chile's main international airport seemed more than a little dubious. Nonetheless, it began to feel as if this Chile was not simply another South American country hovering on a knife-edge between the Developed World and the Third World. It was not an Emerging Nation: Chile had emerged – albeit strongly and fiercely governed. A sense of purpose and organisation had come in with the cool atmosphere. It seemed that the Latin character and the Latin world had become less evident and more dilute as it spread into the temperate parts of the southern hemisphere. The business of living appeared to be conducted at a level well above the surface of chaos. In fact, this long and narrow country – isolated (as it was) by both geography and politics from the world of the 1970s and the 1980s – looked as if it was getting along quite well in the world of the early 1990s. 'Erewhon' – that mythical invention of Samuel Butler which lay hidden across snowy mountains and difficult to reach; Erewhon was doing okay. Shut off from the main population centres of Argentina by being on the far side of the pampas and over the high wall of the Andes; physically sealed off to the north by the altiplano of Bolivia and the chaotic in-fighting of Peru; facing westwards to half a world of water in the Pacific Ocean – this place did not sit astride any of the great commercial crossroads of world trade. And yet it was a country that was getting more and more of those very drinkable Cabernet Sauvignons, Merlots, Pinots and Rieslings on to the world's tables.

Another hour passed. More people for Valdivia and the flight to Patagonia struggled in from a darkness that seemed to be taking an eternity to evolve from black night to pale dawn. Huddled groups began to form – those Patagonia-bound already in their overcoats or wearing thick patterned sweaters. More and more heavy suitcases began to accumulate – each new entrant sliding across the plastic floor tiles to join the jumble already piling up around the check-in desk. The latter remained empty, however, and the conveyor belt behind it was motionless. Fast asleep even – and so far from a sudden stir into life that any progressive removal of bag and baggage to a place behind the rubber-curtained hatchway where a 7.00 a.m. plane stood waiting seemed most unlikely. Perhaps Chile was just another Latin American country after all – airline staff coming when they were ready rather than when their passengers were ready.

In the absence of a uniformed sector, the place was represented by its only other operating staff-member – a rather glum-looking man with a broom who worked his way somnambulantly along and under each row of plastic seats, skirted deftly around the waiting luggage and then disappeared into a dim recess. He reappeared every thirty minutes and began the circuit again. The fact that it was not a particularly pressing job did nothing to alter the cycle of cleaning. Indeed, it was clearly a task several hours ahead of its due position in the timetable of events. There was nothing of the usual litter of cups and sandwich wrappings to tidy away, collect up and bin. There was no coffee, no tea and no breakfast to be had anywhere in Santiago airport. Dawn took a tediously long time arriving in Chile.

At seven in the morning, the sky began to show the faintest sign of approaching day. It was, after all, almost autumn in the southern hemisphere and the sun was not in the habit of jumping to attention in the same way as it did in the tropics. A tentative lightening of the sky slowly grew stronger until a misty scene became visible through the glass doors of the terminal lounge. The vague outline of sunlit hills formed a western rim to the flatness of what soon appeared as the valley in which the airport lay. To the east, through windows on the opposite side of the building, a touch of white glinted from an impossibly high position in the sky. Was it an incoming plane? Nothing had landed since the Lan-Chile flight. It took a few minutes for the realisation to surface that this glinting came from snow – from Andean peaks that were over twenty-two thousand feet in altitude. There were mountains out there which were towering up towards the heights of the Himalayas although reticent to show themselves very clearly in the faintly polluted air of the valley floor.

And Santiago? That air still indicated that the city was not far off but – like La Paz – from the vantage point of its main airport, it was nowhere to be seen.

*

With the day came a certain amount of action. Airline staff emerged and began dealing with the suitcases and the people eager to get to Patagonia; offices opened for currency exchange; a row of cabins became visible in the terminal car park where vehicles could be hired; the world seemed to be readying itself for business; then everything started all at once. It was as if a bell had rung or a switch turned on.

All this suddenness came as a bit of a contrast to the sleepiness of the pre-dawn hours. And, it was a sudden shock – after flying down the length of South America – to grapple with a confusion of dollars before breakfast; a task neither good for the head nor the wallet. The exchange rate in Chile, it seemed, was one US dollar to three hundred and fifty Chilean pesos. That fact was clear enough – except that a Chilean peso was indicated by the same $ sign as a US$. So $1 was exchanged for $350 and – with the fuzzy head of early morning – the alarming concept of hiring a car for $10,000 a day could easily be overcome by the happy thought that $10,000 was only $28! And it was a very nice car (a new 2.0 litre Peugeot) on offer for that very reasonable sum. Sounded like a bargain. I buckled up and slid out of Santiago airport well satisfied with the deal.

Neat estates of incredibly tiny houses – each with a little garden and some with half-timbering on their gables. They looked as if a row of British suburban semi-detacheds had been lifted bodily into the southern hemisphere and shrunk to half-size on the way. Taller and more spacious buildings took over, however, as the road grew closer and grander on the edge of the downtown part of Santiago. The wide boulevard – Avenida O'Higgins – filled with buses and people on their way to work. A strip of lawn interceded between the lanes and then – intermittently – heroic stone figures on horseback stood poised amongst shrubbery. Then the great wooden doors of the city's Franciscan church were passed on the right; the church which hid the votive hopes of the faithful and grateful and the torso of the Hispanic Christ.

Downtown, the misty, smoky early morning light of the airport and suburbs had quickly changed to the bright expectant glare of a Mediterranean morning. It was the light of open café tables, croissants, of coffee – and of breakfast! Hunger pains began to build up. There must be a multitude of places serving breakfast in this big work-a-day city.

The traffic slowed and stopped at a red light. A considerable stream of modern-looking buses and smart cars began to move across and down the intersecting boulevard. I switched on the car radio and tried to keep pace with the news in Chile. Some sort of explosion had occurred in a *polvorineo*. What on earth was a polvorineo? The intersecting boulevard had emptied and the engine of the Peugeot purred quietly under the bonnet waiting for the signal to change from red to green. It was a lovely motor – this Peugeot. At the mid-to-high end of the range. At $28 for a 2.0 litre, some of those smaller cars for hire must only cost $7 a day.

Was that too good to be true? Was that exchange rate calculation right? I suddenly realised there was no comma or dot where a person would normally expect to find one in $10,000 – even if they were Chilean $s. What if they were not Chilean $s but US ones? What if a dot was placed two places from the end and I was being debited $100 day from my credit card! And why was it that deductions like that – once thought of – proved to be some of the most difficult things in the world to eradicate mentally? After a few minutes there was absolutely no doubt about at all – the very nice Peugeot was costing $100 day!

Just something to be lived with, I supposed. It would be a small compensation for its cost if it led me to some food and a place to freshen up.

It did – in a way. After the lights once more gave the go-ahead and the traffic streamed forward, the Peugeot and I spent some unprofitable time around the leafy suburbs on the Andean side of Santiago and then settled into a firmer idea of north, south, east and west. A return was made to the city centre where a large hotel, clearly and expansively offering drive-in basement parking space loomed up at the side of one of the main boulevards. The Peugeot had no hesitation in seeking a temporary haven in its dark recesses.

I had decided as I rose in the elevator that it could by no means be a half-measures breakfast – wherever they put the dots or commas in the $s of the bill. To see anything of Chile meant a journey of at least five hundred miles and who knew what the roads or the roadside facilities might be like to the north or south of this modern city. Once in the hinterland and it could be another Bolivia – bumping along in the dust as the tarmac gave out some one hundred miles outside Santiago and gravel took over. Perhaps – psychologically – it was not just breakfast I needed, it was a down-payment on lunch, dinner, supper and a midnight feast, too.

From the elevator, russet carpet swept off majestically into the public rooms of the hotel. It flowed easily past a reception desk and past the several sub-reception facilities which were positioned on its fringe like tiny terminal buildings hovering near the runway of some deserted early 1950s airport. Then it swelled and flooded around far off clusters of armchairs. Then the carpet swept back once more though a series of normal-sized interior spaces displaying tapestries and carved and polished wood until – with a final flourish and curtsey – it delicately descended a foot or two, swung around (at a safe margin) from the edge of a blue-surfaced pool and announced that breakfast was served.

Tables and chairs were arranged tastefully around the side of this interior pool. Meals were consumed to the agreeable music of Vivaldi. A sumptuous cornucopia-like buffet spilled along a nearby wall – a still-life canvas of a breakfast. Fresh and preserved fruit; cereals; hot rolls; croissants; toast; eggs; bacon; sausages – hot things simmering on burnished platters; cold things filling great glass bowls to their brim. All ready for the eating and all totally neglected. The room appeared empty except for a silent Jeeves-like figure holding a silver coffee pot.

Closer inspection revealed – after the first pangs of hunger had been dampened down – that Jeeves was serving one or two other small groups of patrons hidden amongst the potted palms. Two men: one a blazered Englishman; the other a Japanese salaryman. They talked deals in hushed tones and with a brief manipulation of calculators. Fruit? wine? Tourism? Elsewhere, three middle-aged executives soon gave away their North American origins by their size, suits and haircuts. They were almost certainly in copper. There were no signs of any Chileans other than the staff. Nonetheless, this was again clearly the stuff of the 'First World' and not of the 'Second' or 'Third Worlds'. I ate as much as was humanly possible and hoped that Jeeves worked for one of a chain of hotels.

*

He was, of course, part of a big city scene. But the rest of Chile kept up a reasonable standard. There was one curious quirk about the coffee, though. The hotel seemed to command the only decent coffee pot in the country.

Elsewhere it inevitably arrived in a curiously long-drawn-out sequential process: first a sizeable tin of Nescafé with a spoon dug into the top of the granules; then a container of milk; then an empty mug or cup and saucer and then – no little time afterwards – a jug of hot water?

It wasn't just once this happened on the Pan-American highway which streaked out south of the Santiago and down the central valley – it was a ritual repeated every time and at every place I stopped. Venezuelan restaurants always brought their gin bottle to the table just to show that it was the real import and not some local hooch brewed up in a back alley. Patrons of Chilean restaurants were obviously keen to ensure they were getting Nescafé and not the real thing.

The Pan-American highway proved to be an excellent hard-surfaced road – a road which also kept up a reasonable standard until its end in Puerto Montt. Travelling south on it was to travel down that metaphorical second hand; the arm stretching from London to the River Niger. Not all the way, of course. I hadn't time. But any hypothetical romp though Europe to Africa would have seen the landscape change from green to yellow; from woodland to desert. This antipodean route did the opposite. Going south down the central valley of Chile was heading into the trees and not away from them.

The Pan-American began in 'Italy' – or was it southern 'Spain'? The landscape in which Santiago was set: the pale, dry soil; the fields of vines, maize and sunflowers; the tall Lombardy poplars – perhaps a landscape more of the valley of the Po than of the Guadalquivir but with an unmistakable atmosphere of the warm south. A landscape shaped by the early imports of Franciscan monks. In fact, with the hot, hazy sky of approaching noon it was easy to lose one's bearings and think the car was actually speeding along somewhere like the Via Emilia and not pressing down through the temperate zones of the southern hemisphere. It was the vague outline of high ground to the east which encouraged this illusion; the Andean mountain chain was easy to confuse with the Alpine mountain chain – particularly when distantly glimpsed across those wide fields of brown maize or drooping sunflowers. And the coming and going of the towns of Chile did nothing to dispel the trick: at first sight, across the fields and vineyards, the taller office blocks of Rancagua, San Fernando or Talca looked for all the world like the campaniles of the Veneto.

The road continued through this 'Italy' for a while but moved closer to Milan. Cultivation was intense but the emphasis began to shift to fruit. Peaches, plums, apricots and apples – the ripe products of the season were being collected together and shipped out from modern packing depots ringed by huge stacks of wooden boxes. 'FRUITICOLA', 'COLIFOR', 'UNIFRUTTI', 'FRUTISUR' said the company signs – often set on a neatly manicured patch of well-watered lawn.

Water for such activity was plentiful where it tumbled down from the snows of the Andes. Sometimes a river would be marked by a great swathe of pale gravel and low bushes – a chaotic contrast to the ordered agri-commercial orchards and fruit plantations all around it. Sometimes, in this gravel, flowing water had vanished and only pools marked the route from mountains to the sea. Southwards, as the land became more temperate, there was much more evidence of run-off. Increasingly, swift-flowing torrents heavy with purple-brown volcanic silt or milky-white with suspended rock flour passed through the landscape. Sometimes the glacial silt had been dropped and a clear, sparkling flow would pass under the road. In each case, river-banks were lined by a narrow fringe of brilliant green beyond which continued the pale dry soil and the brown crops of late summer.

With the crossing of the rivers – the Cachapoal, the Mataquito, the Maule – noon came and went. The hot blur of a mid-Chile afternoon began to slip by with the Pan-American continuing to swoop down through the huge farm of the central valley – a farm twenty-five miles wide and four hundred miles long!

'France' was entered somewhere south of the town of Linares. The commercial orchards continued but there was greater emphasis on vegetable crops. Then, south of the town of Los Angeles, the road quietly entered southern 'England' and the first signs of an approaching evening. Fields of wheat and barley; hedgerow alders retaining the full leaf of summer; solitary oaks standing with their broad crowns inflamed by the deepening gold of the sun. Long shadows began to reach over the harvesting in progress. I crossed the River Bio-Bio.

With that river-crossing, came not only the end of the old Spanish Empire but the end of the domains of the Inca Lords. Even the world of Latin America had ended. The Bio-Bio marked a frontier. Beyond lay the woods and rain.

Long before the 'Old West' of North America had been tamed and the Apaches, the Commanches and the others had been pushed by wagon train and railroad track into the margins of twentieth-century history, this boundary to the edge of South American colonialism had been fought over with stockade and fort, horse and rifle, ambush and counter-ambush. Mounted patrols of the seventeenth and eighteenth centuries splashed across the Bio-Bio on reprisal raids into the densely forested country beyond – seeking the 'Apaches of the South'. But these 'Apaches' (the Araucanian or Mapuche Indian peoples) fought in a land very different from Mediterranean Spain, and frequently gained the upper hand in skirmishes and guerrilla fighting amongst the endless tree cover and cool persistent rainfall of the temperate forests. It was as much the climate and weather which had drawn a boundary to the world of the conquistadores and early colonists as the Mapuches. The river was the Rhine of the Roman Empire; the Hadrian's Wall of South America.

But – beyond the Bio-Bio of the late twentieth century – the woods had largely been cleared. Foliage which once hid the Mapuche Indians had been progressively cut back over the previous one hundred years as a wave of (mostly Swiss and German) settlement began in the late nineteenth century. In sufficient numbers and with sufficient determination, axe and plough managed what gun and horse had failed to achieve. The woodlands had became part of Chile.

Now peace reigned over countryside where, in earlier years, the fights between indigenous peoples and the newcomers had taken place. The society of the Araucanian Indians did not capitulate as fast as those further north. In fact, it had been touch-and-go as to who would win – the conquistadores and those early farmers or the war-like inhabitants of the south. The business of city-building and settlement had almost faltered once or twice – even around Santiago with its more open countryside. Those fields of Franciscan vines had been hard-won.

The first of the conquistadores to brush with the Araucanos was Diego de Almagro. After an extremely arduous journey south along the Inca roads and through the desert (and leaving behind him the squabbling Pizarro brothers and the aftermath of the conquest of Peru), he and his 'Men of Chile' searched hard for an *Otra Peru* in these previously unexplored lands; for another empire of gold and fame which they were convinced would surpass even that of the Aztecs and Incas. Why should there not be more fabulous Indian worlds to be met (and overwhelmed with horse, a few cannon, indomitable will-power – and, not least, European disease)? The South American continent of these early days was still a wondrous place. Unknown civilisations could be stumbled upon in the most unlikely places and – along with the gold – offered the opportunity for millions more souls to be converted to Christianity.

But Diego de Almagro and his men grew increasingly disappointed. There was no empire to the south; instead of more Inca riches, he met only the Araucanos, increasing resistance and heavy rainfall. As they travelled back up the central valley in low spirits, there was no fruit or wine of the rich farmlands of the twentieth century to cheer them up. Only (then) a poor, harsh, dry country which offered little incentive to linger. In 1537, the 'Men of Chile' arrived back at Cuzco empty-handed and much reduced in numbers. They had nothing to report but hardship, deserts and wet forests where death stalked from tree to tree.

Land was land, however, and there was clearly enough of it for the taking to induce Pedro de Valdivia south again not long afterwards. This time the conquistadores stayed. The city of Santiago was founded, the nucleus of a slow-growing colonial settlement began, the Mapuches and other Araucanos were slowly pushed back down the central valley and coastal bridgeheads were established into their territory to the south. Valdivia was founded. The stormy island of Chiloe was settled. Fishing started in the cool, dangerous waters which lay at the edge of the Roaring Forties. The patrols across the Bio-Bio began.

★

The Pan-American showed no sign of faltering at the old frontier and the road carried on into the former woodlands as the sun dipped further beyond the hills of the coast range. The wheat began to turn rose-red as – westwards and above a hidden Pacific – the sky became a vast shifting palette of pinks, lilacs, yellows, purples and deep reds. Flaming orange streaked in – and then deep purple. First one and then another of the tints briefly glowed with almost unbelievable intensity until – as is always the way with sunsets – majesty was suddenly replaced by mundanity. Colour was still wreathed across the western sky but its glory was fading by the second. The passage from that point to darkness was brief and sobering. The sun had set on the last land for thirteen thousand miles.

Chile – on the edge of the Pacific – was the home of sunsets. Where else did land pass so far south into a hemisphere that was mostly water. South-western Australia, perhaps, or New Zealand, but the Pacific Ocean was emptier than the Indian Ocean and the Tasman Sea. It was a sunset which (unless it was watched from the deck of a ship plying up from Cape Horn to California – and most now took the shorter route through the Panama Canal), would remain unseen along latitude 39°S for a great distance around the world. That pale pink, purple and flaming orange sky would illuminate no more land until it passed swiftly over the North Island of New Zealand. Everywhere else was water – albeit shallower than the great oceans on the passage across the Bass Strait of southern

Australia – but water, nonetheless. Where there was no land; there could be no dust, no smoke and no pollution. It was a clean, clear sea breeze which came ashore on the Pacific coastline of southern Chile.

Black night in that clear air – and still nowhere near Valdivia and the planned end of the five hundred mile journey. I was growing rapidly and progressively wearier as long stretches of road emptied of traffic. The Pan-American had been left behind in the central valley. This was a quieter route which now climbed into the low hills of the Coast Range.

Midnight approached. No light shone out in the landscape; Coast Range Chile was as deserted as its roads. An Araucanian world beyond the Bio-Bio with the poplar trees and vinefields of the Franciscan monks now seemingly as far away as the sixteenth century. Any trace of the warm south had gone. All around was a 'northern European' landscape of tall grass and forest clearings.

I stopped. On closer inspection, it was not a harsh landscape. Grassland and trees seemed freshly rinsed by recent showers. Puddles lay on the uneven surface of the road – patches of blackness which merged with the dark shadows of nearby trees. There was no moon. Night birds could be heard calling to each other in the woods. The surprisingly moist, soft air flooded with a silence – a silence that was suddenly delightful after those long hours with the sound of rubber drumming on tarmac.

Silent but oddly luminescent. Yet the glow of the last town had been left some distance behind. It couldn't be a glow from Valdivia, either – that town was still twenty or thirty miles ahead. More sensations slipped in as the silence grew stronger – louder! A gentle rustle in the branches of the nearby trees brought with it the faintest trace of the sea.

It was a breeze which surely represented a last faint landward movement of the air which had been crossing eastwards over the Pacific since leaving that North Island so many miles away. I turned westwards but it was impossible to see beyond the black silhouette of the coast range and the pale strip of road leading up to the last crest before Valdivia.

The origin of the luminescence rose above the silhouette. No, the countryside was not being palely lit by some distant town. This was Chile and – in its exceptionally clear air – the southern cone of South America was being bathed in starlight. The land was being lit by the billion suns of the Milky Way.

A Milky Way as rarely seen in more populated areas, however. It was a Milky Way of the desert night or of mid-ocean. A view of the galactic disc encompassing a universe of stars. A real universe. Not stars struggling to send a pinpoint of brilliance through a man-made haze. Stars raw and primordial. Stars clearly stretching away beyond the range of the naked eye. Stars beyond stars: some faintly orange; some faintly blue; some faintly red. A southern hemisphere night sky which was not simply two-dimensional but a black, velvet dome over which a random hand had scattered a myriad of tiny reflective fragments of sparkle. It was multi-dimensional; infinitely deep; infinitely crowded. Above all, a great stream of pale light rose up from the south-west, reached its zenith almost directly overhead and then swept off to the north.

A Milky Way which pointed back to Santiago and the direction from which I had come. A long day's journey that suddenly shrank to nothing in the face of these billion suns. A tiny distance down the southern extremity of a South American land mass; a land mass which was itself insignificant against any kind of galactic yardstick. The great water-mass of the Pacific – that was insignificant, too. Even the Earth itself – just a pale blue planet occupying only the minutest corner of the space which arched overhead and which was crowded with such intense specks of incandescent energy. A tiny Earth but one – on the human scale – which was nonetheless wearying enough to cross when marked out in long miles, in heat and dust, in cold mist, in drenching torrential rainfall. A place wearying enough to travel over but nothing in comparison with what lay above. A place which could not even be seen from 'Sirius', or 'Betelgeuse', or 'Bellatrix' or the 'belt of Orion'. A slowly cooling planet that had no place in the celestial show.

But it was all we humans had to protect us against those roaring blasts of eternity.

⋆

Valdivia: a somewhat reassuring scene of rain-washed streets still inhabited by late-night strollers. A sign for a motel down a side-street. Low buildings arranged around an illuminated reception area. A room that was a little airless but gave out on to lawns from which came the smell of tides and of the sea. The dark shape of gently rising land all about. A Pacific Ocean still remaining elusive but clearly not far away. The Great Water that covered a significant part of an Earth spinning its slow way towards another dawn.

Charles Darwin called in at Valdivia in 1835. The *Beagle* sought relief in its excellent natural harbour after rounding Cape Horn and making some very heavy weather of the passage north along the western coast of Chile. The expedition seemed to have encountered the very worst that the Roaring Forties could deliver. Days of storming seas, blustering winds and incessant rain. So grim had the journey been up from the Horn that the unfortunate purser of the ship (so Darwin wrote to one of his sisters) had '*...been caused to gradually sink under a complication of diseases*'. He sank to such an extent that he ended up on the ocean floor – buried at sea before they hove in sight of the island of Chiloe. There the rain continued. Dry beds and hot meals were in very short supply even in this wished-for landfall. Darwin's strongest impression seems to have been of '*...pigs and potatoes.*'

The *Beagle* pressed on northwards. In letters home, Chiloe was dismissed as a '*...miserable hole of a place.*' Unfortunately, it still seemed to be raining when the ship reached the end of a two hundred mile run to the north and they sought anchorage in the natural harbour of Valdivia. Darwin had more bad news to write home about. Another letter joined the batch to be somehow transported back around Cape Horn to England. Terse commentary of Valdivia being another miserable hole. Seemingly, conditions in the 1830s were '*...just like those of Chiloe.*'

It was, of course, the early ninetieth century when all this rain fell on a largely untamed land. Fifty years or so were to pass before those industrious Swiss and German farmers came on the scene and began pushing back the trees, planting their crops, breeding their livestock and building their timber homesteads. In 1835, the Araucanos still held the hinterland. In Darwin's time, however, these peoples – soon recognising that the settled land to the north was no longer protected by the forces of the king of Spain – battled against the post-colonial soldiers who had taken over the government of Chile.

*

Twentieth century Valdivia did not deserve Darwin's faint praise. It was a little town with a pleasant, fresh atmosphere about it. Buildings – many of a timber which had bleached to a light grey – were a-stir with the Saturday-morning ritual of the Developed World: shopping; selling; delivering; chatting and visiting. People could be overheard asking each other how things had been during the previous week. That universe perceived in the coast range night had vanished into infinite space. The neat and well-trimmed lawns of Valdivia had brushed it into oblivion. A freshening breeze constantly drew the growing life of surrounding countryside into the town's streets: the moving air delicately mixed the smell of fresh-cut grass, of drying seaweed, of freshly exposed salt-flats.

Lord Cochrane had been more enthusiastic about the harbour of Valdivia than Charles Darwin. To a naval man, it was – after all – a superbly protected natural anchorage that had been created where an incursion of the Pacific reached into a valley which stretched several miles inland until it touched the town. A narrowing at the seaward end caused by a closing in of high land had further offered the strategic benefits of a channel easily protected by cannon shot from either shore. Not unnaturally, over two centuries of colonial rule, the Spanish authorities had made much of this natural situation. Fortifications and batteries of heavy guns had been sited at the entrance channel to bear on incoming vessels long before the early nineteenth-century movements towards independence began. The Spanish regarded the harbour of Valdivia as impregnable and had given it the title of 'Gibraltar of the Southern Hemisphere'. It was regarded as the best protected harbour north of Cape

Horn. Its maritime door had remained firmly closed to all those not in sympathy with the aims of the Spanish monarchy.

Cochrane pushed it open in 1817 with barely a shot fired. Hot from the Napoleonic Wars (and from a certain amount of controversy over share dealings in the Britain of George III, he had become Commander of the (independent) Chilean Navy and thus in charge of a revolutionary force which was definitely opposed to the revived colonial ambitions of the Spanish state. Whilst Bolivar was busy in the northern part of the continent, the forces of the Argentinian General San Martin and Bernardo O'Higgins were at work in the southern part. The Britisher Cochrane helped to keep afloat the naval part of their operations. In fact, staying afloat was a job which, hovering just below the horizon off Valdivia, was literally one of his prime tasks – the frigate he commanded had begun slowly to sink. Undeterred (or, perhaps, with little choice), he closed with the land and set about bringing the capitulation of the Gibraltar of the Southern Hemisphere by tricking the officer in charge that he was on official colonial business and had come to deliver the garrison's long-awaited pay.

It worked. A pay-ship was due and the commandant was fooled into thinking that Cochrane's vessel was it, until closer inspection uncovered the ruse. By then it was too late. The fox was amongst the chickens. Cochrane had arranged a series of false attacks and confusing signals. Men in the several forts and batteries all guessed (wrongly) that the others had surrendered. Valdivia was taken.

Then, fortuitously, the pay-ship arrived and was also captured. With money, guns and a secure position in southern Chile covering the route up from Cape Horn,

Cochrane had hammered an important nail into the coffin of colonial Spain. It was the stuff of Horatio Hornblower or Jack Aubrey, but it happened.

*

Gulls wheeled overhead and one of the small yellow fishing boats which rode the slight swell pushing in through the channel at the harbour entrance rhythmically heaved and rolled on its mooring. The partially restored 'Fort of the Pure and Clean Conception of Monforte de Lemos' had the rusty barrel of a cannon pointing with others across to the far side of the channel. Bright sunlight lit the scene. Beyond – out past the darker waters of the narrows – the blue of the Pacific opened up. The ocean heaved with a gentle swell. This was the Pacific that John Keats had in mind. This was better than the disappointment of Salinas. This was how '*...stout Cortés' who... with eagle eyes... star'd at the Pacific... silent, upon a peak in Darien.*'

Except that it wasn't Cortés, it was Balboa!

*

I knew as soon as I landed that there was likely to be some sort of run-in with Pinochet's men.

Valdivia was a coastal detour off the long streak of the Pan-American down the central valley to its end at Puerto Montt. Just as I returned to join the main southbound route, a uniformed figure strode out into the highway and motioned for a stop to be made. His raised hand was not one of those floppy, 'spot-fine' kind of hands; it was a crisp, sharp indication to 'stop or I'll shoot'. Chilean police were not the sort of people to play around with.

He was very polite. Where was I going? Where had I come from? Could he see a driving licence? Passport? A khaki uniform with peaked cap; more military than civilian in style and with a polished Sam Browne belt and holster heavy with pistol. Rather like a British officer of the Second World War.

Chile was not a police state, of course. The general had stepped down in March 1990 after establishing a framework of sound economic progress through twenty years of political stability. Before those years, the government of Salvador Allende had preceded him and had clearly been in a mess. There were strikes, inflation, talk of workers rule and of another Cuba. Something had to be done. But, in doing it, the stern Pinochet did not drop in overnight from some military eyrie in the provinces (like young Lt. Col. Hugo Chavez) and set about putting the capital to rights before dawn. Pinochet was Allende's Commander-in-Chief of the Armed Forces.

That crisp, sharp indication to 'stop or I'll shoot' was probably why the *coup d'état* of September 1973 succeeded. Stirred into the ethnic mix of Chile were not the Italians of Venezuela and Argentina but those late nineteenth-century Germans and Swiss. With that kind of backing, coups were carried out properly and finished off properly.

In 1973, the Chilean military – operating with panzer-like efficiency – carried out the overthrow of the democratically-elected government by thoroughly bombing Allende's Presidential Palace. They had the streets of Santiago and other cities like Concepcion under control within hours. Columns of steel-helmeted troops were soon making their way up and down Avenida O'Higgins. The house-to-house searches quickly started. Allende died in the chaos of the first hours.

The 'finishing-off properly' took three years. When the Far Left had been 'finished-off' it was the turn of the Left. Then the Centre came under observation. Then anyone with the remotest inclination towards Liberalism. It was a three-year period when more than one hundred and thirty thousand Marxists, Socialists, Liberals, university lecturers, artists, writers and musicians were questioned and – more often than not – arrested, interrogated and sent for varying periods to prison or labour camps.

A good few were never seen again.

*

But this was March 1992 and Chile had moved on. So much so that a national referendum had been held with the result that the general had accepted the outcome and stepped down. The country was officially no longer a police state although it was – perhaps – still one where authoritarian rule had assumed a comfortable familiarity. Trains ran on time. The economy was booming. And the big man had only just been tipped to one side by a 55:45 result. A close-run thing with 45% of the population wanting him to continue for another eight years. Democracy had settled uneasily into the driving seat but there was to be no liberal back-sliding. Pinochet made sure he held securely on to the reins by retaining the role of Commander-in-Chief of the Armed Forces as he waited in the wings of power to see what happened.

It struck me as I waited for the return of documentation, that these 'armed forces' could well cover almost anyone with a gun and a Sam Browne belt. Pinochet was probably as much in charge of the unsmiling man who was handing back my passport with a curt indication that I could now proceed as those who drove tanks or fighter aircraft. Close attention to 'National Security' over the past twenty years had no doubt produced a fully integrated database. A brief encounter with a policeman on a quiet highway south of the Bio-Bio was almost certain to find its way back into the general's computerised filing system. I almost began to miss the men with the black notebooks and their income supplements. These guys were for real.

⋆

What a beautiful country lay under the watchful eye of Pinochet's men. The air was Baltic-bright at Puerto Montt as the Pan-American came to its end. Nestling at the centre of breeze-block suburbs was a small town of old wooden houses which sloped away to the edge of a wide expanse of water shielded from the Pacific by the distant island of Chiloe. A town which could easily have been located in some quiet spot in Scandinavia or Canada. Large ships lay at anchor offshore. Puerto Montt formed the first real point of contact with modern civilisation and surface communications after the thousand miles of fjords and outlying islands which had to be avoided on the way north from the Drake Passage. Rounding twentieth-century Cape Horn was still a dangerous business. The Roaring Forties had not been tamed and a lee shore was a lee shore – whether for a reefed-down barque with battened hatches or a modern freighter with a blocked fuel pipe.

The brightness became more muted inland. Not far away to the north-east of Puerto Montt was the Chilean Lakeland; countryside which would have touched the poetic soul of Wordsworth as did that of the lakelands of the British Isles. Between the ocean and the mountains was another face of Chile: green hillsides; quiet roads meandering along the edge of clear waters; water-fowl rising through the haze of mid-afternoon; the scent of new-mown hay; the hum of a distant tractor; gnats hovering above a blackberry bush – an English peacefulness hidden away in the 'Southern Cone' of South America.

English – or European? Two cycle-campers in lederhosen peddled past as if to question any nationalistic claims to sole ownership of tranquillity. They disappeared eastwards – moving slowly across this quiet end-summer landscape in the direction of the snow-capped cone of Mount Tronador (which Wordsworth would not have recognised). A few more miles up that road was the Andean frontier with Argentina.

The Chilean/Argentinian frontier was not one of those dramatic frontiers. Cities and busy cross-continent lines of communication had all been left behind. Southwards in this narrowing, empty tip of Latin America was only Patagonia, thick wet forests and difficult mountain country of glaciers and fjords shared by both Chile and Argentina. The lakeland crossing was one of the last routes between the two countries before things became too difficult – here was no steep climb up through rocky defiles to edge past the icefields; no chilly officials stamping their feet and waving through the occasional car before fleeing back to the comfort of some overheated shed. The frontier road wound slowly through leafy woodland until it met a gate and a wooden chalet. Outside the chalet, a minor traffic jam had collected.

Why not nip out of Chile, have a brief look at the Argentinian ski resort of Bariloche and nip back again before beginning the northward return journey to Santiago? After all, doing so (with a British passport) in March 1992 and under the presidencies of Aylwin and Menem was a lot easier than it would have been ten years earlier – in March 1982 when General Pinochet ruled on one side of the Andes and General Galtieri on the other side.

I considered and then decided against the venture. The traffic jam was caused by some very careful and very thorough attention to documentation. The men in Sam Browne belts were busy at their task of national security again and looked a little too grim-faced and serious to be met twice in the course of an hour or two. I started back for Santiago.

*

I don't think I was meant to see the van in the Plaza de Armas. It was a funny time to be transferring prisoners or collecting the weekly wages for the civic authority's office and maintenance staff. Eight o'clock on a cool, grey Sunday morning in coastal Concepcion – Chile's third largest metropolis and a city with a long history of working class union and political activism. Mines and steelworks were somewhere in the vicinity although the air smelt more strongly of fish than coal-smoke. The van was armoured, had barred windows and was the only other vehicle in the large square. As I drove the Peugeot towards it, armed police with sub-machine-guns jumped out and raised their barrels. Other police seemed to be carrying out a search through a nearby apartment block. There was a distinct air of tenseness – as if they were expecting attack or retaliation. The Peugeot became the subject of intense scrutiny as it drew close.

Not a wise time to hang around. I accelerated past. Something was happening which outsiders were not welcome to witness. It was an incident more unsettling than any number of those paramilitary patrols darting in and out of the traffic in downtown Bogotá; a lot more unsettling.

Much flagging down and checking took place on the Pan-American highway leading back into the capital. It even began to become commonplace and it was interesting how many of those moving south warned those of us heading north that we were due to meet another police car. A sudden flash of headlamps and – sure enough – not far ahead would be a uniformed man about to step into the highway with outstretched arm and with a crisp, sharp indication, which it would be folly to ignore, insist that the selected vehicle pull to the roadside for inspection.

It became so frequent that I felt morally bound to flash southbound drivers when they were about to encounter a police check. This was not a wise move. At the end of a long bridge, the familiar figure of a Second World War British Army officer stepped into distant view and, with a crisp, sharp indication, signalled that he had something to say to me.

'*Buenos dias.*'

'*Documentation, por favor.*'

'*Extranjero?*'

'*Su pasaporte, por favor.*'

'*Por que usted viajerente en este pais?*'

I became aware that there was a skimpy, disinterested way of flicking though a passport and a through and potentially serious way of flicking through one.

'Why are you in Chile?' he said, during a pause in the latter process when I realised that he had stopped at the various East European and Chinese stamps that had accumulated on some pages. Feebly explaining that I was on my way to Santiago, I hoped that the Cuban stamp was tucked away in some more remote spot.

He looked intently into the back of the Peugeot and continued in good English.

'You are a foreigner, *señor* – a tourist. Why were you flashing?'

I shrugged. There wasn't much of an answer to that. He continued looking serious but presumably couldn't think of how to pursue matters further. A mild warning about cruising in the outside lane was given and I was waved on.

On reflection, it must have been the *polvorineo.* Newspaper stands in Santiago were full of big headlines with the words 'SABOTAGE' featuring very strongly. The day before I had landed in Chile, the general had been up in the far north visiting an army installation. Part of a small armaments dump had accidentally exploded hours before his visit. This was the 'polvorineo'. Any remote possibility that it might have been some attempt of the Far Left, the Left, the Liberals or the Centre to rock the boat a little was taken very seriously. Presumably – behind the scenes – the armed forces had been put on full alert.

Later, the country stood at ease and the Press tried for a few nervous laughs. A cartoon appeared showing a long-legged figure in fatigues (Pinochet was a very tall and athletic man) lounging in an army deckchair and under an army sun umbrella. 'Chief,' said a minion, 'previously saucepans being banged (*caceroleo*) were a sign of trouble; now its a polvorineo!' ... Ha, ha...

It was a kind of humour that grew less and less funny the closer you got to it.

*

Santiago. Sunday evening in a Catholic country. The evening promenade in the Plaza de Armas (another one). Shady trees, fountains, rather dried-up lawns and copies of classical Greek statuary. A good atmosphere of fun and relaxation. Dwellers of the inner city drawn to one of its cultural focal points. People turning the general hubbub to their own good fortune: bootblacks shouting for custom; lottery ticket-sellers festooned with numbered chits; balloon-sellers tied to a riot of reds, blues and yellows swaying above their heads; peanut-hawkers; loving couples impeding the slow surge of the crowd as they embraced; clusters of arguing families; old men fiddling with tickets and walking sticks; old women passing on confidential information; prams, parents and candy-floss. Bible groups to be avoided.

A small, stocky man with closed eyes and a huge bushy beard moved about in a tight circle of watching people – some of whom strummed guitars. I took him to be blind at first since he moved like a kind of puppet from one side of the crowd to the other, chanting as he went. The guitars grew louder as the man swung to a finish holding a bible high in the air. The crowd said 'Amen' and a collection box was handed round.

A gale of laughter came from the far side of the Plaza. People were sitting in terraced rows arranged crescent-like in front an expanse of pavement. The standing figures of late arrivals completed two large circles. In the middle of one, a man in a violently coloured suit strutted around whilst speaking a kind of 'Burns Night' oration in fast, staccato Spanish. It was not a prayer meeting. Roar after roar of laughter came from the assembled crowd when he touched on any point of amusement. He was probably talking about polvorineos.

The other circle lay quiet but all associated with it were looking intently into the empty space at its centre. No figure was visible in this space – only a powerful voice could be heard.

'*Este es mi trabajo, este es mi trabajo,*' intoned the voice.

Over the sea of heads was only a glimpse of bare flagstones. Still nobody seemed to be in the circle but the voice was obviously emanating from somewhere within the ring of people. Something else was said in Spanish and the crowd suddenly erupted in applause and laughter. A witticism had broken the serious mood. The humour finally allowed me to lean forward far enough to catch sight of the speaker. A small, twisted man was surrounded by his appreciative audience – his misshapen body propped up crookedly in front of an empty wheelchair. A vivid animated face contrasted strongly with his bent form. He himself was not particularly old but one or two 'helpers' who proffered their battered trilby hats at the audience were. It was clear from their dress that this Sunday night show was their means of a slender income.

The animated face – casting about for the subject of another witticism – suddenly caught my eye.

'*Quel pais, quel pais?*' he shouted out with a mischievous look on his face.

Two hundred people turned to find out what country.

'*Quel pais?*' insisted the little man. There was no escape.

'*Ingleterra.*' I shouted but he didn't seem to hear.

'*Canadiense?*' he said.

'*No, Ingleterra.*' I shouted more loudly. Nearby members of the audience also began to shout '*Ingleterra, Ingleterra, Ingleterra,*' into the centre of the circle. At last he chose to hear. All eyes turned back to him for the next remark.

'*Aiae, Ingleterra,*' he said. '*Señora Magereet Tatcher.*' An expectant laugh rippled around the crowd.

'*Un secreto para Señora Magereet Tatcher,*' he suddenly cried with what I hoped was mock seriousness.

The crowd rippled with laughter again and looked curiously in my direction. It was a joke but you could never be sure whether someone out there wearing a Sam Browne belt might not have a sense of humour.

'A spy. Chileans beware! She has taken Las Malvinas back! Now she wants Isla Pascua.'

Easter Island. That raised a really good laugh. I hoped *Señora* Tatcher had put a few extra coins in his trilby hats. After all, she and the general were good friends.

★

Plaza de Armas was not the only place where the citizens of Santiago were being entertained. Leading off it, the Paseo Ahumada was where high-spirited promenaders also surged around the many stalls and pavement displays. Ties, trinkets, toys, tapes and a hundred other bits and pieces were on offer. At the Café Haiti, men propped up against its chrome and plastic bar sipped their coffee thoughtfully as the young women who operated the espresso machines behind the counter twisted or turned in their tight, red, figure-hugging dresses. The scene repeated itself in the Café Caribe. Sex appeal came in two colours in Santiago: it wore red in the Haiti; yellow in the Caribe. Few looked down at their coffee and checked whether it was black or brown.

★

A light brown. Or, perhaps, more of a dusty ochre. The plane from Santiago wheeled down towards a coastline of parched dust and bleak, waterless hills above a cliffed edge. An aircraft gliding above a landscape which seemed impossibly far from the green-flanked harbour of Valdivia and the 'Fort of the Pure and Clean Concepcion de Monforte de Lemos'. Even the vineyards and the Lombardy poplars were more than six hundred miles to the south.

A sprawl of white buildings marked the appearance of Antofagusta. A vastly different town. In the Valdivia and Puerto Montt of southern Chile, it was unusual to see a day or a night without rain; up here – at this northern end of Chile – it rained about once every four hundred years.

The aircraft began its final approach and the ground grew closer. How could humans live in such a burnt and blasted land? Dust and stones alternated with stony dust: no grass; no shrubs; no trees – not even a cactus. The plane touched down on a tarmac strip and taxied to a modern terminus building. This could be only the briefest visit to the Atacama desert – a short day. I hired a car and set out for the inland town of Calama and the oasis of San Pedro de Atacama – a return journey of nearly four hundred miles through one of the driest places on Earth. Not just Earth – it was said that travelling to the San Pedro was the closest anyone could get to a visit to the surface of the planet Mars.

The desert did not begin outside Antofagusta; it began before the last garden-less houses of that coastal town had dropped behind. Dust, the glitter of broken glass and dry stones rising into those ochre-coloured hills seen from the plane – gradually climbing away from the coast and into the parched hinterland.

Once a few hundred feet of altitude had been achieved, a railway line drew close to the road and began to accompany it across the desert – the same railway line which, in fact, had left the dust of Challapata to cross the *Salar de Uyuni* and the Western Cordillera and begin the long and steep descent to this dry spot. It had exchanged that inhospitable high altiplano for this equally inhospitable coastline of dust and salt pans. Only the altitude had changed. In Bolivia, coarse grass and scattered reed beds had softened some of the aridity of the altiplano. Here, in northern Chile, there was nothing.

Nothing but mirages. Railway track and road breaking up as – straight as a die – they marched to the far horizon of brownish-grey dust. Shards of quivering light replaced the certainty of dark tarmac and rusty iron rails. And from time to time – coming out of those shards – a blacker form shifted and twisted in the hot air until it approached close enough to take on mass and solidity. Suddenly, as if holding back for the final passing, a speeding truck would burst out of the desert air as it hurtled by on the road down to Antofagusta – an accompanying blast of hot air sending a fierce patter of tiny stones dancing on the tarmac and leaving a brief-lived momento of its passing.

Otherwise, the land was totally devoid of life. Even the tattered wreath of artificial flowers which hung below the sign of Alfredo Molina had faded and half-disintegrated – part of it drooping to join the few rusty cans which littered his resting place.

Then a faint trace of sulphur began to be noticeable as the road started to cross a great empty bowl in the landscape called *el Pampa del Indio Muerto.* The 'field of the dead Indian'. A lifeless valley of death – everywhere brown-grey in colour and with wide and level patches streaked by a dirty-white crusty rubble looking as if it had been clawed out of the surrounding dust and then abandoned.

Compounds of nitrates, sulphates and salts made up the rubble – minerals soluble and unstable in the presence of water and only able to exist on a surface completely untouched by rain.

No rain. No water. No life. The field of the dead Indian had nothing to support even the lowest form of being. And yet, barely a century ago, on this hazy, sulphurous surface people had lived and worked in sizeable mining communities of up to ten thousand souls. No drastic climatic change over the period from the 1890s to the 1990s had made things worse now than it was for them; those people toiled in this same corrosive atmosphere of the 'field of the dead Indian'.

Strange roofless structures began to hover in the vagueness of the distant mirage. As the empty road and the deserted railway line (both accompanied, rather reassuringly, by the pipeline carrying water to the town of Calama and the huge copper mine of Chuquicamata still sixty miles ahead) pushed deeper and deeper across the dust bowl, the homes of these vanished workers started to appear in view.

How could anyone live in such alien surroundings? Could humanity really come to terms day after day with a place totally devoid of life-giving moisture? And were these roofless barracks really only a hundred years old?

To the unknowing, they could have been thousands of years old. Millions even. The homes of alien beings. Of a long-lost civilisation whose members – generation after generation – had watched their world dry up and their culture shrivel and then pass away to leave nothing but a few walls to greet the final catastrophe. The classic end of science fiction – when the slow spin of their now-empty planet became finally engulfed in the furnace maw of some nearby sun.

'Beam me up Scottie – there's no one left.' The rows of low buildings stood on the dust and stones clothed in an eerie silence. If there had been any movement in the hot and slightly poisonous air, their ghostly walls and blank windows would have sighed with despair. There was no incentive to penetrate deeper amongst the rough ochre-coloured vertical surfaces. This was a ghost town with the ghosts still in residence. No scrap of wood or metal remained – nothing remotely human in purpose or origin had survived from the time when '*OFICINA ANITA*' had been one of the focal points of the considerable late-nineteenth-century nitrate mining industry. It was a place to leave well alone. Oficina Anita still pulsated with hardship and despair.

Yet, from such desolation came the means for abundant and renewed life elsewhere. In their time of peak production at the end of the nineteenth century, this place and these northern Chilean deserts gave the world of agriculture a huge supply of mineral fertiliser.

It was a grim life of labour for those who endlessly hacked at the hard-cemented cocktail of caustic salts in the *Pampa del Indio Muerto* – lugging the dusty products to the waiting railway waggons; earning just less than the cost of a week's food in the company store; downing the company booze to break the monotony of the browns and greys and dirty-whites; sliding slowly and remorselessly down an endless slope of debt.

Sounded like slavery and probably was. The mining and transportation of the South American nitrates industry was dominated by Britain. It was from amongst the low barracks of Oficina Anita and elsewhere that the foundations of resistance came; the foundations of Chile's twentieth-century socialist and communist parties. From this hardship were schooled the grandparents of the people who – before September 1973 – democratically elected Salvador Allende as the only Marxist president the world had seen and hoped for a fairer world. But perhaps the mistake had been to apply a nineteenth-century solution to a twentieth-century problem.

Beyond the ruins of Anita, the road snaked out across the last twenty or thirty miles of the '*Pampa*' before climbing through some fringing hills and then setting off towards another bowl of dust. A larger bowl where even the traces of the nitrate industry seemed to have faded out. Brownish-grey dust stretched far into the distance – the monotony only broken in one place by a curious pale green lichen which covered a small area where the land began to rise into ochre-coloured hills.

The lichen wavered in the heat and then took on more character as the road, the railway and the water-pipe all began to head more directly towards it. The lichen was Calama – the pale green was foliage. Dwarfed by the total desiccation all around it, humanity flourished with its houses, churches, cafés and trees at this tiny oasis in this fierce dust-desert of the Atacama.

⋆

Tall trees shaded the main square of Calama where, on seats in front of a simple white church, the old men of the place gathered. Women passed by with shopping bags. Taxi drivers hung about for business. Once inside the town – and even more so – once inside the Café Bavaria which stood on one corner – it was impossible to imagine the raw harsh lands beyond the few shaded blocks of this small, lively community. True, a huge opencast copper mine was just up the road and provided income and much of the *raison d'être* of the town but it was still a shock to emerge from the shelter of humanity and leave it behind once more for the lifeless bare hills reeking with sulphur.

To my deep dismay, the water pipeline had vanished. It carried water to Chuquicamata and not the unimportant village of San Pedro to which the route now steered. Losing a water pipeline in such a desert was like discovering that the triple plexiglass had suddenly disappeared from your cabin window in mid-flight. I hadn't realised how reassuring it was until the Atacama closed in and it had gone.

But it was a slightly different desert which came into view on the road from Calama to San Pedro de Atacama. The land was rising and a rugged landscape of grey and ochre dust began to open up on either side of the route. Although still half-buried in grey dust, outcrops of a pale red and orange rock had gradually come to dominate the scene. Height brushed away the desolation which surrounded Oficina Anita.

Nonetheless, as this road to San Pedro continued on its journey over this rising land – the *Cordillera Domeyo* – it might just as well have been crossing part of the Depressio Hellespontica of the planet Mars and beginning a winding passage up the lower flanks of Olympus Mons!

Calama hung in the rear view until it once more dissolved into a pale green lichen faintly discolouring the rim of a grey dustbowl. Ahead, San Pedro was still a considerable distance off. The climb continued.

It did not take long for a renewed sense of penetrating deep into an alien world to begin to erupt with a greater vengeance. It was the feeling of being totally alone on the surface of a dead planet. Of being outside the limits of human existence. Any small sign of life would have helped to dispel this sensation; some scrubby little desert weed or a spiky ground plant here and there. But there was nothing – no psychological anchorage points to prove that this was familiar Earth which was still being traversed and not some raw and red surface a million light years from home.

The Old Testament. It was like finding oneself in the aftermath of one of those Old Testament catastrophes where the hapless Children of Israel have yet again crossed an angry and vindictive Jehovah and their lands have been well and truly smitten. '*Ye mountains of Gilboa, let there be no dew, neither let there be rain, upon you, nor fields of offerings: for there the shield of the mighty is vilely cast away.*'

Perhaps the only way to stay on course was to look for a bit of humour in all the desolation. Passing drivers had obviously come to the same view. Somewhere up in the cordillera, a sudden and unexpected flash of brilliant green at the roadside proved to be a small bush about three or four feet in height. '*DAME AGUA*' said a hand-printed sign on a stick – 'Give me water.' A funny place, this lonely desert: dead men wished you well and plants asked you for a drink!

It was not so soulless after all. Nobody talked to you on some bleak, dripping moorland and it was pretty desolate up on the night-time altiplano of Bolivia. In fact, in a curious way, the sterility of the Atacama possessed a kind of grandeur. The stark absence of life amongst its plains and hills was a reminder of the fragility of the living process in the grander scheme of things. The view of that universe was back again. If no one watered '*DAME AGUA*' for a week or two, there would not just be one less plant; there would be no living organism for miles and miles around. If life faded away on Earth, the void around it would be filled with desolation – perhaps limitless.

★

But life was tougher than that. It had survived at San Pedro de Atacama since Man first probed these southern deserts. It survived, even though – unlike Calama – it had no twentieth-century water-pipe leading conveniently past it. San Pedro was a natural oasis in a place which had become so bleak that it defied reason as to how it could occur.

San Pedro sat at the foot of the steep rise of the Andes into the Western Cordillera – mountains as dry as the land which lay all around. It was a part of the Atacama which had once more turned its harsh and inhospitable face and hidden its aspect of grandeur. Partly, the bleakness was enhanced by the fact that the hard surfacing of the road which led towards the oasis had inexplicably stopped where the route plunged towards an empty moon-like surface called the *Llanos de Patiencia.* Tarmac became rough white stones and much patience was required to press on. Southwards from the 'fields of patience' lay the terrible sixty miles of salty dust that was the *Salar de Atacama* – a place reported as receiving more solar radiation than any other spot on earth. Eastwards, the familiar winding gravel-coated bends were beginning which led on far above San Pedro to a border crossing and the Bolivian altiplano.

★

San Pedro was old. Much older than the nitrate and copper-mining around Calama. An Inca trail had led to its tiny drop of life-giving water. It was the way Diego de Almagro and the 'Men of Chile' had come and it was the way that Pedro de Valdivia travelled south. Before cars and trains and planes, that passing from one tiny oasis to another (and praying to God that no misfortune sprang out of the dust and stones and left a traveller stranded in between them) was the only land route down through the western deserts of South America.

I couldn't linger in San Pedro de Atacama to find out where the mummified bodies were. It was Monday afternoon and I had to be at the office in Venezuela on Tuesday morning!

★

From Santiago to Lima – four hundred and fifty years after Diego de Almagro's disappointed struggle back out of the country that was to become Chile. An evening view of the bone-dry western seaboard of South America from the air – the same view as that of the morning whilst landing at Antofagusta. The Atacama seen comfortably from the cabin window of another brand-new Lan-Chile Boeing 767. Seen as dinner was being served. Ice-cold water available at the press of a button.

There was no ice-cold water available when the conquistadores struggled across the dust. Even three centuries later, not much had changed when Charles Darwin made his way though in May, 1835. Itching and dry-mouthed, he wrote in his diary of '*...a country very miserable, so burnt up and dry that the mountains are as bare as a turnpike road.*'

Darwin had as hard a time of it on this spell ashore as he had experienced when the *Beagle* fought its way north up through the Roaring Forties some months earlier. Here on the Tropic of Capricorn, the spare horses and mules of his party could only carry a small amount of food owing to the places where they had to '*...traverse for a day and a half without a drop of water (and) where it was necessary to travel slowly so the animals remained in good condition.*' And, for their uncomfortable overnight stops and meagre suppers, they had to carry '*...a bed, kettle and a pot, a plate and basin*' since these halts for the night inevitably had to be a case of '*...bivouacing in the open air and at some little distance from (any) house where we (can) buy corn and grass for the horses... it was impossible to sleep in houses on account of the fleas.*'

As much as in the 1830s, the fleas at the oasis settlements were there in the 1500s to trouble those who travelled across the South American continent. In the 1500s, too, were all the other mundane irritations: the constant difficulty of provisioning men and horses; the slow hours in the saddle or on foot; the burnt-up and miserable country; the days without a drop of water; the smell of sulphur in the southern wastelands. Also, the fear of the unknown – the fear that with that taint of sulphur they might be drawing ever closer to the very Gates of Hell.

Indeed, it could have been no light task stamping the seal of the Spanish Crown on the face of the New World. It was a task which – in many ways – was a tale which still remains untold in its entirety. Of how they really felt when, further north and in the thin air and biting cold of mountains higher than they had ever imagined could exist, those small parties of conquistadores faced the thousands of armed warriors of civilisations they had never dreamed possible. How it felt to be down on the plains or in the rainforest, when they were wading through vast snake-ridden swamps with pinched bellies and had to maintain constant alertness for the whistle of a poisoned arrow. How they had doubts as to whether strange foods would sustain them or agonisingly kill them. How comrades disappeared and the party got smaller and smaller in an unknown land. How they were uncertain of the way forward and fearful of the way back.

They were just a few horsemen and foot-soldiers moving over the Inca road system and past weird temples and strange practices. And, in the north, when they came across the skull-racks in Yucatan or in the lake city of Tenochtitlan – how did the minds of those physically tough men cope with their grisly discovery as they moved deeper and deeper into an inhospitable continent? It was the early sixteenth century – there was no safety net; no rescue parties; no radios; no mail service; nothing to place it all in perspective.

How did it feel to be always hearing about *El Dorado*? Chasing after that elusive city of dreams that lay at the end of the trail, over the next hills, across the next pass, on the other side of the next swamp. Gripped with gold fever and yet able to organise large-scale mining and lay out and construct cities. Destroyers – stamping of the seal of Catholic Europe across the face of South America's mountains and plains, islands and rainforests with cruelty and murder. But they must have seen cruelty in the ritual sacrifice, too, and the often arbitrary deaths suffered by Indian peoples from one end of the continent to the other as they worshipped insatiable gods. Whatever they thought as they saw and did these things – they colonised a continent. All in the short space of a lifetime.

The *Santa Maria* ran ashore in Hispaniola on Christmas morning, 1492. Fifty years later, a Latin culture had been transposed on the South American land mass. It survives as strongly in the twentieth century as it did in the sixteenth and from Cape Horn to the United States' border (and beyond until the latter part of the nineteenth century). Those cities of Latin America which they constructed: each with *plaza grande, casa del gobierno* and *casa episcopal* at the centre of a rectilinear pattern of streets; they are still there. Santo Domingo in 1496; Havana in 1511; Mexico City in 1521; Quito in 1534; Lima in 1535; Bogotá in 1538.

Chile lay at the outer fringe of this massive explosion of energy. With the founding of Santiago in 1541, the limit had been reached and the expansion down the western side of the Americas halted. The Spanish empire came to a stop at the banks of the Bio-Bio. There was, of course, a slow move into the interior from the Portuguese and Spanish settlements on the Atlantic coast – but that was later.

The mould was cast between 1492 and 1541. In those fifty years, 'South America' became Latin America.